Italy to Argentina

Travel Writing and Emigrant Colonialism

TULLIO PAGANO

Amherst
College
::::: Press

The complete manuscript of this work was subjected to a partly closed ("single-blind")
review process. For more information, visit https://acpress.amherst.edu/peerreview/.

Published in the United States of America by
Amherst College Press
Manufactured in the United States of America

Library of Congress Control Number: 2022948899
DOI: https://doi.org/10.3998/mpub.12758341

ISBN 978-1-943208-54-8 (print)

ISBN 978-1-943208-55-5 (OA)

CONTENTS

Introduction:
From Genoa to Le Havre with a Pot of Chestnuts

Because I already lived in Argentina / Who knows what my
name was in Argentina / And how I lived in Argentina?
— Francesco Guccini, *Argentina*

The small town of Bogliasco, just five miles outside Genoa on the Italian
Riviera, is twinned with Chivilcoy, a much bigger city located about 150
miles east of Buenos Aires in Argentina. The first time I heard about
Chivilcoy, I was interviewing Luciano Siri, an older gentleman who lives
in Sant'Ilario, a village perched on the hills above Genoa overlooking the
Mediterranean. When Luciano's father settled in Sant'Ilario in the 1920s,
it was inhabited mostly by farmers who tended the properties belonging to
wealthy Genoese ship owners, like the Pencos, whose villa is still standing,
and the Marsanos, a family of merchants who owed their prosperity to
the intense commerce that developed in the nineteenth century between
Genoa and the Rio de la Plata.[1] Many farmers also worked in the shipyards
as *camalli* (dock workers) in the port. Others were *naviganti* (sailors), like
Marcello Siri's father-in-law, whose last name was Costa, like the Genoese
owners of the famous company Costa Cruises. Life was hard in the hills,
since they all worked *al terzo*, meaning that they could only retain one-
third of their harvest — for the most part olives. The Siri family was an
exception because they owned their own land in Sant'Ilario. Like many
other families, the Siris came originally from Cisiano, another small village situated on the northern side of the mountain.[2] Siri's grandfather
was expected to serve in the military, like all men of his age. At that time,
after the Italian unification, the army conducted a long military campaign

against the *briganti* in southern Italy. The *briganti* were impoverished farmers, like those in Sant'Ilario, who became outlaws to escape the draft and heavy taxation and engaged in guerilla warfare in the Apennines of Campania, Abruzzi, and other southern Italian regions. Luciano's father did not want to go fight against people that he perceived as very similar to him. When I interviewed Luciano and referred to southern peasants as "briganti," he corrected me, saying they should be called "partigiani" instead, like the patriots who fought against the German and Fascist armies in the mountains of Liguria during the Resistance. My father, a good friend of Luciano and his family, was one of them. Luciano's grandfather left with three other friends from Cisiano: they went to the French port of Le Havre and boarded a ship going to Buenos Aires. They could not leave from Genoa because they would be arrested, so they took a bag of dried chestnuts and a pot and started walking. Chestnuts were the main staple for the people of the Apennines. Once dried, they are light, nutritious, and long-lasting. Since the Middle Ages, peasants of the interior would sell them to ship owners, who used them to feed their crews during the long voyages at sea. Luciano's grandfather managed to get to Buenos Aires, jumped on a boat, and went up the river Paraná until he reached Paraguay, where he stayed for about ten years. Luciano told me that he lived with a Native American woman who healed him when he became sick with yellow fever. He was told that he would die if he were to get infected again, so he decided to return home. After serving in the Italian army—even after ten years he could not get out of it—he got married and bought some land around Cisiano, where he tended to his chestnuts, as he had before departing.

The story of Luciano's grandfather is typical of many families who lived in the mountainous region of Liguria. The Rio de la Plata represented an important resource, although located thousands of miles away. Many of the inhabitants of the nearby village of Sessarego, situated at walking distance from Sant'Ilario, above Bogliasco, settled in Chivilcoy, where one of the main streets is named after the Ligurian hamlet where so many people who settled in Chivilcoy were born. Edmondo De Amicis, the famous Italian writer whose work I analyze in the following chapters, wrote that at the turn of the century in the town of Santa Margherita—now a fashionable seaside sea resort like Portofino—many children playing on the beach and the nearby alleys called each other with Spanish first names.[3] Both Sant'Ilario and Santa Margherita have become exclusive destinations for the new upper classes, who built their residences next to the villas of the old Genoese aristocracy, like Beppe Grillo, the famous comedian and politician, founder of Movimento Cinque Stelle.

In the nineteenth century, Liguria was a very poor region, and its inhabitants were among the very first to migrate to the Americas. Many of the ships that carried Italian emigrants along the Paraná River from Buenos Aires to Rosario, Santa Fe, and beyond, all the way to Paraguay, like the one where Luciano's grandfather probably boarded, belonged to Genoese sailors, who had settled in the famous neighborhood of La Boca, named after the fisherman hamlet of Boccadasse, in Genoa. Although the signs of mass migration are scattered throughout its urban landscape, when I was growing up in Genoa I was not aware of the many connections with Argentina, probably because in Liguria, like in the rest of Italy, emigration belongs to a past that everyone prefers to forget. One of the most important and central boulevards in Genoa is named Corso Buenos Aires. Next to it is Via Montevideo, which owes its name to the capital of Uruguay, situated on the opposite shore at the mouth of the Rio de la Plata. At the end of Corso Buenos Aires, in Piazza Tommaseo, there is an equestrian statue, which I always assumed was dedicated to Victor Emanuel II or another hero of the Italian Risorgimento.[4] Only recently did I found out, however, that the man on the horse is Manuel Belgrano, one of the founders of Argentina, whose family came from Oneglia, a town in the Riviera di Ponente, the western Riviera. The beautiful staircase in Liberty style, called Scalinata Giorgio Borghese, is also named after a Ligurian man from Rapallo, on the Eastern Riviera, who in 1729 became one of the founders and the first *regidor* (governor) of the city of Montevideo. Giorgio changed his name to Juan Burgues, as many humble Italian emigrants did when they arrived in the Americas.

A central question discussed in this book is reflected in these two Latin American figures of Italian origins, whose national identity becomes the site of a struggle: On the one hand, the Italian authorities often seem to consider Manuel Belgrano and Giorgio Borghese as evidence of the strength, courage, and resilience of those Italians who ventured to the Americas, dating back to Christopher Columbus, a native of Genoa as well. On the other hand, these two men are representatives of a humble Italian diaspora, which scattered its people across the globe, to be assimilated by other nations, losing their language, their name, and any connection with the motherland. The monument created during the Fascist era may be interpreted as a last, desperate attempt to reclaim these South American heroes and reinsert them within an Italian nationalist genealogy. They become, in other words, the expression of what Mark Choate has called "emigration colonialism," a strategy used by Italian governments since the late nineteenth century to turn emigration and the loss of human capital that it necessarily entails into a source of empowerment, through which a "greater Italy" that would extend beyond its national boundaries may be created.[5]

Conquest through Emigration?

In contemporary critical discourse, the terms *diaspora* and *colonialism* are usually juxtaposed. The former derives from the Greek *dia speiro,* meaning "to sow over." Although originally used to describe the spread of Greek civilization throughout the Mediterranean, the connotations of the term were usually negative, indicating a dispersal, a loss of origins, as in the Jewish diaspora. Colonialism, on the other hand, derives from the Latin *colon,* signifying farmer, and implies the transfer of a population to a different territory, where the new group settled, while maintaining a strong political allegiance to the country of origin. More recently, cultural critics have begun attaching more positive meanings to the word *diaspora,* arguing that the act of scattering seeds to which the word's etymology refers may be seen as a productive process. Modern technology makes it possible for "diasporic subjects" to remain in close contact with each other and the motherland. Thus, "dispersal" may become a means of empowerment, as Johnathan and Daniel Boyarin, authors of *The Powers of Diaspora,* have successfully argued.[6] Moreover, the phenomenon of globalization associated with multinational capitalism, which tends to "scatter" workers all over the globe, has contributed to a further reevaluation of the significance of diaspora and its relationship with migration studies.

The case of the Italian peninsula is especially complex, because one may argue that throughout its history Italy has experienced many diasporas, ranging from antiquity to the present time, as Donna Gabaccia has shown in her successful book *Italy's Many Diasporas.*[7] When I began studying the phenomena of Italian diaspora and colonialism, I saw them as juxtaposed, or at least clearly distinguished. After all, the movement of Italian Nationalism, which was the precursor of Fascism, originated in opposition to both Socialism and the "scandal" of mass migration.[8] As I continued researching, however, I started seeing indications of continuity between the economists, anthropologists, journalists, and politicians who supported "free" emigration and the nationalists who opposed it. The terms *emigration* and *colonialism* are not clearly separated, as I had initially thought; instead, they join to form what at first sight may seem an oxymoron. The common goal pursued by otherwise opposed nineteenth century Italian groups—liberals who encouraged emigration to Argentina and nationalists who sought to create an Italian empire—was conquest.

When Italians started arriving in great numbers at Rio de la Plata, the region was still in the process of being "colonized," especially the interior, where the dominant mode of production was pastoralism. English capital and Italian (and southern European) labor constituted the two forces that brought about what Walter Mignolo has called the "internal colonization" of Argentina, which radically transformed its landscape and caused the extinction and the definitive marginalization of the native population.[9] This process would not have been possible without the support of the Argentine hegemonic classes, the "Creoles" who saw European immigration both as an indispensable vehicle for the modernization of the country and as an opportunity to get rid of their "second-class" status with respect to the European elites they were trying to emulate.[10] Thus, humble Italian men and women whose families had been starved and exploited for centuries in their own land, when they set foot on American soil, often turned into avid "proletarian *conquistadores*" pushing back the natives and depriving them of their own land, culture, and identity. Ironically, many of them were patriots who had fought bravely in the Risorgimento against the foreign powers that had governed the Italian peninsula for centuries.

One of the first texts that opened my eyes about the phenomenon was a short story by María Luisa Ferraris titled "El Malón," describing a scene similar to what one may expect in a classic Hollywood Western movie, with a young Piedmontese couple barricaded inside their house in the prairies, awaiting with fear the incursion of a band of "savages" who may kill them and destroy their possessions, as was occurring in the surrounding farms.[11] The story is told from the point of view of the woman, who reminisces about her previous life in the Langhe, in the northern Italian region of Piedmont, while her husband stays awake the entire night by the window with his carbine, ready to shoot any intruder. *La vuelta del malón* (The return of the Indian raid) is the title of a famous painting.

I saw it for the first time at the National Museum of Fine Arts in Buenos Aires. It depicts a group of Native Americans returning from a raid: one of them is holding a partially naked white woman while others carry severed heads in their saddles. The artist suggests that they also attacked a church, because one man is waving a crucifix in the air and others hold chalices and other religious objects. The name of the artist is Angel della Valle, the son of Italian immigrants who completed what many critics consider his masterpiece in 1892, to be exhibited at the World Columbian Exposition in Chicago the following year. When the painting returned to Buenos Aires in 1894, it became an essential piece in the commemoration of General Julio Argentino Roca's brutal military campaign against the Native population, presenting it as the culmination of the conquest of America in 1492. As Laura Malosetti Costa argues, the painting effectively inverts the symbolic terms of conquest and plunder, transforming the colonizers into victims and implicitly justifying the massacre of the indigenous people, shown as ruthless savages who have no respect for human life and the most sacred religious symbols.[12]

The other text that made me question my previous assumptions about the Italian diaspora is a poem by Dino Campana, titled "Buenos Aires," describing the arrival of a ship full of Italian immigrants in the Argentine port. In the text, the author uses the term "ferocious" to characterize the migrants, as they get ready to disembark and start their "conquest." The image of those Piedmontese families fighting the Native Americans in the *pampa* was totally unexpected and stuck with me, as did Campana's portrayal of the emigrant as ferocious. In contemporary Italian literature and popular culture, emigrants were usually represented as victims, marginalized and meek individuals forced to leave their country. Instead, the Italians who settled in the interior of Argentina were authentic "colons," that is, they were sent there by the local government to accomplish what was described as the "conquest of the desert."

To illustrate the similarities between late nineteenth-century liberalism and nationalism, I decided to focus on a variety of texts, organized in chronological order. Although the main focus of the book is travel writing, I included economists who never traveled to South America but whose ideas helped shape the discourse on emigration. I start by analyzing a little-known book by the Ligurian economist Jacopo Virgilio, published in 1868, who strongly supported "free," "spontaneous" migration to Rio de la Plata.[13] Virgilio was a patriot who had fought in the Risorgimento and saw the emigration in that region as a new and more profitable form of peaceful colonization. Although he never traveled to Argentina, his work represented an important theoretical point of reference for those who did go. The author I examine in chapter 2 is Paolo Mantegazza, a doctor, anthropologist, traveler, and eclectic intellectual who spent several years in the region in the 1850s and 1860s. I focus on two books that in my opinion complement each other in interesting ways. The first is a travel narrative titled *Rio de la Plata e Tenerife: Viaggi e Studi,* first published in 1867. The other one is a philosophical epistolary novel titled *Il Dio ignoto*—although the author calls it a *poema*—in which one of the protagonists, Attilio, embarks on a ten-year adventure in Argentina, becoming first a successful entrepreneur and successively a *cacique,* or chief of an Indian confederation. Mantegazza was a very prolific and somewhat controversial author whose texts have recently attracted some critical attention, even though no one, to my knowledge, has ever analyzed in any depth his fictional and documental writings on Argentina.[14] Mantegazza, like Virgilio, was a steadfast liberal who upheld the ideas of Charles Darwin (with whom he corresponded) and went to Argentina with the deliberate objective of becoming rich. During his first journey, he married a Creole woman from Salta and even tried to create his own colony in the region, which was to be inhabited by "moral and hard-working" men and women from the regions of Piedmont and Lombardy. His views of the native peoples of Argentina are extremely racist and amply justify and support the internal colonization that was being implemented by the local government at the time. In his epistolary novel *Il Dio ignoto,* Mantegazza unleashes, through his male hero Attilio, an authentic delirium of colonial control that makes the reader question the principles of universal progress and brotherhood on which the peaceful colonization of Rio de la Plata was supposed to be founded.

The third chapter is devoted for the most part to the Italian novelist and journalist Edmondo De Amicis, especially famous for his sentimental, patriotic novel titled *Cuore* (Heart). De Amicis was invited to lecture and write about Argentina in 1884, when Italian emigration was at its peak.[15] In my analysis, I show how De Amicis's view of emigration changed through time: from the classic "anti-emigration" poem "Gli emigranti" (1880) to the more complex and articulated representation in his reportage *I nostri contadini in America.*[16] In my reading, I concentrate on the military metaphors used throughout the text, and I juxtapose De Amicis's romanticized portrayal of the Argentine *gaucho* with the more realistic representation of Italian colons in the region of Santa Fe, the heart of the so-called *pampa gringa*. De Amicis was, like Virgilio and Mantegazza, a staunch supporter of free, spontaneous migration. I show that in his writings the descriptions of patriotism among Italian emigrants are used to promote a nationalist agenda in the motherland. Although the Piedmontese author did not openly support military-based colonialism, a careful reading of his text shows that colonialism always looms in the background, obscured by more positive terms like *development* and *civilization*. In De Amicis, as well as the other Liberal authors, "Colonialism is a like the shameful member of the family—it's always there, people know about it, but they prefer not to mention."[17] It is something that cannot be avoided, when the goal is spreading prosperity, democracy, and freedom to the world, as Mignolo puts it. In my analysis, Italian colons became the proletarian soldiers of the capitalist army that invaded and recolonized Argentina, whose high officers were English and other northern European capitalists. Their "ferociousness," to use again Campana's poetic term, may be seen as a precursor of the rapacious method displayed by contemporary multinational corporations like Monsanto and its political allies, responsible for the destruction of the environment and the poisoning of many inhabitants of the *pampa*.

In chapter 4, I start by focusing on a book by another liberal economist, Luigi Einaudi's *Il principe mercante* (1901), whose protagonist is an Italian entrepreneur, a "prince-merchant" who "conquered" the South American market with his textile products, developing a wide and powerful network, not only in Argentina but in many other nations too. While other cultural critics see a strong opposition between Einaudi's approach to emigration and nationalist authors like Luigi Barzini, Giuseppe Bevione, and Enrico Corradini, who visited and wrote about Argentina in the same decade, I argue that they all share a similar "colonial" outlook, where the migrant workers are perceived as "soldiers" to be guided by their Italian superiors toward the conquest of new, undeveloped markets in the Latin American continent. Barzini remarked that Italian emigration is like an army with a multitude of soldiers but without officers, arguing that emigrants were left without any support from the mother country and especially without capitalist entrepreneurs who could direct them. Both Barzini and Bevione were journalists sent by major Italian newspapers to investigate the real conditions of Italians in Rio de la Plata. While Einaudi presented a glowing picture of Argentina, the two reporters who followed him were much more critical about the political and judiciary system, which often discriminated against foreigners and Italians in particular, whose massive presence in Argentina caused great anxiety among the hegemonic classes. The Argentine government began to impose more restrictions on immigrants, who were no longer portrayed in positive terms by the local press. On the contrary, as Eugenia Scarzanella has shown, Italians were often described as "malagente," bad people.[18] In Corradini's nationalist novel *La Patria lontana*, set in Rio de Janeiro, both the Liberal and Socialist protagonists are humiliated and defeated by the "Herculean" Piero Buondelmonti, who has inherited from his mentor, Ercole Gola, a strong sense of patriotism. The novel ends with the return of Italian emigrants to their motherland, where they will fight in the upcoming conflict against the Ottoman empire. Thus, military colonialism is replacing the peaceful one advocated by Corradini's Liberal opponents.

Argentine society at the turn of the century was characterized by social and political conflicts, with Italian political activists playing an important role in the organization of the first labor unions and strikes. Thus, in the fifth chapter, I examine the writings of Anarchist authors who encouraged Italian emigrants to form broader alliances beyond the Italian diasporic community. Pietro Gori and Errico Malatesta were two internationally famous Anarchists who escaped to Argentina after the Italian army killed hundreds of workers during the protests that took place in Milan in 1898. I concentrate especially on Pietro Gori, a lawyer and legal scholar and specialist in criminology who investigated the Argentine carceral system and founded an important academic journal in Buenos Aires titled *Criminalogía Moderna*. Gori became enormously popular both in Italy and in the Americas (he also lived in the United States before going to Argentina) for his unique style: his lectures were authentic performances, combining historical and political analysis with music and acting.[19] I unravel the intriguing convergences between Gori's revolutionary political activism and the controversial legacy of Cesare Lombroso, founder of modern criminology, whose theories were widely studied and applied both in North and South American universities.[20]

In the sixth and last chapter, I analyze the travel writings of Cesare Lombroso's daughter Gina, who visited Brazil, Uruguay, and Argentina with her husband, Guglielmo Ferrero, and published a book based on her observations, *Nell'America meridionale* (1908). I explore to what an extent Socialist thought at the turn of the century was still informed by the racist theory developed by Lombroso and his Positivist disciples. I also discuss how the Italian anthropologist's ideas about women and gender influenced his daughter's writings on Argentina, where women had reached a higher degree of emancipation.

In the epilogue, I fast-forward to Vanni Blengino, a cultural critic whose books have been instrumental for my research. Blengino, who unfortunately died shortly before I began reading his works, was a professor of Latin American literature in Rome and an internationally admired cultural critic. A native of the Langhe region in Piedmont, Vanni migrated with his family to Argentina after World War II when he was still a young adolescent. He worked in his father's bakery, went to school, and studied philosophy at the University of Buenos Aires. In the Argentine metropolis, he was exposed to a wide range of ideas that contributed to his development as an original transnational scholar. His memoir—titled *Ommi, l'America!*—published in 2007, constitutes a thoughtful reflection on what it meant to be an immigrant to Argentina in the postwar period and shows how stimulating the intellectual climate was in the American metropolis. Blengino recounts that his return to Piedmont after living in Buenos Aires for several years was a true cultural shock. He had difficulties communicating with his old friends, who seemed so closed-minded and provincial with respect to what he had experienced living in the multicultural capital. His autobiography shows that the journey to South America, although it did not bear the financial rewards that his father had hoped for, represented a unique opportunity his for intellectual growth. As opposed to the writers I analyze in the book, who visited and wrote about Argentina at the turn of the nineteenth century, Blengino's story shows that the most fruitful way to "conquer" another culture while maintaining one's *italianità* is by letting oneself "be conquered" by it, without fear of being assimilated. Blengino did not cease being "Italian" when living in Buenos Aires; on the contrary, his Italian identity was enriched by his experience and, by continuing to study and research Argentine history and Italian immigration, he was able to offer his students and readers truly unique insights into both cultures.

CHAPTER ONE

Free to Leave: A Liberal Economist Looks at Emigration

There are so many Genoese, and so scattered throughout the world, that everywhere they go and stay, they create another Genoa.

—Anonimo Genovese, thirteenth century

Jacopo Virgilio (1834–1891) was an important liberal economist from Chiavari, a town in the eastern part of the Italian Riviera, and one of the most eloquent supporters of free emigration during the post-unification period. Emigration to the Americas had a huge impact on Liguria and the town of Chiavari in particular. To understand Virgilio's ideas, it is important to bear in mind that his native town is situated at the threshold between the Mediterranean, with its many opportunities for global maritime commerce and economic expansion, and an impoverished and harsh mountainous interior, the Fontanabuona Valley, which constituted through the Middle Ages and Renaissance a preferred itinerary for the merchants who moved between the rich Po Valley and the Ligurian coastline.[1] As he was growing up, Jacopo saw the farmers on the hills around Chiavari and Fontanabuona constantly building and maintaining their small terraces supported by stone walls, where they cultivated olives, citrus fruits, and vegetables. As he climbed toward the interior, olive and citrus orchards gave way to chestnuts, the tree on which the Italian peasants of the Apennines had always depended for their survival. The town of Chiavari, on the contrary, based its relative prosperity on maritime commerce, being closely associated with Genoa, the capital of the homonymous republic that controlled the long and narrow strip of land called Liguria, which stretches from southern France to Tuscany. Walking through the nicely preserved historic center, one cannot avoid noticing a series of elegant villas, built in an eclectic style that is different from the traditional architecture of the area. People from Chiavari called them "le ville degli Americani," the Americans' villas, because they were constructed by those who, after making their fortune in the American continent, returned to give back to their community and display their economic success. People from the region usually went to South America: Argentina, Uruguay, Chile, and even Peru. The commercial and cultural ties between Chiavari and Argentina were so strong that until the 1970s in the small town of the Italian Riviera there was an Argentine consulate.

In several articles published in the 1860s in the prestigious journal *Il Politecnico,* founded by Carlo Cattaneo, one of the most prominent figures of the Italian Risorgimento, Virgilio criticized those who tried to pursue agriculture in Liguria and instead encouraged its inhabitants to embrace other activities connected with the naval industry: that was the future of the region, as was evident by the many shipyards that were being built not only in Genoa but also in many smaller Ligurian towns, like Chiavari, Varazze, and Camogli. In a short text published in 1910 and dedicated to Santa Margherita, a coastal town next to Portofino, Edmondo De Amicis wrote that through the old town one could hear mothers calling back their children playing in the streets and on the beach with Spanish first names. He remarked that those who have Spanish words in their mouths have money in their pockets.[2]

Virgilio opens his book, *Delle migrazioni transatlantiche degli italiani e in ispecie di quelle dei liguri,* with a general overview of migrations: they have always occurred throughout history and are a "powerful and providential instrument, aimed at proportioning the population...and spreading the seeds of progress and civilization among less cultured people."[3] Migrations and colonization are closely related, and often indistinguishable, as powerful nations tend to conquer other areas of the globe in which they can extend their influence and create new colonies. Jacopo identifies what he calls the "modello romano," followed in modern times by Spain, Portugal, and Holland, where the government promotes and protects its colonies and exercises control over them. This method, in his opinion, "was not only fruitless, but in fact almost always caused ruins and disasters."[4] The migrations that Virgilio advocates are the ones carried out by the Greeks and especially the Phoenicians, a people that closely resembled the Genoese: "Phoenicia, on a strip of land with a dense population enriched by navigation and commerce, needed to disseminate across a wider area the excess of its multitudes."[5] Phoenician colonies were created throughout the Mediterranean and the Black Sea by private initiative," not by government intervention. This method, based on "individual transmigrations," is the most successful and bears long-lasting results, which tend to unfold and develop over a longer period of time: "Emigration thus happens freely, spontaneously, although with slow progression; and the results obtained are infinitely more advantageous and lasting."[6]

Greek and Phoenician colonies could develop freely, without any government interference. Thus, "the greater the autonomy, the stronger the bonds of affection were felt,"[7] because those who leave their country always retain the desire for products of their origins, as the memory of the homeland urges them unconsciously to consume the merchandise from the places where they were born. On the contrary, when colonization is based on the spirits of conquest, intolerance, and tyranny, it is bound to fail, as was the case for the Romans, the Portuguese, and many others. The true and best migration is the one based on freedom, without any government interference, as it was happening in the Rio de la Plata at the time when Virgilio was writing.

According to statistical data gathered by the economist, around 580,000 European individuals migrated to the Americas every year, but the actual numbers were probably higher. The Germans were the largest group, over 200,000, and Virgilio—who had at heart the development of a powerful Italian naval industry—hoped that the Italian government would do something to attract these migrants to the Italian ports of Genoa and Livorno. He thought that Germans possessed the ideal characteristics to succeed abroad: they had a strong and resolute character; they respected the laws and private property; they were sober, courageous, patient, hard-working, attached to their families; and they integrated easily with Anglo-Saxon people, although they had more difficulties assimilating in Latin America. In second position, according to Virgilio, were the people from Liguria, Piedmont, and Lombardy, who also adjusted very easily to new environments. Moreover, they could learn the Spanish language more quickly than the Germans and had "a lively intelligence, affability, a spirit of economy, order, and sobriety."[8] Unfortunately, he thought, they lacked the sentiment of cohesion and self-esteem that characterized the German emigrants and did not have the same desire to read and enhance their education (15). Interestingly, Virgilio wished that the Italian authorities would do something to block those "groups of buskers who certainly do not contribute to making us gain esteem among serious and hardworking peoples."[9] He referred to the barrel-organ players who were being recruited by agents to perform in the streets all over Europe and even in the Americas. Many of them were children (called *birbanti*) from impoverished families who either loaned or sold them to an agent. Often, they ended up working for criminal organizations, who exploited them, much like today with the illegal migrants from Africa who may be seen begging on the street corners in many Italian cities.

Virgilio criticizes those who claim that the wealth of a country is based exclusively on the density of its population. Capitals are equally important, and in Italy at that time they were not available to lessen the miserable conditions of the peasants, who continued to reproduce incessantly. The only remedy, for Virgilio, was "to leave free the gates for migration....It is carried out from the place where life has become more difficult and is directed toward the districts where it is easiest."[10] Thus, trying to limit or block emigration is "the most unjust and harmful act that can be perpetrated by a government."[11] Virgilio quotes numerous intellectuals who shared his views, including Gerolamo Boccardo, a famous economist from Liguria, like himself:

> Unfortunately, there are countries where the means of subsistence are overwhelmed by the mouths that need to be fed: endless districts rot under the encumbrance of their native fertility, and countless urban populations suffer in cramped spaces and the misery of forced inactivity. These two undeniable and obvious facts are enough by themselves to reveal all the incalculable importance of emigration, which is needed today and is destined to serve more in the future as a vehicle for the propagation of wealth and civilization on the earthly planet....All that the government has to do is remove the obstacles that stand in the way of emigration; it must favor societies that protect emigration and leave emigrants and immigrants perfectly free, leaving the consequences of the choice and methods of this economic emigration to individual responsibility.[12]

Nevertheless, other Italian economists thought otherwise and considered the population as the most important resource for the nation. If people leave, the result is a loss of human power, thus the country will be impoverished. Virgilio quotes a memo from the Ministry of Interior, dated January 23, 1869, addressed to Italian mayors and prefects, ordering them to give permission to emigrate only to those individuals and families who have a guaranteed job or sufficient means of subsistence (29). The memo states that in New York at the moment there are "more than sixty thousand unemployed workers who live in idleness and in the most squalid poverty" (29).[13] In Algeria, another important destination for Italians in those years, the conditions "are made harder and more unbearable by famine and cholera in many of those districts."[14] Virgilio observes, however, that most emigrants do not go to New York and Algeria; instead they prefer the regions of Rio de la Plata, where they find more opportunities. He also quotes an article from *Eco d'Italia*, an Italian American newspaper, dated March 27, 1868, showing that European emigrants preferred to settle in rural Virginia, where they applied to obtain land and establish agricultural colonies. Virgilio regrets that the Italian ministry does not distinguish between North and South America. Whereas in previous years the United States offered "lucrative contracts" to Europeans willing to fight in the U.S. Civil War, after the end of the "fratricidal struggle" the incentives have become almost insignificant (31). Virgilio wonders how the minister of a liberal democracy would want to limit individual freedom. If he is not trying to dodge the military draft, "a man, when he so desires, can go into the world as he pleases, wherever he desires, since by doing this, he exercises one of the most simple, yet fundamental individual rights" (33).[15] Other countries tried in the past to intervene in a similar way, including China, England, France, and Portugal, but according to Virgilio they always failed, and once the governments realized the ineffectiveness of their laws they repealed such measures (33). Virgilio observes that the Italian government does not consider as a valid document the letters that family members and relatives may write to those who had remained in Italy, inviting them to come and help in the family business. As a result of these new policies, many Italians are forced to depart from foreign ports, like Marseilles, Le Havre, and others, thus depriving the Italian shipping companies of much-needed revenue. Virgilio is thinking especially of those firms based in Liguria, since "the emigration by sea in Italy originates almost entirely from the port of Genoa."[16] Virgilio quotes the Genoese newspaper *Il Corriere Mercantile*, where one reads that "Liguria created truly important colonies in various places, and above all in the vast region of the Plata, which benefit both the region and all of Italy and respect the independence of the indigenous Hispanic peoples."[17] These colonies are destined to a great future, although they do not have the same political structure of those created by Spanish-Americans.

To undermine the argument of those who saw emigration as a possible cause of national impoverishment, Virgilio shows that between 1864 and 1866, the Italian population increased by an average of 200,000 each year, whereas emigration was less than 20,000. Moreover, he claims, many emigrants return to their mother country, send large sums of money to their families at home, and, most importantly, contribute to keeping the maritime trade between the colonies and the peninsula alive (43). Virgilio thinks that Italian emigration should be at least double. In fact, many workers in Italy are paid so little that "they are not even able to provide themselves with healthy and sufficient nutrition."[18] In the South, the living conditions are even worse, where peasants very rarely can afford eating wheat bread, and meat appears on their table only two or three times a year. Their houses are nothing but "filthy and rundown dens, more suitable for beasts than men. And their clothing is nothing but a disgusting mass of rags."[19]

Governments should not be surprised of the rise of *brigantaggio*, a popular uprising that was affecting southern Italy after the unification: "Neither bayonets nor hurried executions will manage to cleanse those provinces of such terrible leprosy."[20] Brigandage is the offspring of poverty and the growth of capital, a greater distribution of land, and the gradual increase of wages and economic education may help defeat it. The living conditions of the peasants are not better in Emilia Romagna, Tuscany, Lombardy, and even in Virgilio's own region of Liguria, which he described so vividly in an article published in *Il Politecnico* in 1862, titled "Delle condizioni economiche delle Province Liguri." The main problem, in Virgilio's opinion, is the small amount of capital that Italy invests in agriculture: whereas in England the investment is forty liras (*franchi*) for each hectare, in Italy it is less than four. Only an increase in capital investment may make agriculture more profitable, but unfortunately the capital is not available in Italy. Virgilio writes that there is "a wave of restless, unemployed people looking for places where they can profitably work."[21] The government had just implemented a new "tassa sul macinato" (tax on ground wheat), which impoverished even more Italian peasants. As a result, the incarcerated population is increasing: a real "army" of eighty thousand people that cost taxpayers a huge amount of money. Virgilio argues that if emigration were to double,

> wages would rise by balancing the price increase of commodities...the trade between our ports and those lands where our migrants prefer to go

would augment, leading to a greater consumption of national agricultural and manufactured products, which would benefit the maritime commerce, one of our few vigorous sectors, and would increase the sums that the colonists send home each year. Ultimately, the number of those who return to Italy to enjoy the fruit of their honorable labors would rise as well.[22]

Virgilio is convinced that emigrants usually do not change their habits when living abroad and continue to use products that remind them of their mother country: "this fact explains the sizeable transports that the Genoese ships make to the ports of South America with products from Piedmont and Lombardy."[23] In other words, the economist foresaw that migrants are instrumental in the propagation of "Made in Italy" products throughout the world.[24] Like other contemporary authors, the Italian economist uses the "organic" metaphor when discussing the Italian diaspora, comparing the nation to a living organism: "Emigration acts in the nations as the circulation of blood in the human body; it is not only a relief for populations that are too large, but it is also an essential condition of prosperity, well-being, and wealth."[25] Virgilio writes that Ligurians consider Buenos Aires and Montevideo as true colonies, because eighty thousand Italian citizens are scattered in those areas, where they trade intensely. Emigration is a source of prosperity for the Italian Riviera, because the colons "alleviate our country, which is overly inhabited in proportion to the means of subsistence, initiate trade with the homeland, make navigation prosperous, send more than a million [liras] to their relatives every year, and return rich to the country they had left as poor."[26] He concludes with the observation that Ligurians in the region of La Plata have been carrying on, with their parsimony and their industriousness, "a peaceful conquest" (56).

Unfortunately, Italian landowners want to limit emigration, so that the day laborers' salaries "decrease to the level of those received by Chinese *cool*, Indian *Sudra*, Russian and Irish peasants, and *Cafoni* of southern Italy."[27] The landowners are afraid when they see peasants leave their native country and return to buy land and houses, treating the old masters as equals and often surpassing them with their possessions. These landowners, Virgilio continues, "would like to keep the peasantry tied to the earth as the serf was in the Middle Ages, and in a condition not too different from that of a beast."[28] Therefore, they constantly complain about the lack of labor. Because of emigration, they claim, the countryside is becoming deserted. Thus, they spread rumors of terrible shipwrecks, epidemics on board the ships, inhumane treatment, and so forth, hoping to discourage peasants from leaving. Sometimes, they even convince journalists to write articles against emigration, which they call "the gnawing cancer of Italian agriculture," while the ship owners are compared to "merchants of human flesh who carry out the trade of whites."[29] Virgilio admits that some ship owners and captains occasionally mistreat migrants, but those are rare occasions, because the health authorities ("Sanità marittima") perform frequent inspections to make sure the emigrants' rights are respected and the proverbial honesty of Ligurian ship owners and captains ensures that complaints are very rare. In fact, Virgilio points out that Neapolitan peasants often prefer to depart from Genoa instead of other Italian ports. In a footnote, Virgilio quotes an article of *Il Corriere Mercantile* stating that several hundred Neapolitans were wandering through the city waiting to board a ship. Apparently, they had already paid an agent for the trip, who told them to be patient because their ship was not ready yet, and we do not know if they ever managed to depart. The article underlines that ship owners are not responsible for these unfortunate situations, and the author hopes that the government will monitor more closely brokers who mistreat their clients. In particular, the most severe punishments should be applied against those who hire "musician boys, for whom there is no protection."[30]

Virgilio dismisses the argument that emigration may depopulate Italy, because emigrants are always fewer than the ones who would like to leave their country. In order to embark on such a long and expensive trip, individuals need a small amount of capital. Thus, truly poor people are unable to leave, and "It is from this mass that the worms who gnaw at modern society swarm. It is in this multitude that idleness and vagrancy find a perpetual nursery."[31] In other countries, including Germany and Switzerland, the government offers financial support to those who wish to migrate but lack the economic means to do so. "Emigration Societies," whose purpose is to assist emigrants, are being developed in many European nations, but Italy does not have anything similar to help alleviate the sufferings of the most impoverished and numerous classes (66). Virgilio quotes a member of the Medical Academy of Turin who wrote in 1860 that the Genoese already have true colonies in Montevideo, Buenos Aires, and many other cities in Argentina:

> Many thousands of Sardinian subjects in those distant regions have their minds and hearts turned to their motherland, and with work and industries they procure sizable assets, until, having reached a mature age and

having obtained the necessary conditions of fortune, they can return to the soil on which they were born; and here they wait in peace and relative prosperity the end of a life spent in part in faraway lands.[32]

In Liguria, many families were able to survive the most recent economic crises thanks to the help they received from the Americas: "entire towns rescued from poverty and hunger...because their aid came from the Americas, where there is no family in the Riviera that does not have some relatives" (69).[33] Camillo Cavour, the Italian prime minister, had foreseen the importance of emigration for the economy of the new nation and hoped that the port of Genoa could attract more people from Switzerland and Germany who were transiting through other ports in northern Europe. In Virgilio's opinion, Italians should aim toward Argentina and the Rio de la Plata region, because in other areas in Central America and Brazil the tropical climate makes it very hard for Italians to adjust; in North America, where the climate is more similar to Italy, the land concessions are now limited to extremely remote areas in the Far West. Argentina, on the contrary, offers opportunities both in the cities and in the countryside. In Bahia Blanca and Patagonia, south of Buenos Aires, the government assigns large portions of land to those who apply. Furthermore, the soil is extremely fertile and does not require—as in North America—preventive tillage. Those who wish to pursue pastoralism don't have to build expensive stables, because the animals may live outside in every season. For seven or eight years the soil remains productive without needing to be fertilized. In the region of Santa Fe, the administration provides food to the colons for an entire year, and livestock is repayable at a very reasonable interest. Ships transport migrant workers at no charge along the rivers from Buenos Aires to Santa Fe. Finally, in Argentina Italian emigrants enjoy "maritime, commercial, and industrial liberty; and political, civic and religious freedom,"[34] and foreigners don't have to serve in the military. In "Bocca" (the famous Genoese neighborhood in Buenos Aires discussed in chapter 3),

it is a wonderful thing to see that swarm of workers, some intent on *saladeros* or *barraccas*, warehouses of products, others anchored in the river or engaged in forge works or working as carpenters and caulkers, necessary professions for the repair and construction of those fleets which are always in motion, now pushed by the wind, now by the current, and now dragged by horses.[35]

Virgilio quotes extensively from Paolo Mantegazza's book *Rio de la Plata e Tenerife, Viaggi e Studi,* whose first edition came out in 1867. The famous Italian anthropologist and congressman was extremely fascinated with Argentina and the Rio de la Plata and thought that Italy could find nowhere more suitable land for its emigrants than in Rio de la Plata. He observed that in the city of Buenos Aires, 45 percent of the European immigrants were Italian. Furthermore, many professors at the University in Buenos Aires were Italian, and so were the doctors throughout the city. The climate, according to Mantegazza, was very similar to southern Italy, and the quality of the air and water were excellent. Meat was so abundant, he remarks, that with the leftovers that are given to the dogs, one could feed all the poor people in Ireland. In Argentina one may see many Italians who in their own country would have led a miserable life and "go confidently to the new lands and find wealth and happiness there."[36] Unfortunately, many Italian journalists and public officers tried to discourage emigration to Argentina, thus damaging not only the individuals and their families but also the Italian economy, which would greatly benefit from emigration. Virgilio argues that when the Italian peasants returned to their native regions, they acted as a stimulus for those who remained, who wanted to emulate them. The returning emigrants acquired in the new country a different, more entrepreneurial mentality and brought back to their villages "those seeds of continuous activity, of commercial calculation, of industrial prudence that are typical of men who have always lived amid business."[37] Thus, the returning emigrant may contribute to refashion the "Italian race": "he will have a considerable influence in tempering the Italian race more suitably."[38] According to R. De la Ville, consul of Argentina, the worst defect of Italian people was their laziness and lack of productivity, but when these individuals were transplanted to the Plata region, awed by the feverish activity of their compatriots, they developed a strong desire to improve their condition through productive labor, thus becoming extremely hard-working and industrious. Italians in Argentina were very successful: in addition to shipping, livestock, and commerce, most faculty members of humanities and sciences at the University in Buenos Aires were Italian. The first chair of economics in Argentina was held by an Italian, and many architects, painters, and sculptors came from Italy as well. The consul observed that almost all the vegetable gardens that provided the city of Buenos Aires with fresh produce were owned by Italians and that most of the coastal and fluvial navigation was managed by Ligurians. Virgilio concludes with a quotation from the war minister of France, who explained to the Parliament that every individual who is transplanted to Algeria costs to the state about 8,000 liras, half of what it would cost to support these colonists on French territory. Therefore, it makes no economic sense to colonize either internally or externally. Instead, the governments should let people settle wherever they prefer, as happens with the "free or voluntary colonization," which Virgilio defines "alla ligure," Ligurian style (90).

The Italian "peaceful colonization" extended beyond Argentina and included the adjoining nation of Uruguay. In Montevideo in particular, Italians controlled entirely the maritime and fluvial commerce. The consul of Uruguay stated that "from the deep-sea ships to the small boats in the harbor, from the shipowners, consignees, and shippers, to the captains, sailors, and carpenters...all belong to one or the other Rivieras of Liguria."[39] He noted that Ligurians usually settled there with their families, and they did so in part to dodge the mandatory military draft, which at that time could last several years. Virgilio calculated that about twenty thousand Italians were in the Plata region to avoid the draft. If the Italian government were to promulgate an amnesty, one third of them would probably return home, thus bringing with them significant capital that the new nation badly needed. Uruguay was a country with lots of potential. Unfortunately, the native population neglected "industries, contenting themselves with accumulating the riches that come from the natural gifts of that country with little effort."[40] The air quality was excellent and the soil extremely fertile, creating a healthy environment for both humans and animals. In fact, the wools from Uruguay were among the most valuable on the global market. Unlike the *pampas* of Argentina, in Uruguay the terrain is not completely flat, and the gentle hills of that landscape may have reminded Italian emigrants of their native country.

The main reason Italians preferred to settle in the Plata region was the relatively high salaries, which allowed a family to set aside a part of their income and save enough money to start a business of its own. Both governments and private citizens created agencies that helped new immigrants cope with the initial problems they might encounter, like the Sociedad Protectora de la Emigration, established in Buenos Aires in 1855. Unlike what happened in many English colonies, where the immigrants were lured into signing contracts that forced them to work for very low salaries, in the Plata region the public administration made sure that new immigrants were not exploited. In Montevideo, a government agency received the requests from the landowners of the interior and put them in touch with the new immigrants. The Oficina Central de Immigration in Montevideo published detailed information on the job market and offered free legal assistance to the labor force, protecting their interest against those employers who might try to take advantage of the newly arrived. Workers were in great demand, in both Uruguay and Argentina, and this contributed to creating a market that was favorable to new immigrants. Virgilio mentions an article that appeared on March 14, 1867, in *La Tribuna*, a newspaper from Montevideo, comparing the salaries and cost of living in the Plata region and Europe that leaves no doubt as to where workers would find more favorable conditions. The Consul of Argentina in Milan, Paolo Stampa, had tried to inform the Italian public about the real economic situation in his country, but many protectionist Italian businessmen and landowners protested, and the local authorities were forced to intervene and suspend his activities.

Toward the end of the book, Virgilio deals more explicitly with the main reasons that motivated him to write. Liguria, he confesses, is the Italian region that benefited the most from emigration, and "our country owes a large part of its wealth to it" (100). The constant flow of emigrants to South America contributed to give "impetus for shipbuilding, an industry that rewards those employed by it with high wages."[41] In addition to mariners and officers, many other economic sectors benefited from this situation, including insurance agencies, brokers, and those who provided food for passengers and crews. In 1867 alone, one hundred ships left from Genoa for the Rio de la Plata, carrying not only passengers but also all kinds of merchandise, including olive oil, pasta, rice, and wine destined in great part for the local Italian population. Shipyards all over Liguria benefited from this boom, with 130 ships currently under construction. These results are to be attributed, for the most part, to emigration: "Emigration made possible, thanks to passengers who paid for their tickets, for ships to go the Argentina, when the demand for our products was still small."[42] Emigration gave the first impetus to trade, and in many cases Italians in Argentina helped finance the construction of new and larger ships, creating a constant exchange of people, goods, and capital between the two distant shores. After considering all these statistics, Virgilio states: "There is no solid maritime trade, if first there is no emigration and numerous establishments of fellow citizens abroad."[43] He suggests that the export of wool from Uruguay and Argentina may contribute to developing new woolen mills in northern Italy. At this time, Italians purchased most of their wool clothes from England, Belgium, and France, for a total of over 80 million per year. Thus, he concludes: "Without colonies, there is no real trade, there is no thriving navy, no industrial activity, and therefore no prosperity of the State."[44] The history of Genoa, which in the Middle Ages had created colonies throughout the Mediterranean and beyond, shows that to develop a robust trade with other countries, it is necessary to be present in the territory: the ports that attract more trade are those where there are more emigrants.

The Italian economist strongly opposes any direct state intervention, similar to what France and Portugal attempted to do: "If Italy had a direct dominion over Montevideo and Buenos Aires, all the prosperity of those colonies, all the advantages that our nation currently derives from them, would vanish."[45] Virgilio agrees that Italian emigrants need government assistance in those countries where the principles and freedom and justice are not respected, but in the Rio de la Plata region Italian citizens are welcome and find there the most favorable conditions to settle and prosper. Nevertheless, the love for their country remains strong, and the ties between the Italians abroad and their mother country are not severed. The great number of returning emigrants and the constant flux of capital from Rio de la Plata toward Italy show that Italy is not forgotten, and the love for the native country is often enhanced by distance. Thus, in conclusion, Virgilio dismisses the "imperialist" model that Italian nationalism and Fascism would try to implement through colonialism during the first half of the twentieth century. He quotes the famous Italian patriot and liberal thinker Cesare Balbo, who thought that the epoch of English-style colonialism had come to an end. On the contrary, "the glory, the gain of the mother nations, does not lie in keeping their daughters in political and commercial dependence, but precisely in having common blood, names, languages, and customs in them" (112).[46]

The appendix of Virgilio's volume includes a section devoted to "La questione dell'Emigrazione nel Parlamento Italiano" (The question of emigration in the Italian parliament), with speeches delivered by various congressmen. The first one is Ercole Lualdi (1826–90), one of the most important industrialists of Lombardy. He strongly opposed Cavour's and Virgilio's liberalism because he thought it would destroy Italian industry and vehemently criticized emigration, which he saw as having reached truly saddening proportions (117). He feared that "if we go at this rate, we will lack the men necessary to work the land and develop the industry."[47] The congressman Antonio Arrivabene (1801–77) responded that emigrations are more beneficial to the country and should not be limited, except those that concern minors, which he called "tratta dei bianchi" (the trade of whites; 120). He denounced the associations that recruited children in the Italian countryside, where for a few liras they bought children aged seven or eight or up to fifteen and sixteen. These children were brought to London and New York, where they lived in horrible conditions and were treated like slaves. Since begging was prohibited in those countries, they were given an organ-grinder to play all day long, with the expectation that people would give them money. If they didn't bring enough of it to their masters, they were beaten and left without food. Another representative, Stefano Castagnola (1825–91), agreed that the exploitation of children must be stopped, but he argued that there is a different kind of emigration that is very beneficial to the country. Castagnola (who also was from Genoa) observed that if the region of Liguria today finds itself in a state of relative prosperity, that is due in no small part to emigration (123). He added that most emigrants, as soon as they manage to save enough money, return to their mother country. Usually, no one leaves his or her homeland with the intention of never returning, as Congressman Lualdi argued.

Another important document included in the Appendix is an excerpt from the letter that Paolo Stampa, consul of Argentina, wrote to the director of a newspaper in Treviso, a city in the Veneto. Stampa states that the peasants who arrived in Argentina were assigned several hectares of land and a substantial sum of money, which they were required to return—only in part—after four years. In addition, immigrants were transported free of charge from Buenos Aires to the province of Santa Fe. There, the worker shared the crop in equal parts with the landowner. Both men and women were very well paid in Argentina, including seamstresses and domestic workers. A female factory worker in Italy was paid on average forty cents a day, while in Argentina she received no less than five Italian liras. The cost of food was very reasonable, and Stampa remarked that no hospital in Argentina ever turns down a person who needs care: "Medical assistance is free and more than satisfactory."[48] Virgilio includes some passages from the Constitution of Argentina, stating that "Foreigners enjoy in the territory of the confederation all the rights of the citizen…they are not obliged to accept citizenship…they may obtain citizenship after two years of unin-terrupted residence in the confederation."[49]

In conclusion, Virgilio's voice was one of the most eloquent and authoritative in promoting emigration toward the Rio de la Plata region. His words were echoed by Paolo Mantegazza, who traveled extensively to South America and even attempted to create his own colony in the region of Salta, in northern Argentina, where he also met his future wife. Mantegazza embodied, I believe, the characteristics described by Virgilio in his book: a doctor by training, he showed the entrepreneurial features necessary to succeed in Argentina. He admired Argentine political lead-ers because they reminded him of the chaotic but exciting times when Italy was still being unified and politics was not a professional career but a passion that one would pursue for a limited time while cultivating other intellectual interests, like poetry, philosophy, and the natural sci-ences. Italy had transitioned too rapidly from the lyrical, romantic poetry of Risorgimento to the rational, objective prose of post-unification. The search for truth was replacing the idealistic impetus that had inspired the men and women of Risorgimento. Just a few years after unification, the country seemed already old and the intellectuals who had fought on the barricades, like Mantegazza did in Milan against the Austrians, sailed to America hoping to find not only economic opportunities but also a chance to reinvent themselves, away from the restraints that seemingly did not exist in a young "barbaric" country like the one that Domingo Faustino Sarmiento had depicted in his seminal book *Civilization and Barbarism*.

CHAPTER TWO

The Anthropologist as Entrepreneur: Paolo Mantegazza's Real and Imaginary Journeys to South America

> *Wretched is the country that does not have its own distant*
> *land, where violent and impatient people can migrate; where*
> *the comets of civil society can err, where the mentally and*
> *physically sick can restore their health.*
>
> —Paolo Mantegazza, *Rio de la Plata e Tenerife*

In this chapter I examine two works that Paolo Mantegazza (1831–1910) wrote shortly after Italian unification in 1861. The first is a travel book titled *Rio de la Plata e Tenerife: Viaggi e Studi,* published in 1867. At that time, Mantegazza was a member of the Italian Parliament, a professor of pathology at the University of Pavia, and one of the most prominent figures in Europe's scientific scene.[1] The second is titled *Il Dio ignoto,* an epistolary novel published in 1876 in which the narrative is split between two protagonists: Attilio, a young Italian lawyer, recounting his ten-year journey through South America to his friend Giovanni, who has recently graduated from medical school and has instead decided to remain in Italy and to pursue a career as a physician and researcher. I argue that the fictional text allows the reader to discover the profound and partially unconscious motivations that inspire the young doctor to travel to South America in the first place. As Fredric Jameson shows in *The Political Unconscious,* when the author's ideology is articulated in a novelistic form, the ideological conflicts are fully developed and ultimately reconciled in a truly utopian fashion.[2] The style of Mantegazza's first book takes a more factual approach because it was not only meant to entertain his bourgeois readers but also to inform Italian emigrants, entrepreneurs, and politicians about the opportunities that the Rio de la Plata region had to offer. In *Il Dio ignoto*, on the other hand, Mantegazza could fully articulate, through the actions of his fictional hero, the complex and often contradictory ideologies that inspired the Italian "conquest" of Argentina.[3] The dream of subduing the indigenous populations while affirming the superiority of European civilization displayed in Mantegazza's work made me rethink the initial hypothesis that had guided my research, based on the juxtaposition between diaspora and colonialism.[4] As I hope to demonstrate, there is a continuity between turn-of-the-century liberal intellectuals like Mantegazza and Virgilio, both strong supporters of "free" emigration, and those Nationalist and Fascist authors who instead preferred military-type invasions. The link, I would argue, is the racist ideology, camouflaged as scientific discourse, that permeated even the most progressive Italian and Western scientific discourse at the turn of the century.

Mantegazza is less known to English readers than his fellow student Cesare Lombroso (1835–1909), but both men studied and taught medicine at the University of Pavia for many years and shared a similar vision of human nature.[5] While Mantegazza traveled extensively through South America, where he witnessed the extermination of what he considered inferior races, Lombroso made similar observations while working as a doctor in the southern Italian region of Calabria, where the Piedmontese army was conducting a ruthless military campaign to eliminate the *briganti*, mostly impoverished peasants who revolted against the newly created Italian nation. "Brigante o emigrante," either brigand or emigrant: those were the choices that southern Italian peasants faced after the unification, as Francesco Saverio Nitti explained in a famous essay.[6]

In a letter dated April 20, 1854, the young doctor wrote to his friend Luigi Medici that he did not want to go South America to practice medicine but "to attempt a financial enterprise that I hope will be very successful."[7] Inspired by the German naturalist Alexander von Humboldt, Mantegazza thought that the best way to know the world and human nature was by studying "la società viva" (the living society) and "viaggiare tutto il mondo" (traveling the whole world), instead of reading books in his own studio.[8] More than ten years later, in the introductory essay of *Rio de la Plata e Tenerife*, titled "Fede di nascita del libro," Mantegazza explains what motivated him to undertake that journey and write about it. The paragraph is worth quoting in its entirety:

Italy has already had close commercial and colonial ties with the Argentine Republic for many years, and we would like to see them made even more intimate and warm. In that country there is a great future for those among us who were born into the slums of our cities or who were suddenly afflicted with an economic or moral disaster. The change of climate alleviates much suffering, as does emigration purge and heal many people. Wretched is the country that does not have its own distant land, where violent and impatient people can migrate; where the comets of civil society can err, where the mentally and physically sick can restore their health. When emigration is not an escape, neither is social revenge, nor hunger; it is a remedy that maintains the power and agility of the spirit and body of nations; and Italy cannot find a more suitable land for its emigrants than in Rio de la Plata. The beauty of the climate, the profound sympathies of Argentines for us, and the long traditions of many centuries call us to the lands blessed by the genius of Columbus and by one of the most attractive smiles of the southern hemisphere. Indeed, we see that forty-five percent of European emigration to Buenos Aires is Italian; and if you consult the latest figures from the National Register of the State of Buenos Aires you will see that Italians live long lives in those districts. Many who would have dragged apathetic, poor, or dissatisfied lives here in Italy have rebuilt themselves with new energy in those countries, living rich and blessed lives in the new world. I am not speaking of the few who are sick in the brain or heart and emigrate to flee from themselves, as they always blaspheme and curse every land in which they live and every sky they live under. My book is neither an indiscriminate praise nor an expression of contempt of an intolerant foreigner; it is the simple and straightforward expression of the truth; and to the most scrupulous sincerity of the traveler, I uphold myself as an honest man's right. I hate a panegyric even when it is directed at the sky or to the earth; even when it is inspired by passion and not greed.[9]

Argentina is presented as a hospitable country blessed with a gentle climate, where Italians who were either born in unfortunate conditions or were struck by a moral or economic downfall may find a second life. The emphasis is both on the necessity and opportunity of remaking Italians: "rifatti a nuova energia" (rebuilt with new energy) is the expression Mantegazza uses. Just like a change of climate may heal a weakened organism, emigration may "purge and heal many nations." The metaphors used by Mantegazza are the same that one finds time and time again in other contemporary European authors, based on an "organicist" interpretation of society. When the body of the nation is sick, it needs to expel those elements that prevent it from establishing a healthy equilibrium: it is a therapy that keeps the nation vigorous and young. However, one also notices in Mantegazza's introduction some of the contradictions that characterize the Italian philosophy of emigration at the turn of the century: on the one hand, Argentina is viewed as a welcoming country; on the other, Mantegazza cannot avoid describing it as a sort of "dumping ground" for those who were born into the slums of poverty. At best, it becomes a place where "gli ammalati nel sangue o nel cervello" (the sick in blood or mind) may find a "guarigione" (recovery) and be born again.

In the preface of the novel *Il Dio ignoto*, Attilio is depicted as a talented individual who in Italy may have lived a "vita sonnecchiosa" (apathetic life), while in Argentina he became extremely successful. His motivation to leave for the American continent, as he explains to his friend, is the desire to explore new places and create his own life:

> I have two strong arms and the courage to do anything. The unknown fascinates me; the unknown exhilarates me; the thought that after landing in America I will not know where to go, or how to earn my bread, tempts me greatly. And then here I would not fit; our country is unhappy....You cannot climb high without courting our tyrants, and the life of the clerk nauseates me, and that of the lawyer I do not like. I have had many misfortunes in my family...I need to go far, far away.[10]

Contrary to Giovanni, who believes in God, Attilio thinks that one should create his own ideal on earth, and Argentina is the perfect place to pursue that goal, because it is a virgin land, "non ancora guastato dagli uomini e dagli Dei" (not yet spoiled by men or by Gods; 9).

In the preface of *Rio de la Plata e Tenerife*, Mantegazza advocates an emigration that is not characterized by "fuga," "fame," and "vendetta sociale" (escape, hunger, and social revenge), but in the same paragraph he suggests expelling the poor, the violent, and the restless. During the years of mass migration, even the most liberal and progressive Argentine intellectuals and politicians who had strongly supported European immigration accused the Italian government of discharging on the shores of the Rio de la Plata the scum of Italy: individuals who could not make a valid contribution to Argentine society but on the contrary were the source of its most pressing moral and political problems.[11] Furthermore, Mantegazza's introduction reveals another problem that will continue to resurface in the decades to come: the idea that Argentina represents for Italy a "terra lontana e quasi sua" (distant land and almost ours), which will be the source of many misunderstandings and conflicts between the two countries. In the eyes of liberal intellectuals like Mantegazza and Virgilio, emigration was a valid alternative to colonization and imperialism: an outlet, or *valvola di sfogo*, for countries that were experiencing demographic growth and, often, violent social conflicts. Nevertheless, the "peaceful" expansion that emigration seems to embody often conceals a desire to silently conquer a land that even progressive scientists like Mantegazza could not help depicting as inferior and therefore needing to be civilized. The references to Christopher Columbus and the echo of "long traditions" mentioned in the book's preface that are luring Italians to travel to the American continent are ambivalent because, as Tzvetan Todorov and other cultural critics after him observed, the Genoese explorer embodied the beginning of a "long tradition" of exploitation and extermination of the native population.[12] Nevertheless, the existence of "vincoli di parentela" (bonds of kinship) between Italy and Argentina that in Mantegazza's view are bound to become more and more "intimi e caldi" (intimate and warm) suggests that the Italian anthropologist aims to go beyond the narrow boundaries of the recently unified nation that inspired the men and women of the Risorgimento and create a "greater Italy." The diaspora toward Rio de la Plata that he is promoting seems to point to a socialist utopia of universal brotherhood. As we will see, Mantegazza was critical of socialism and communism, because in his view they would deprive individuals and society of their most precious gift: liberty.[13]

Mantegazza argues that the result of these intense commercial exchanges, "vediamo poi tradotta dinanzi ai nostri occhi nei marmorei palazzi di Genova" (we then see it translated before our eyes into the marble palaces of Genoa; 11), at the time the main Mediterranean port from which Italian goods and emigrants were departing for South America. The author's political views, based on the principles of *laissez faire* capitalism, emerge very clearly when he states, on the same page, that the commercial exchanges between Italy and South America will continue to increase, provided that "dagli individui si voglia fare e dal governo si lasci fare" (people are willing to do it and that the government allows them to; 11). In other words, the Italian government should stay out of the business of emigration, as the liberal economist Virgilio—quoted approvingly by Mantegazza—advocated in his publications. The Italian doctor adds:

> Nor does the exchange of two nations that know and value each other begin or end in commerce. We still have the exchange of sympathy and affection: we already have in Italy many Italian citizens who owe half their blood to Argentine women; and in Buenos Aires we see in the people a large vein of blood that is ours and the best. These are the seeds from which universal brotherhood will be passed on to our later grandchildren.[14]

Mantegazza practiced what he preached: during one of his trips to South America he married Jacobita Tejada de Montemayor, a fifteen-year-old girl from a wealthy family in Salta, a city in northern Argentina, with whom he had five children.[15]

One final consideration needs to be made about the passage quoted above: Mantegazza's claim that his book is "la semplice e schietta espressione del vero" (the simple and straightforward expression of truth). To understand the importance of this statement one must realize that he was writing in the age of "Verismo e Positivismo" (Verism and Positivism), Vittorio Spinazzola argued in his seminal book on the movement the Italian literary movement of Verism and its connections with French Positivism.[16] Thus, Mantegazza shows a desire to go beyond "ogni panegerico" (every panegyric), even when it is "inspirato dalla passione e non venduto" (inspired by passion and not greed). In other words, he is acknowledging that the age of Romanticism that characterized the Risorgimento is finished and that the "poetic" idealizations of that epoch must be replaced with a more objective and "prosaic" observation of reality. When, in the same years, Giovanni Verga and Luigi Capuana began theorizing what a new Italian "Verist" literature might look like, they both used the same concepts evoked by Mantegazza: "sincerità" and "vero" (sincerity and truth).[17] Interestingly, truth is one of the ideals advocated in the final pages of the novel *Il Dio ignoto*. Although neither Attilio nor Giovanni pursues it, the narrator presents it as the missing element of a new religion based on *buono*, *bello*, and *vero*:

> You embraced the good, you who have the most compassionate and peaceful heart, you who have found the angel of goodness. I am more sensual and embraced the beautiful. God for God; deserving of each other. It is a

shame that there is no third friend or brother, who adores truth; because in this case, sublimating our three religions to an Olympic ritual height, we could say that we worship only one God, the ideal, manifesting itself in three entities: the true, the good, and the beautiful.[18]

I would argue that Mantegazza shared with contemporary writers like Verga a similar objective: expanding the mental horizon of bourgeois readers by making them realize that even individuals who are socially and culturally distant from them ultimately share the same common humanity. Verga accomplished that objective by portraying Sicilian society through a popular narrator whose worldview is similar to the peasants of his native land. Mantegazza's "quadri di natura umana" (pictures of human nature) scattered throughout the travel narrative aim at "farvi sentire compassione per l'indiano che è pur nostro parente; amore per il creolo che è nostro fratello" (making you feel compassion for the Indian who is our relative; love for the Creole who is our brother; 12). Whereas statistical data are necessary to fulfill the need for objective and scientific knowledge, and descriptions of natural landscapes are indispensable to make the audience recreate in their own imagination exotic places that they would never be able to visit, the portraits of human nature "satisfy the other burning need of the heart to know and love many human beings, who under other skies and in other lands are born and die like us and suffer and hope like we do." There are, however, limitations to how far one's love for a common humanity may stretch. As I show in the following pages, despite the idealistic view displayed in the introduction, Mantegazza—like most of his contemporaries—believed that human "races" should be understood in a strictly hierarchical order and that indigenous Americans, although similar to "Caucasians," could not be placed at the same level as their European "cousins."

Observing and Theorizing Latin American Culture

Mantegazza's Eurocentric view is reflected throughout the book, which provides a personal overview of Latin American culture aimed at justifying what I call the "re-conquest" of the continent. While Mantegazza acknowledges that the new nations that were currently developing in America were based on the extermination of the native populations—an "original sin" that continues to loom over them and cannot be easily erased—the gaze of their citizens is focused on the future that progress will bring about, not on the past:

> In the cradle of South American society there is an original sin, and after three and a half centuries its fatal influence is still felt: on that cradle, however, shone a radiant beam of courage and freedom, and that glory always shines in the history of those people and more than ever illuminates their future.[19]

Thus, Mantegazza's vision is diametrically opposed to Walter Benjamin's angel of history who, propelled forward by the allegorical storm of progress, has his face turned toward the landscape of destruction that it is constantly piling up behind at his feet.[20] His vision also differs from Giovanni Verga's who in the same years was constructing his great narrative cycle on the metaphor of the "vanquished" who were being submerged by the "tidal wave" of progress.[21] Indeed, the feature that the Italian doctor admired the most in Americans is their faith in progress and their ability to reinvent themselves and their societies.

According to Mantegazza, the inhabitants of South America inherited from their Spanish ancestors a sense of courage, independence, and self-reliance that was difficult to find in Europe:

> Those who conquered a new world had to have the tenacity to want, so strong in character and tenacious in opinion, to leave their rich treasures for the children of their children....In America every man is more individual than we are and, dare I say, there is a greater number of brilliant and talented men there than there are in many of our European countries.[22]

Since they usually received very little from their governments, Americans were supposedly forced to rely on their own strength and resources to succeed. Climate, however, also played a major role in the formation on the national character, as many European philosophers had argued, from Herodotus to Montesquieu: "Dove il sole dardeggia infuocato, molta parte dell'umana attività andò esaurita nelle lotte contro il calore" (Where the scorching sun darts, much of human activity was exhausted in the struggles against the heat; 20). In northern Europe, where the climate is more forbidding, people tended to be more industrious, while the inhabitants of regions gifted with warmer temperatures supposedly became "natu-rally" lazy. Lombroso's disciple Alfredo Niceforo used a similar argument when he presented his own theories in the famous book *Italiani del Nord e Italiani del Sud*, published in 1900.[23] Another factor that was said to shape the character of South American people was the coming together of differ-ent ethnic groups: indigenous Americans, Africans, and Europeans pro-duced a variety of physical traits that could not be found in Europe. The supposedly main feature of South Americans, however, is summarized by Mantegazza in one phrase: "una vivace e indolente gaiezza" (a lively and indolent gaiety; 24), the consequence of living in a natural environment that is usually plentiful and generous and does not require a lot of effort to secure its fruits. His views reflect what the Argentine thinker and statesman Faustino Sarmiento had written about twenty years earlier in his influen-tial book *Facundo*, which Mantegazza almost certainly read: "The fusion of these three families has resulted in a homogeneous whole, distinguished for its love for idleness and incapacity for industry....The American races live in idleness, and demonstrate an incapacity, even when forced, to apply themselves to hard, uninterrupted work."[24]

Americans refused the concept of inherited nobility of which Spaniards were so proud and replaced it with a new form of aristocracy based on individual strength and intellectual abilities: "the mixing of human races has created a new aristocracy in America and has founded new hierarchies that rest on one solid basis: that of the organism, that of the brain struc-ture."[25] Despite the mixing of different ethnic groups, a "natural" hierar-chical distinction between the three main races remained, according to Mantegazza, which shows his internalized racism. When slavery was abol-ished, the African and native population remained in a subaltern condi-tion, unable to reach a higher level of civilization. Although the notion of nobility was for the most part eradicated by the revolutions that led to inde-pendence from Spain and replaced by a more democratic vision of society, the hierarchical racist view persisted. As Mantegazza writes: "the poorest white man laid bare in the face of nature can immediately persuade every-one that he is superior to the prognathous Negro and the muddy Indian."[26]

Mantegazza claims that the adjective most commonly used in South America to describe a white person is "decente." The term endows the individual with "a blazon of nobility that makes him equal to the president of the republic and makes any ambition possible."[27] Even if some of his ancestors were African or Native American, that does not matter, provided that he "looks white" and is therefore able to conceal any sign of "black" or "yellow" ancestry (27). At that time, a true Argentine bourgeoisie did not exist. People were divided into two main categories: "decentes" and "cholos," a mix of European and Native Americans. A *cholo* may become a *decente* if he is white enough and capable of concealing his origins with a proper education. Mantegazza, however, believed that racial distinctions in America were just a temporary phenomenon that would become obsolete as people continued to marry across racial lines: "When the continuous intertwining of families will have made American society only one color, the aristocratic criterion of blood will also disappear, and only ingenuity, money, and honesty will distinguish men from one another."[28]

In a society where aristocracy has lost most of its prestige, education becomes crucial: Mantegazza remarks that Americans were eager to absorb and imitate, often in a superficial way, every new custom from the European continent, especially France. Whereas Europeans desired to discover the uncontaminated nature of the American continent, Americans wanted to travel to Europe and experience the tumultuous life of its modern cities. While in Europe poetry was being challenged by the rise of the novel, poetry continued to occupy a prominent position in America.[29] In Vichian fashion, Mantegazza argues that poetry is the genre that best suits a young nation, as the individual sentiments are more directly and freely expressed, regardless of the formal literary training one may have received. Every American nation has many poets, according to Mantegazza, who are usually "fecondi, facili e ricchi d'ispirazione e di cuore" (fertile, simple, and rich with inspiration and heart; 34). Prose, on the other hand, is less cultivated, and even when Americans wrote historical narratives and legal documents, they tended to adopt a poetic style. Also on this subject, the Italian traveler seems to reflect the ideas of Sarmiento, who argued that the poetic inclination of Argentine people originates from the physical features of the landscape: "There exists, then, an underlying poetry, born of the natural features of the country and the unique customs it engenders. Poetry, to awaken, needs the spectacle of beauty, of terrible power, of immensity, of expanse, of vagueness, of incomprehensibility....The result is that the Argentine people are poets by character, by nature" (*Facundo*, 60–61).

Mantegazza also observes that whereas in Europe politics had become a profession to which its practitioners were expected to devote all their time and energies, American statesmen enjoyed more freedom and were free to pursue many other interests: the president of Argentina at the time, Bartolomé Mitre, was a poet, historian, and general.[30] The main requirements for a young individual who wanted to start a political career were energy and courage. Thus, it was not unusual for a forty-year-old man to become president of his country. Members of the Parliament were not selected according to their social status and education, as in Italy. On the contrary, one could find doctors, shopkeepers, and even priests in the Argentine Senate. The first requisite was passion: "passion is the first spring of political action, as it must be in every young society."[31] Mantegazza was fascinated by the absence of bureaucracy and the many opportunities that young and gifted individuals enjoyed in America. The disregard for questions of social distinctions seemed to him to be an incentive for young emigrants to take risks and become more productive, thus contributing to economic advancements that would not be possible in a country like Italy. Another important characteristic of American society noticed by Mantegazza was the high position of women: "New balances were created in those countries and women found a more dignified position that better conforms with their nature."[32] Thus, in his view, women in American societies were bound to play a prominent role, both in the domestic and public sphere.

The first chapter of *Rio de la Plata e Tenerife* ends with an allegorical description of "la donna *porteña*," using the familiar term *porteño/porteña* to denote the inhabitants of Buenos Aires.[33] I use the term *allegorical* because the portrait constructed by Mantegazza does not describe a real woman but an idealized emblem of the most promising characteristics of Argentine society. This ideal woman that Mantegazza constructs represents an antidote against the Romantic heroine famously portrayed by Gustave Flaubert in *Madame Bovary*, published in 1856. He writes that the "la donna *porteña*" has Andalusian and French blood in her veins and possesses the art of seduction that Arab men appreciate in a woman. She is not as fragile as European upper-class women of that time. On the contrary, she is used to living outdoors, and her body has been fashioned by the strong winds and harsh sun of the *pampa*. She has strong hips from riding wild horses; she is the natural fruit of America, embellished and refined by a touch of European culture. Her eyes exude authority and self-confidence; her body is both strong and sensual. Argentine women are cultured: they play musical instruments; speak several languages; and enjoy fashion, theater, and promenades. "La donna *porteña*," according to Mantegazza, "embellishes the world around her with the happy gaiety of those who know they are powerful; seduces with confident grace; conquers with courage and holds firm the conquest with her beauty. She is a Greek Venus enhanced by modern civilization."[34] The Argentine woman dominates men with her perfection and plays a major role in society. Her social influence can and should increase because her role is to channel Argentina toward the cult of beauty and grace and away from profit and material wealth, which seemed to dominate everyone's mind in the American metropolitan capital. In conclusion, "la donna *porteña*" possesses all the natural qualities of a creature used to living in harmony with nature but is endowed with the refinements of a culture that is strong and vibrant and does not show the signs of physical and moral decadence that were beginning to emerge in Europe. The American woman envisioned by Mantegazza is both sensual and innocent, powerful and compassionate, cultured and refined, but has not lost the "sapore agresto della natura" (rural flavor of nature) that persists, pure and uncontaminated, in Argentina. "La donna *porteña*" is an allegorical construction that contains in her physical features and in her character all the regenerative qualities that Mantegazza saw embodied in Argentine culture. She is the cure for Western societies that were entering a period of decadence. With her strength and beauty, the *porteña* woman is capable of stirring men and her country toward higher goals. She is a secular and more sensual version of Dante's *donna angelicata* and conceals, underneath her stunning beauty, "il vero e il buono, che soli danno la vita" (the true and the good, which alone generate life; 42), because beauty is only capable of inspiring but cannot generate anything. "La donna *porteña*," Mantegazza suggests, would make an excellent wife and a caring mother. She would always nurse her own children—while at that time in Europe upper-class mothers preferred to hire wet nurses from the countryside. She is in touch with her own inner feminine nature, and even though her culture is not as sophisticated as in northern Europe, she is more balanced and capable of evolving and perfecting herself, like the societies of the Rio de la Plata.

Mantegazza used—probably unintentionally—a beautiful hendecasyllable to define Buenos Aires, a city of "belle signore, fango and *saladeros*" (beautiful ladies, mud, and *saladeros*; 48). *Saladeros* are the cycloptic slaughterhouses where hundreds of animals were killed and processed every day to obtain meat products for shipment overseas. Mantegazza's psychological portrait of *porteños* resembles how the aforementioned Italian anthropologist Alfredo Niceforo categorized southern Italians:

The inhabitants of Buenos Aires are lively but volatile, intrepid in struggle and tireless in rest. Lovers of all that shines, they excite easily and with even more ease do they forget. Of rapid and violent passions, they do not even know greed by its name. They are too obedient to the rule of fashion. Of awakened talents, there are already many first-rate poets in the country. Their character, full of small vices and great virtues, is one that lends itself to the hopes of the future.[35]

After dividing Italians into two different "races," *arii* in the North and *mediterranei* in the South, Niceforo presents a description of their *psicologia* that shows how certain cultural stereotypes were still deeply rooted in the scientific community at the turn of the century:

The brown Mediterraneans, inhabitants of Southern Italy, have, as the main principle of their psychology, an enormous excitability of their *ego*. They don't walk, they run; they don't move, they break in; they always have a fury to start and end, they love speed, noise, instability. They exaggerate everything....They have everything in relief, the gesture, the look, the word, the style, the exclamation; they quickly conceive because their *ego* flashes rapidly over everything, almost in a state of overexcitement, but they do not scrutinize anything; they are hypertrophic in their sentiments and intermittent in energy.[36]

The protagonist of *Il Dio ignoto*, Attilio, was not impressed when he saw the Argentine capital: "Buenos Aires seemed to me like a herd of dirty sheep, grazing in a sad and boundless plain."[37] Mantegazza's hero is an idealist, and although he eventually became financially successful in Argentina, he is disappointed to see how the inhabitants are so concentrated on making money:

Here they are all merchants, a republic without freedom and without justice, pride without science, sensualism without sentiment. Everywhere I see nothing but desecrations: the church defiled by speculators, the temple of letters desecrated by mediocre people and merchants; the sanctuary of the heart prostituted by cynicism and skepticism. I hoped to find another world, more poetic, more cheerful, more sincere, and instead I find the emaciated skeleton of a corrupt society, which covers the skinned bones with the pomp of luxury and the coarse enamel of imitation gold. Here too I find no faith or enthusiasm…but man is everywhere and always an animal so hypocritical and superficial![38]

The feverish atmosphere of the American city, however, ends up contaminating the idealistic lawyer, although initially he does not understand the reason for such an intense and continuous quest:

> I am inert by nature and habit, but all of a sudden I wake up and feel inside me a true explosion of projects, one more grandiose than the others, and it seems to me that my body may crash, like the crater of a volcano, which yields to the burst of lava and lapilli. And so, I throw myself head on to the conquest…to the conquest of what?[39]

The fictional protagonist of Mantegazza's novel shares with the author a strong fascination for Argentine women. He remarks that young women enjoy more freedom than in Italy. As a result, he claims, they develop a strong set of moral values and a sense of independence. They freely choose their husbands, without following their parents' orders, and before getting married they often had numerous male friends, as opposed to young Italian women, who don't have any direct knowledge of their partner before the wedding:

> Here morality is much greater than among us: young women, not bringing dowry to their husband, know they are loved for themselves only; and they freely choose their groom, without being forced by the parents to endure a tyrannical yoke. They love after having had many friends; they choose after having seen many men intimately, after having studied many characters; and it is for this reason that, after having given their hand to the groom, are always faithful to their life's companion. With us instead, how many times does one transition from the ferocious virginity of the monastery to adultery—of course passing through the gateway of matrimony.[40]

After a few weeks in the city, where his law school degree turns out to be worthless, Attilio finds a job as a clerk in a *saladero* located in the Italian neighborhood of La Boca. These processing plants were described as gruesome by European observers: every day, several hundred animals are killed and processed on the premises and at the end of the day the newly hired clerk prefers to return home on his horse because he cannot stand the smell of the slaughterhouse. Attilio falls in love with Dolores Perez, the beautiful daughter of the owner, a wealthy man of Spanish descent, but soon realizes that he will never be able to marry her unless his social status changes radically. Thus, he departs for the interior, which represents for a European man something similar to the Far West:

> I want to throw myself on a horse through the desert; I want to know the Indians and dominate them and have them make me their leader, I want to conquer the Pampa and Patagonia and return them to Argentine civilization. With the halo of *cachique* or General or legislator, I want to ask Dolores' parents for her hand in marriage.[41]

In the Heart of America: The Discovery of the Interior

Although he finds it difficult to be away from his love, Attilio realizes that if he wants to discover the real America he should not stay in Buenos Aires, because the European influence is so strong in the city that it is hard to detect the real American spirit. He finds a job opportunity in the province of Entre Rios, a region that became increasingly important as a link between Argentina and Brazil. Attilio is overwhelmed by the beauty of the landscape, so different and richer than the ones he had seen before, and he does not hesitate to compare it to an earthly paradise:

> Here, on the other hand, I was in the middle of an earthly paradise, and the trees, all new to me, were so beautiful that I could hardly choose the one that may offer a hospitable shadow for my meditation. The village seemed like a tiny thing in the middle of the gigantic nature that surrounded it, and the houses of men looked like children's games next to the *ombus, talas, fiandubays, and algarrabos*, which were the setting for them. And also the grass of the meadow was different from ours, so that the meadow seemed more like a forest, and the woods like a forest of giants made for a world bigger than the one in Europe. And on the flowers of that grass flew new butterflies and insects I had never seen before, and on the branches of the trees lay birds of every color, and the hummingbird, the true gem of the aerial world, rapidly flew to the *corollas* of the *palams*, from which it sucks the sweet nectar with its tongue.[42]

In *Rio de la Plata e Tenerife*, Mantegazza also chooses to focus on the province of Entre Rios, one of the most fertile and promising areas of Argentina. He quotes Domingo Faustino Sarmiento, founding father of Argentina: "Quel paese sarà un giorno il paradiso terrestre, il centro del potere e della ricchezza, la riunione più compatta di floride città" (That country will one day be a terrestrial paradise, the center of power and of wealth, the most compact meeting place of flourishing cities; 55).

The father of Attilio's girlfriend Dolores in *Il Dio ignoto* is a practical man, and when he learns that the young Italian man is an idealist in search for his "unknown god" he comments that he should look no further, because the new god is money:

> My dear mister Attilio, you are a great poet searching for the Unknown God, where you will never find him. For me, without much poetry or effort, I have found and had him for a long time. The Unknown God is money, the force of all forces, power of all powers.[43]

Despite his idealism, Attilio cannot resist the lure of becoming rich and powerful: "I feel invaded by the industrial genius and by the thirst for immediate earnings; and I enjoy finding myself in full harmony with the atmosphere around me."[44] By the end of the novel he will realize that the unknown god he was looking for is beauty, but initially he is persuaded that wealth is superior:

> There is perhaps only beauty that compares to the power of wealth, or comes close to matching its seductions, but it is too fleeting; wealth instead outlives even beauty and youth, it lives as long as we do and more than us, because it survives us and is passed on to the children of our children from its chalice full of inexhaustible sweetness.[45]

Attilio is attracted by the mysteries of the Buenos Aires Stock Exchange, where wealth is continually created and destroyed,[46] but he does not want to pursue financial speculations because he prefers the feeling of power that only modern industry can give to the entrepreneurs who embrace its challenges. The industrialist is like a military commander who leads the docile proletarian soldiers to the conquest of new global markets. Thus, in the mind of the Italian lawyer-turned-entrepreneur we see the emergence of two parallel images of conquest: the *cacique* who subdues and controls

the ferocious indigenous tribes of the interior, and the capitalist who trans-
forms the European immigrants into "un esercito di operai pacifici e tranquilli" (an army of peaceful and calm workers).

> I adore industry, big industry; the manufactories, in which hundreds of
> workers under the guidance of my gaze and gesture transform the mate-
> rial to create a new source of wealth for the country. I adore this art of
> guiding an army of peaceful and calm workers who, singing in chorus,
> bless the work in a healthy and well-ventilated workshop; I adore the com-
> ing and going of bales, commissions, buyers and sellers; I adore the power
> of being at the head of one of the first industries of the country, perhaps
> even creating it, and then to generate ten or one hundred others.[47]

Attilio is a lawyer and a humanist, but he also studied chemistry, and it is
his scientific background that enables him to create a new technique to preserve and ship to Europe the precious animal fats that are extracted from
the cows butchered every day in the *saladeros*. His invention rapidly trans-
forms him into a wealthy and famous man. Thus, he may finally marry
the beautiful, rich, and spoiled Dolores, who, "like her brothers, like her
fathers,...too will have children who will continue the pleasant traditions
of a brilliant idleness, happy and without a care in the world."[48] Attilio's
quest seems to follow the traditional trajectory from rags to riches: the god
of money of his father-in-law will give him the happiness he was searching
for. His beloved Dolores, however, suddenly dies of a heart attack and the
young Italian entrepreneur, desperate and heartbroken, takes on another
adventure in the interior of the country: "And I gallop, gallop, gallop, completely immersed into this infinite desert of yellowish grass, which surrounds me everywhere."[49]

Far from getting lost in the *pampa* and becoming a *gaucho*, as happens
to Enrico Mruele, the young Italian professor from Friuli whose story is
narrated in Claudio Magris's philosophical novel *Un altro mare*,[50] Attilio
undertakes his own "conquest of the desert"[51] based on the assumption
that the European "race" is superior and therefore its emissaries are enti-
tled to take over the territories that belong to the native people:

> Race; which is the safest, fairest, and most tyrannical criterion for assign-
> ing seats to the spectators in the great amphitheater of this sublunar world.
> The Argentine Constitution declares all citizens of the Republic equal

before the law; but alas, how many crowns of laurel and thorn does the world distribute every day without the law and even outside of the law! The mulatto and cholo can boast of being judged by the same judges, and put in the same prisons as white Americans and Europeans, but a mocking grin is enough, a "you all," a "you"; a nod of the head or a gesture of the hand is enough to mark them in the flesh, as if it were with a scorching iron, with the tacit and unreleased sentence that is on the lips and in the eyes of all: remember that you have black or yellow blood in your veins....Erasing these laws of the human heart is useless, because they are written in fiery characters in every fiber of man, and as long as the heart is made as it is today, the human hierarchies will change shape and move their center of gravity, but they will always be one of the fundamental cornerstones of every human society.[52]

The Gaucho, Symbol of a Vanishing Civilization

The people who inhabit the "campagna" of Entre Rios are *gauchos*. The term, Mantegazza explains, was originally used in a derogative sense, referring to what he calls "la feccia del popolo" (the scum of the people), born from the intermingling of different ethnic groups, but later the word referred to all the people from the countryside, who were totally different from those who lived in the cities. Although occasionally the two groups came together to defend common interests, they remained separate, as it happens with water and oil (64).

Mantegazza's portrait of the *gauchos* in *Rio de la Plata e Tenerife* is one of the most memorable parts of the book. Like most European travelers, his description of their lifestyle is ambivalent, showing great admiration for their independent and noble lifestyle, their courage and the total disregard for money and practical matters. On the other hand, the *gaucho* is the symbol of a vanishing culture that must disappear, if Argentina wants to become a modern nation:

Separated from friends and cities by immense distances, he has no other means of joining the common consortium of men than his horse; living on flesh that runs free and wild across the plains, he has no other means of obtaining food than his horse: true Arab of America, he has in this noble animal the most indispensable tool of life, a source of wealth, an inseparable friend while resting and working; in war and in peace. The *gaucho* spends more than half of his life in the saddle and often eats and dozes off in the saddle. On foot he walks poorly and drags his heavy spurs, whose immense wheels prevent him from walking as we do, he seems like a swallow forced to stay on the ground. A few years ago, the beggars of Buenos Aires were still seeking alms on horseback; and more than once I have seen the *gaucho* mount his horse to go to the back of the courtyard to draw water from the well.[53]

Mantegazza writes that as soon as a boy can stand on his own feet, he is placed in the saddle in front of his father and never leaves that place until he dies. As a result, the *gaucho*'s physical structure is profoundly altered by his being constantly on the horse: "The lumbar muscles and the others that keep the torso erect are so developed that they make onlookers perceive as monstrosities what for him is natural."[54] According to Mantegazza, every *gaucho* despises agriculture and all other forms of activity that would force him to stand or sit down. His clothing is very primitive and reflects his innate desire for freedom. The coat is a piece of textile roughly cut in the middle, the famous *poncho*. Instead of pants, he wraps another large piece of cloth around his waist, thus leaving his thighs free. On his legs, he wears *botas de potro*, rudimentary boots made from the skin of horses' legs. His house is equally primitive, usually a simple shed made of branches and reeds called a *rancho de totora*. The *rancho de estanteo* is a bit more elaborate, made of tree trunks plastered with mud. Some *gauchos* live in a *rancho de adobe*, built with bricks baked in the sun. The floor of the house is the same as the terrain that surrounds the dwelling. Being so simple, the *gaucho* can build his own house by himself in a short amount of time and leave it without regrets if he decides to do so. Inside, he has all the bare necessities: a simple table and a chair, an *aseador* to roast the meat, and a pot for his *mate*. Sometimes the bed is replaced by the saddle. The door is made of loosely connected boards or by a cowhide stretched on a wood frame. Often the *gauchos* do away with it. While they do not care at all about their dwelling, their horse is the object of the greatest attention and veneration:

> The *gaucho* often accepts the immense sacrifice of work to set aside some money and spend it to decorate his idol, so that often his house is without doors and without seats; but the reins of his *parajero* [honorific word that distinguishes a racehorse] are loaded with silver.[55]

As mentioned before, Mantegazza claims that *gauchos* are not interested in money. He quotes an expression that he heard people of the interior say multiple times: "For what does one want money? What I want is the friendship of men....I look for money to serve my friends...Money is made to spend."[56] *Gauchos* are not concerned with money and property in general because they live simply and are always certain to find hospitality and work whenever they need it: "The cruel question of hunger in that country is nonexistent. The poorest *gaucho* in the world will never lack a horse, and his people's hospitality will give him a roof and a *trincha de asado* everywhere he goes."[57] The personality of the *gaucho*, according to Mantegazza, is a mix between the haughtiness of the Spaniards and the profound love for freedom that was thought to be typical of Native Americans. A sense of almost natural equality characterized their society, which disdained wealth and social status. The sense of submission that was so common among Italian peasants would be inconceivable in the Argentine *pampa*, where men are free to move as they please. Family relations were also extremely loose. Only about 50 percent of the *gauchos* were formally married, and it was very common for a man to abandon his wife and children: "ciò che non fa gridare al tradimento e non fa spargere una lacrima" (That does neither make one scream at betrayal nor even shed a tear; 77). Mantegazza writes that women are free to marry again whoever they want. While men often forget about their children when they leave their wives, women continue to love and care for them. In fact, orphanages did not exist in the interior, and it was very difficult to convince any mother to give up her children for adoption. Young women are not concerned about their virginity, and promiscuity is common, even among young girls. Mantegazza writes that in the *pulperias*, the typical general stores of the interior, girls often offer their sexual favors in exchange for a piece of cloth or any other merchandise they may fancy. Reading Mantegazza's account, however, it is not clear how women and their children managed to survive in a society that was so unstable and nomadic. In *Facundo*, Sarmiento explains that their society was entirely dominated by men, while women did most of the work: "The women keep the home, prepare the meals, shear the sheep, milk the cows, make cheese and weave the coarse material with which they make clothing. All the production of the home, all the domestic chores is the woman's job, all the burden of work in on her" (56).

From 1829 to 1852, Argentina experienced Juan Manuel Rosas's brutal dictatorship, and Mantegazza describes Rosas as a *gaucho* of the *pampa*.

Although he was born and raised in the city and had wealthy parents, he preferred to stay in the country, and when he eventually returned to Buenos Aires, he started his own *saladero* and surrounded himself with a group of violent men. The new republic at that time was still unstable, and the Native Americans' raids took place very close to the city. Rosas was nominated "governador de la campaña" and managed to stir the people of the countryside against the city. In 1830 he was elected governor of Buenos Aires and gradually established a dictatorship. Mantegazza describes him as a coward and opportunist, but also as an intelligent and determinate man:

> Juan Manuel Rosas, or how his henchmen have called him at various times, the illustrious restorer of the laws, the hero of the desert, the father of the homeland, the column of the federation, the defender of American independence, the Washington of the south, the Norman prince, is a more than robust man, of masculine and profoundly sculpted features, with sunken eyes full of life. He has the agility of a squirrel and the force of a lion, and a tenacity for life that will make him die old and still strong. The arrogance of will served by low instincts is the moral formula that represents him; and in him the high intellect not cultivated by education was always fully wasted in service of tyranny.[58]

Mantegazza is convinced that dictatorships like Rosas's could develop in the American continent because it was so far from "civilized" Europe. He believes that modern ships and railways are the most powerful instruments of civilization and the progress brought about by the new immigration from Europe will inevitably lead to more democratic forms of government. A strong contrast still exists between the city and the countryside. When the author visited Santa Fe, which would become one of the main centers of the *pampa gringa*, the city was still undeveloped and exposed to the incursions of "savages." The *pampa*, however, is their territory. Even the word is indigenous: "significa piazza, terreno piano, grande pianura" (it means plaza, flat land, large plain; 330). Mantegazza is both fascinated and terrified by the desolate vastness of the landscape:

> The Pampa both terrifies and moves you with the sensuous idea of infinity, but in a very different way from the sea. At sea you almost always have before your eyes a boundless mass of water in front of which you seem to

be a piece of straw; but you still see the waves, which move, now agitated and foamy, now slow and lazy; you hear the wind screeching between the masts of your ship and inflating its sails. You move above a mobile ground, and although it gives you the impression of of an inexorable monotony, you still see a picture of life within which you are an active, reactive, combative part. —In the Pampa, on the other hand, you touch an infinity that does not move....Always the same light, always the same grass; the same earth; the same infinite circle that encloses your sight.[59]

At the time of his visit, the *pampa* was relatively safe, but until a few years earlier the colons were often sieged for several weeks by the Native Americans, relying only on dried meats and their domestic animals to survive. General Justo José de Urquiza, who was instrumental in defeating the dictator Juan Manuel de Rosas, signed various treaties with the Pampas and Araucano groups, thus making the territory more accessible.

An Italian Dream of Conquest

In *Il Dio ignoto,* Attilio joins Colonel Mansilla in an expedition to the land of the Indian *Ranqueles.* Mantegazza recreates the events depicted by Lucio Victorio Mansilla (1831–1913), an officer of the Argentine army, in his famous book *Una excursión a los indios Ranqueles,* published in 1875.[60] The colonel had been sent by the government to sign a treaty with the chief of the Ranqueles, known as Mariano Rosas, a name assigned to him by the general and dictator Juan Manuel Rosas. The book he wrote was praised by critics and received the prize of the International Geographical Congress of Paris in 1875. The fictional Italian hero, impressed with Mansilla, repeatedly praises his intelligence, courage, and physical appearance. The colonel embodied a modern, enlightened version of the Spanish *conquistador.* He was convinced, in fact, that when dealing with the indigenous populations, intelligence and diplomacy were to be preferred over pure military strength. In Mantegazza's portrayal of the military man one may notice how he captured his imagination:

He is a beautiful man of thirty-five, with a thick and long head of hair, with big and very black eyes: he bears a mustache, which merges into a black and shiny beard like silk, and which falls on his chest. He is very proud of his beauty, and wears a fantastic uniform, half-Indian and half-European, which seems to be deliberately made to enhance the elegance and agility of his Apollonian body. He has a scarlet scarf around his neck, a white poncho, from which the sleeves of a red uniform come out: he wears leather trousers and shiny grenadier boots with two large silver spurs. He's always smoking *cigarritos* and always takes mate, at any hour of the day or night, giving it up only when he sleeps or eats.[61]

In Mantegazza's fictional account, Attilio accompanies Mansilla to Rosas's *tolderia* with many gifts for the *cacique*, because he does not believe in engaging right away in a battle. Instead, he is convinced that "con essi giova meglio una politica accorta, piena di energia e di simulazione, perchè essi alla lor volta sono gli uomini più accorti e più dissimulati, ch'io mi conosca" (With them it is of more use to have a shrewd politics, full of energy and simulation, because they in turn are the shrewdest and most disguised men that I know of; 276). Even when the Native Americans become bellicose, he remains calm: "The savage twirled his long spear in the air and threw his blasphemies in the face of the Christian; the other, the civilized man, made his moral vigor felt with only his intelligence and a flash of his eyes."[62] The colonel shows a deep knowledge of the culture and is very careful in respecting the tribal hierarchies and customs. To reach the *tolderia* of the great chief Mariano Rosas the expedition must go through territories that are controlled by other *caciques*, like Ramon, described as a link between the so-called civilized races and the savages. The son of a Native American and a Christian from the Villa de la Carlota, he is tall and well built, has grey eyes, almost blonde hair, a high forehead, and a dignified demeanor. He dresses like an Argentine *gaucho*, loves Christians, is a goldsmith by profession, sows wheat, and rules his tribe with an iron fist (289). Once again, having some European blood in one's veins is a sign of superiority. Under Ramon's rule, indigenous communities began growing wheat and other cereals, which is traditionally considered a prerogative of civilized people. Food historian Massimo Montanari recounts that in ancient Mediterranean cultures people who grew wheat and baked bread considered themselves superior to those whose diet was mainly based on animal products.[63]

Mantegazza used Mansilla's narrative as a starting point, but he further developed it by making his character Attilio the new hero. After long negotiations, the two main Native American chiefs agree to sign a treaty of nonbelligerence with the Argentine nation, but Mariano Rosas requests that one member of the expedition remain with them for at least one year, to make sure that the agreements will be respected. Attilio volunteers to stay for at least two reasons: he is still heartbroken over the loss of his beloved Dolores, but he also wants to pursue a very ambitious plan: becoming a great chief and bringing about a reconciliation between the Native American and the Argentine governments, thus ending a conflict that had been going on for centuries. But his plans also conceal a desire to conquer, through his superior intellect and rhetorical skills, a population that he essentially considers inferior. No longer attracted by his father-in-law's monetary "unknown god," the pursuit of power becomes his new goal:

> I wanted to become an Indian through and through, dreaming of the glory of power, after having seen how arid the vanities of wealth are. I dreamt of making myself loved and feared by my companions, of dominating them with my courage and intelligence, of attempting their reconciliation with the other nearby tribes, forming a vast Confederation of the Pampa, independent from the Argentine government, but treating it as a friend and establishing itself as a free civilization alongside the Republic of the Plata. If money appeared to me only an instrument, power seemed enough by itself and the goal to which I aimed seemed to me enough to absorb all the energies of my thought, to appease all the passions of my heart.[64]

Attilio fully embraces the lifestyle of the Ranqueles and gradually gains their respect. On one occasion, using only his knife, he kills a gigantic jaguar that was threatening the village. His new life in the *pampas* has an intoxicating effect on him, and the feeling of freedom he experiences is accompanied by a delirium of power:

> When in those infinite deserts I felt the wind whistling in my long hair, tied around my head with only an Indian *vincha*, and felt the wild *pingo* that carried me trembling in a passionate thrill of motion, and his neighing and the stamping of his hoofs were the only sounds of that desert, wide and melancholy, I felt I was carried out of myself, and that I was double, triple the man; I felt transformed into one of the fantastic gods in Scandinavian legends.[65]

The Italian lawyer becomes such a skilled *gaucho* that the villagers bring the most untamable animals to "Don Attilio." When taming wild horses, Attilio applies the same technique that he uses with the Native Americans, carefully blending violence, strength, and generosity: "col terrore misto alle carezze lo facevo mio servo e mio amico, e con una carezza o un grido lo facevo tremare e sudare" (With terror mixed with caresses I made it my servant and friend, and with a stroke or a shout I made him tremble and sweat; 380). Both Dolores's father and the Argentine government, informed by Colonel Mansilla about his accomplishments, send Attilio money and precious merchandise that he liberally dispenses among the village chiefs, thus achieving the title of "honorary cacique."After bringing about a reconciliation between the Ranqueles and the Araucaras, Attilio reaches out to the most "ferocious" *cacique*, Calfucurà, nicknamed "il tigre del deserto" (the tiger of the desert), and after many unsuccessful attempts he manages to convince him to become part of the confederation. When he reaches the shores of the Rio Negro, where the three chiefs have agreed to meet, he experiences a sensation of power similar to when he was taming wild horses, which derives from his ability to control and manipulate these powerful men through his superior intellect. There are in total two thousand warriors at the historic gathering:

> Amid that infernal uproar, which seemed like a sabbath of shamans, in the heart of the field there were four men, who directed all those chaotic elements and in whose fire all the disheveled energies converged, which could either bring the fire of war to all of South America or usher in a new era of peace and civilization. Of those four men, three were Indians, one was European, and without ingenuity distinguishing me from their hierarchy, I placed myself first among them, and presided over them according to my inclination, contrasting the cruelties of one·to the dissimulation of another, and making in each one flash the sweet hope that he would one day be first among them.[66]

Throughout his stay with the Native Americans, Attilio also restrains his sexual desire, another way to discipline himself and control his emotions. Mariano Rosa's fourteen-year-old daughter is madly in love with the Italian lawyer and visits his room every night, covering him with kisses. When he first realizes that Katriel is interested in him, he is surprised, because he had never considered her a woman but only a wild creature belonging to the animal kingdom:

She didn't even seem like a woman to me, and even now she doesn't seem like a human creature for which you can feel tenderness or the desire to hold between your arms; she seems to me more like a gazelle, a guanaco, a little deer: anything but a woman. That simultaneously shy and fierce look of hers, that bronze color, those red cheeks and chin, those black moles on the knob of her face make her appear to me like a doll, an imaginary idol, something curious and strange…nothing else.[67]

After three long years, Attilio finally gives in to her passionate love and asks Katriel's father for his permission to marry her. Although he does not love her, he is moved by her total devotion and admires her great moral integrity and intelligence. Furthermore, a marriage with Rosa's daughter would help him realize his political goals of creating a federation and convincing the Native Americans to embrace agriculture and thus abandon, at least in part, their nomadic lifestyle:

When, between a man and a woman the mind can neither hold hands nor intertwine like the bodies do, nothing is left of love but voluptuousness, which is a fleeting thing; and when it is excessive, even boring. At times, however, to tell you the truth, I must add that my Katriel's moral stature and the great ambition for power that I felt within, to which I brought so much sentiment and thought, made her dear to me.[68]

Go North, Young Man!

Although both Mantegazza and his fictional hero Attilio feel superior to the uncivilized inhabitants of the pampa, they show respect and even admiration for both *gauchos* and native Americans because they are proud individuals who value their freedom and independence above anything else. As the anthropologist continues his voyage north to Corrientes and Paraguay, he encounters people with totally different psychological features, for whom he only shows contempt. Mantegazza offers an intriguing overview of the history and culture of Paraguay, calling it "un paese di schiavi" (a country of slaves) and "La piccola China Americana" (The little American China; 179). The inhabitants are courteous and hospitable, despite the sufferings they had to endure. For centuries, the country went through countless struggles and civil wars that prepared "the most propitious and fertile terrain for one of the most unprecedented and monstrous tyrannies of modern times."[69] The explanation that Mantegazza gives for the emergence of this oppressive dictatorship is, once again, racial: "the free and proud blood of the Castilian was diluted in Paraguay with the pale, drained blood of the Guaraní, born to serve and graze herds."[70] Thus was the cynical tyrant José Gaspar Rodríguez de Francia (1766–1840) able to manipulate his people how he wanted, almost like clay. Francia was so profoundly egotistical that he never got married, did not leave any offspring, and was hated by his people. The only two things that may save Paraguay and restore its freedom are a revolution and education, but Mantegazza doubts they will come because, as he puts it, the natives are "razze slombate ed eunuche di forza morale" (weak and eunuch races without moral strength). Ultimately, every nation is responsible for its own government: "degna della sua libertà e colpevole della sua abiezione" (worthy of its freedom and guilty of its degradation; 220). In the chapters of *Rio de la Plata e Tenerife* devoted to the Jesuit missions in Paraguay, Mantegazza remarks that missionaries brought peace and prosperity to the region even though they restricted individual freedom. The missions lasted until the end of the eighteenth century, when Charles III expelled the Jesuits. The Guaraní did not react, and Mantegazza blames the Jesuits for their passive behavior, since they did not teach their subjects the importance of freedom. Instead, they extinguished their vital energies with "una pastoja di comunismo" (a mash of communism; 214). Interestingly, Jesuits did not teach the Guaraní people how to speak Spanish, but they learned and perfected the indigenous language because they wanted the natives to become independent from Spain. The inhabitants were still grateful for all the help they received from the missionaries. Even when the book was written, according to Mantegazza, if a man was lost in the region and declared himself a Jesuit, the indigenous people would protect and help him. The author also includes diagrams comparing the number of inhabitants at the time of the missions. The demographic decline was astonishing: large missions that prospered with the Jesuits have become insignificant villages.

Throughout his travels to northern Argentina and Bolivia, Mantegazza notices a strong contrast between the beauty of the landscape and the abject conditions of its inhabitants. Salta is depicted as the most beautiful province in Argentina. People live very simply because nature is generous and provides them with whatever is necessary: they don't have to work, so they became apathetic. The author wonders: "And why would they ever occupy themselves with agriculture and industry, when nature sows and cultivates for them, heats the air, and prepares food for them? As long as the *algarrobo* is loaded with fruits, they will never lack food or beverages."[71] The inhabitants of the region spoke a Quichua language, like the one spoken in Peru, because they were in contact with the Incan empire.

Occasionally, the representation of the cities encountered along his journey seems almost surreal, as in the case of Tucumán:

> After so much going and so much following of the hills and plains, of the winding and narrow valleys or open in free fields; after a long silence of human voices, the capital of a province appears unexpected to you, a true finder of civilization, which seems to you laid down by the capricious hand of chance in the middle of virgin and wild nature. In fact, entering through those dusty streets, you suddenly hear the busy noise of the screeching workshops and the confused clamors of a human beehive, and to the trumpeting of your postilion you see coming out from the doors lovely ladies dressed in the style that female vanity and the inviable precepts of the distant French metropolis imposed on them.[72]

Tucumán was nicknamed "giardino della repubblica" (garden of the republic) for its luxuriant vegetation, although locusts posed a constant threat. Nearby is a place called "monte des naranjas" (orange hill) that in the spring spreads its perfume all over the area. The city is also featured in *Il Dio ignoto* as the idyllic location where the hero Attilio goes to recover from the wounds received in a bloody battle with the Native Americans.

Mantegazza remarks that the province of Salta belongs more to Peru than Argentina. "In Trancas voi avete lasciato l'ultimo gaucho. L'uomo del campo che voi trovate più al nord è un *arribeno* [uomo dell'alto] ed egli chiama quelli delle provincie meridionali *abajenos* [uomini del basso]" (In Trancas you have left the last *gaucho*. The man of the field that you find further north is an *arribeño* [highlander] and he calls those of the southern provinces *abajeños* [lowlanders], 381). His characterization of *arribeños* is not flattering:

> The *arribeño* is an Argentine Bolivian, or a Bolivian Argentine, which is why, serving as a passage to these two types of Americans, he unites and confuses them. His impassivity, his dark and gloomy air, seem to you a

paradox in the middle of that paradise of sky and flowers that surround him. At every moment you feel invited to sing and shout, to bless nature and kiss a land so joyful with light and perfumes, and you see yourself in front of a motionless creature that always seems dissatisfied, with an air of perpetual distrust. Truly, in that moment you are drawn to say that the man from the Salta countryside is the worst of all creatures from that country.[73]

The Italian anthropologist is so critical of the natives of Salta because they have almost no European ancestry: "Meanwhile, you may be pleased to recall that this man is a bastard product of the Indians who were subjects of the Incan Empire and that the drop of European blood which ran down his veins, can scarcely be detected."[74] Only a few drops of European blood are present in the inhabitants of the area; not enough, according to Mantegazza, to enhance their status in the hierarchical scale of human races. On the contrary, the Europeans of Salta managed to maintain completely intact their "racial identity" and are hardly distinguishable from continental Spanish. "In the province of Salta the whites are Spanish or almost Spanish, and in them you find culture and good heart; all of the virtues and defects of the Iberian man from which they derive."[75] In other words, there was very little "cross-contamination" between the two groups. In the Andean regions the separation between native population and *creoles* was sharper than in other areas because the European invaders focused exclusively on the exploitation of the natural resources. In *The Idea of Latin America,* Walter Mignolo writes that the colonization of "Latin" America and the exploitation of the natives were based on the principle of the "expandability of human life that, under the concept of inferior human races, justified the demand for increasing productivity in the mines and the plantations" (Mignolo, 47).

Salta, the capital of the province, is depicted as a pleasant city with nice architecture, many churches, and a splendid climate:

Salta is an ancient city that has perhaps 10,000 inhabitants and offers us a somewhat different appearance from its Argentine sisters, with its Baroque Spanish balconies, roofs covered with tiles instead of terraces, less regular streets which violate the monotonous, eternal squaring off of the other cities in the confederation....Salta rightly boasts of having in its province all the climates of the world united by short distances; so that ten leagues from the capital is the ice with which ice cream is made, and to the same distance in the south Campo Santo offers its sugar, bananas, and delicious *chirimoya*.[76]

The city of Salta was a natural link between Argentina, Peru, and Bolivia: the local merchants would buy horses from the pampa, train them on rocky terrain, and sell them at a higher price as far north as La Paz and Lima. They also smuggled silver; purchased coffee, cocoa, and coca leaves from Bolivia; and traded them on Argentine markets. That is how the city acquired the nickname of "porto seco" (dry port). At the higher elevations, people grew wheat, quinoa, corn, and even grapes, while in the valleys the cultivation of sugar cane yielded excellent results.

Unexpectedly, in the chapter devoted to Salta, Mantegazza mentions for the first time his father-in-law, Saturnino Tejada. The author married his daughter but does not mention her explicitly until the end of the book, when he narrates the preparations to sail back to Italy from Rio de Janeiro on a ship that turns out to be contaminated with yellow fever. He praises the gorgeous territory where the city is located, which offers everything, but is very critical of the native people, or plebs of the region:

> The plebs of Salta are among the ugliest I have ever seen. It seems that the worst specimens of the European, Indian, and Negro races have joined hands to form a stunted and monstrous family...you see before you wretched creatures that seem destined by nature to drag a life that is poor in both energy and pleasure, and which will be cut short in time. And yet, upon entering the well-to-do houses, you see coming before you refined, beautiful *señoritas* with long eyelashes and Andalusian eyes, and you are presented to honorable *caballeros* with noble and disdainful posture; and in all families you read the countenance of a full and robust life.[77]

The anthropologist maintains that the separation of the European and the native races is more pronounced in Salta than elsewhere in Argentina: "In Salta the plebs and the rich truly form two different nations living under the same roof, but they have different origins and different destinies written on their face."[78] And he adds: "Where Spanish blood has remained pure and where wealth has fought against disturbing factors, you find good health and life: where instead many wretched germs of human blood fermented in an impure crucible, physical and moral atrophy was born, the harbinger of a certain death of the poor race that has arisen."[79] These observations blatantly contradict what Mantegazza stated in the introduction, that the mixing of different human races should produce good results and lead eventually to "universal brotherhood." In the above passage Mantegazza is portraying the process of "internal colonization" that took place after Creoles gained independence from Spain. Although the elites embraced Republicanism and Liberalism—the same ideologies shared by Mantegazza—they excluded and marginalized natives and people of African descent. As Mignolo points out, racism continued to shape the life and institutions of the new nation-states in South America. While embracing the ideals of modernity, the new ruling classes demonized "entire populations by portraying them as inferior human beings, if human at all" (88).[80]

The fascinating landscape and the abundance of untapped natural resources help turn the young doctor/anthropologist into an entrepreneur. Mantegazza, concluding that the only way to lead the region toward progress and modernization is through colonial expansion, sees in the region of Oran, of which Salta was the capital city, many possibilities for economic development. Thus, before leaving Salta he presented a detailed proposal to the governor, Don Martin Guemez, which was examined and authorized by the House of Representatives and subsequently published in the local newspaper, *Comercio*, on December 25, 1857. An Italian translation of the contract is included in *Rio de la Plata e Tenerife*:

Art. 1: Doctor Paolo Mantegazza is obliged to bring thirty Lombard or Piedmontese families from the agricultural class to the province of Salta within the fixed term of two years starting from 1 January 1858. Each family will consist of at least four individuals of both sexes. Art. 2: These families will be chosen from among the healthiest and most moral and among those that are especially dedicated to the cultivation of mulberry, wheat, and other cereals. Each family will leave Italy with a capital of 1,000 pesos (5000 francs) which will belong to a Lombard or Piedmontese agricultural company. Art. 4: This sum will be used for transport. From Montevideo to the mouth of Bermejo there are 300 leagues, and 227 from this point to Oran, for a total of 3,030 kilometers all navigable by steam engines and ships of sufficient capacity. This, therefore, is how families can go from the ocean to the foot of the Andes in the heart of the American continent and begin agricultural work in the place where they will settle. Art. 5: The government of the province will grant to the colony, according to the law of public lands, 54 square leagues of land, of which six are at least on one or the other bank of the Rio Bermejo. Art. 6: Of these, one will be given to each family, leaving two for Dr. Mantegazza, who will be able to choose them from all the surfaces of land granted to the colony. Art. 7: The anonymous Bermejo company (a shipping company) is obligated to transport the colony free of charge from Buenos Aires to the banks of Bermejo, on the condition, however, that the supreme national government grants it the exclusive privilege it has requested. Art. 8: The provincial government is obligated to deliver to Dr. Mantegazza, or whoever represents him, the sum of 2,000 pesos (10,000 francs) for travel expenses, as soon as he does what he proposes to do, that is, as soon as he provides the 30 families of which Article 1 speaks to the province. Art. 9: If, after two years, Dr. Mantegazza does not fulfill the aforementioned stipulations, this contract will remain without value or effect, and can be extended for two years, given that he provides to the government just reasons that prevented him from executing the stipulations within the time limit indicated. Art. 10: Two copies of this contract will be signed. One will remain in the archives of the general secretariat, and the other will be delivered to Dr. Mantegazza. Salta, December 19, 1857. Martin Guemez, Governor. Pio José Tedin, Secretary. Doctor Mantegazza.[81]

Mantegazza wanted to select a small number of families from the regions of Piedmont and Lombardy who are "morali" (moral) and "laboriose" (hard-working). Once again, his racial prejudice is perpetrated in the document: the families that would colonize the region must come from northern Italy, not from the "barbarian and uncivilized" south. The choice is ironic because southern Italians would find in northern Argentina a warm climate like the one where they grew up. In the entrepreneur's view, the new colony would contribute to the development of the local economy while representing "un'eccellente speculazione" (an excellent investment; 402). An important element of the project is the possibility of arriving to Salta by boat, though the river Bermejo:

From Montevideo to the mouth of Bermejo there are 300 leagues, and 227 from this point to Oran, for a total of 3,030 kilometers all navigable by steam engines and ships of sufficient capacity. This, therefore, is how one can go from the ocean to the foot of the Andes in the heart of the American continent.[82]

The anthropologist gives detailed information that may be used by future emigrants. The best soil to cultivate sugar cane is the one that has been recently cleared, or *esmontado*. That operation, he remarks, may be done by Native Americans at a very low price. Another remunerative plant is the orange, which in this region can yield large amounts of fruits per year. Tobacco represents an excellent crop too, in addition to rice, wheat, and corn. A plant that processes hide of cows, horses, and other animals would be very profitable as well. Mantegazza describes cattle raising in detail, explaining all the by-products that can be derived from cows, like sego (tallow), dried meat (which can easily be sold in Bolivia), cheese, and soap. He notices, however, that in the long run agriculture is much more sustainable than cattle raising: "The raising of cattle is an immense resource for the country, but the land that gives grass to one hundred cows and supports a family, when cultivated can provide sustenance to a hundred men for a hundred centuries."[83]

Since the climate is so diverse and the land so fertile, the cuisine of Salta is much richer than in the rest of Argentina. Gastronomy for Mantegazza was very important; in fact, he was one of the first Italian intellectuals to understand the importance of Pellegrino Artusi's book *La scienza in cucina*, which became the foundation of modern Italian cuisine. He thinks that progress and technological innovations will end up making products from all over the globe available on our table:

> Only the Arcadians and the sentimentalists and metaphysicians, people who are sick in their body and mind, can be disgusted by the kitchen: for the doctor and philosopher one must pass through the kitchen to get to the workshop, the laboratory and the hospital; and in the general movement that brings people together and gives way to human activity, there is also a gastronomic brotherhood that enriches tables with the treasures of the whole earth.[84]

In Salta, people utilized many types of animals, like cows, sheep, chickens, pheasants, and delicious fish from the rivers. Nevertheless, the diet was not so heavily based on meats, as elsewhere in Argentina: "The Argentine of the north is carnivorous but does not forget that he lives in the land of the Incas, tireless and skilled farmers. He does not disregard legumes, roots, and vegetables like his southern brother."[85] Although people made bread from wheat, the cereal they appreciated the most is corn, which was available in many different varieties and was even used to make beer. Some types of corn were so sweet that Peruvians used to extract honey from them. Mantegazza also notices that, although in some areas people lived almost exclusively on corn, *pellagra* was not common, as it was in northern Italy. In the mountains, they also ate lots of *quinoa*, mostly used in soups. Mantegazza was so fond of it that he tried to introduce it to Italy, but the plants did not fare well because they require a dry climate and mild temperatures. His favorite dish from Salta is a soup called *chupi*, which incorporates many local products:

> In the national soup of Salta and Bolivia, the *chupi*, you have a true museum of the three realms. It is the eclecticism and pantheism of the pot: in fact, you find there, as representatives of the inorganic realm, salt and water; the vegetable realm gives you pumpkin, pepper, cabbage, turnip, parsley, coriander, apple, onion, leek, and I don't know how many other plants; while animal life is worthily represented by many little pieces of fresh meat or *charqui* (from the *quichua charqui*, dry meat, or very slim person) and fat. And all this warm, aromatic, and spicy gastronomic Olympia is certainly one of the glories of Saltan and Bolivian cuisine.[86]

The Salta province is situated at the edge of the extinct Incan empire, of which Mantegazza gives a fascinating description, praising its many technological innovations and efficient social organization. His overall judgment of that ancient civilization, however, is negative, because in his opinion it represented a form of despotic communism:

> Nowhere was there a more rigorous and simple agrarian law, and nowhere was there a more despotic communism. No one was poor in that empire, no one begged; but progress was closed in a chrysalis, it was halted. Freedom, the sacred spark of the human family, was extinguished…in the vast territory of the Peruvian empire five republics are colliding, full of vices and passions, but with fertile seeds for a future without end. The magic circle that made so many millions of men immobile is broken; and if the bloodiest anarchy agitates and divides the descendants of Pizarro, they are nevertheless men who go forward and progress indefinitely. Freedom always heals its own wounds, no matter how deep and cruel they seem. Despotism in all its forms breaks the most powerful impulse that animates and moves the human family.[87]

Despite the terrible massacres and destruction that Europeans caused in South America, the Italian scientist is convinced that capitalism is the great motor of history and that European civilization is the only one capable of propelling humankind forward on the road toward progress. Michel Chevalier, a French historian who traveled to America in the 1830s, wrote: "Spanish American seem to be nothing other than an impotent race, without future, unless it receives a wave of rich and new blood coming from the North, or from the East" (quoted in Mignolo, 78). Economic disparities are unavoidable, he thinks, because the entrepreneurs of modern capitalism are, like the Spanish conquistadors centuries earlier, motivated by profit, but he is also confident that the laws of free market will bring more benefits in the long run and will manage to activate all the animal spirits that are still dormant in South America. Emigration from the most "laborious and moral" regions of Italy, as Mantegazza was proposing, will benefit both the Italian emigrants and their host countries. In his view, the destiny of Native Americans is to vanish and be gradually absorbed by the great wave of European immigration. Thus, the dream of "universal brotherhood" presented in the introduction seems to conceal a hegemonic objective, predicated on a vision of humankind that is irremediably racist:

> The Indian of South America is a man of little sensibility, unhappy with himself; he is despondent, silent, distrustful, and coldly cruel; but sometimes tender and passionate; he is a tenacious lover of freedom; but is unintelligent and inactive; he is voracious for opportunities but temperate by necessity or by inertia; from civilization he learns nothing but vices; impassioned by the pleasures of intoxication. He is superstitious without being religious; immoral as a result of his unintelligence; he is incapable of reaching a high development of culture and is destined to be crushed and washed away by the great tidal wave of European civilization.[88]

Essentially, according to him, the indigenous people are not capable of achieving a higher level of civilization without the help of their superior European "cousins." The native cultures are denied their own identity in his writings, as they are destined to be crushed and devastated (*travolti*) by the great tidal wave of European civilization (*il torrente della civiltà europea*). Mantegazza places the Native Americans a step above Africans in his racial hierarchy, but believes neither of them should be considered Europeans' brothers:

The Indian is higher than the Negro in the human scale; he is more intelligent than him and his feelings are richer in form; but our African brother inspires us with greater sympathy because he is rowdier and content; and is a more outgoing talker. The Negro is a humanized monkey; the Indian is a white man who mulls over the pain of the past or on a vengeance of the future. The Negro amuses us without intending to; the Indian scares us or makes us feel compassion. In front of both, we feel that we are distant relatives, perhaps even cousins; but never brothers.[89]

Mantegazza rejects the theories of those European philosophers who idealized the noble savage, of whom they often did not have any direct knowledge:

The philosophers who long for the free and naked civilization of the savage while sitting in their armchair amid the sophisticated pleasures of civilized life should take a run in the Argentine Pampa or go to Corrientes....I would like to ask them if those poor mud-colored creatures, naked or covered with filthy rags, with thin muscles, loose and greasy hair, and devoured by a throng of insects, are representatives of primitive innocence and freedom: I would like to know if those stupidly sad faces await a ray of light from heaven or from the works of their overseas philosopher brothers.[90]

He concludes that the destiny of native Americans is either to be assimilated or extinguished. It is the same assimilationist ideology that inspired Captain Richard Henry Pratt, founder of the first Indian Industrial School in my current hometown of Carlisle, Pennsylvania, who famously declared: "Kill the Indian in him, and save the man."[91]

And of these men who occupied such vast continents, and who in such richness of nature were the poorest creatures, what has European civilization done? It has made a vast cemetery. The Indians, by coming into contact with us, had to suffer the tyranny of this dilemma: either be educated or extinguished.[92]

The Jesuits tried to educate them but failed, because the process would have taken hundreds of years, while Spaniards wanted their gold and silver right away. In conclusion, he states, "The luckiest of all were those who, due to the flexibility of their temper, yielded to servitude and survived so much destruction due to their number. These ones blended with the victors, giving to them a large wave of their blood and sometimes even their tongue."[93]

Whereas his colleague Cesare Lombroso thought that the shape of one's cranium was the key to understand human psychology, Mantegazza believed that the history of a people remained somehow transfixed in their physical features, thus transcending the passage of time:

> And who does not, even nowadays, read in the sad, serious, reflective, and apathetic physiognomy of the Quichua, the history of their past, of that imposed communism which then resulted in a very ingenious form of despotism, later copied with much fortune by the Jesuits in their missions in Paraguay and Brazil?[94]

Human faces are like open books where the features of the natural and cultural landscape have inscribed indelible marks:

> The time and events of life write their memories. No physiognomy is livelier and more mobile than that of the Negro; none is more immobile and colder than that of the pampa Indian. The Guinea Negro at the slightest spark of joy or pain that shakes him, moves all the muscles of his face and shakes and writhes, and shouts and cackles like a monkey; the Pampa Indian instead stays seated and bent over in the shadow of his horse, and with his hands on his knees and his head in his hands remains motionless for hours in the middle of the grassy desert which, almost like an ocean of land, surrounds him on every side.[95]

The most interesting and complex physiognomy is that of the European:

> In no race is the expression of the face more noble and elevated than in that which governs and directs human civilization in these times. It is neither the spasmodic contractions, nor the quick motions of the Negro, more ape than man; nor does it have the bleak passivity of the indigenous Americans. Passions are painted on our face from the most violent to the slightest fluctuation of a sweet feeling, and always in an appropriate way that measures the intensity and mode of action. The creations of genius, the bitterness of doubt, the thousand varieties of moral needs created by the luxury of civilization find a perfect expression in the European physiognomy.[96]

For Mantegazza, beauty is something absolute; it does not depend on cultural perceptions:

> I firmly believe in absolute beauty, and without wishing to make a dissertation here on the origins and criterion of beauty, I recall that many Indians of America, who without ever having studied aesthetics find our women much more beautiful than their wives, and take as many prisoners as they can, often cutting the soles of their feet so they cannot flee.[97]

A Different Kind of Paradise: Tenerife

Mantegazza's journey to South America ends with a touch of suspense, because upon arriving in Rio de Janeiro he finds out that the English ship that should take him back home has been contaminated with yellow fever. In the bay, small vessels with a black flag go from ship to ship to pick up the dead and the sick, mostly whites, since the fever seemed to strike mostly people from northern Europe, while Black people were almost immune. This is the first time in the book that the author (indirectly) mentions his wife: "The idea of embarking on an infected ship with a young bride who had always lived in countries where malaria and yellow fever are known only by name gave me more than fear; but horror."[98] On their ship there were thirty sick persons, and after ten days of navigation the number became forty. During the trip, twelve people died and were thrown into the ocean before getting to Tenerife. When they finally arrived, everyone was confined in a *lazzeretto* (leper hospital), where they were quarantined for nine days. The final chapters of the book are devoted to Tenerife, which Mantegazza describes as an earthly paradise. The valley of Orotava is the place that fascinated him the most, for its mild climate and beautiful landscape:

> The delightful valley of Orotava that lies in front of us, and the peak and ocean form a picture where the contrast of a completely sweet nature enclosed between the gigantic mountains and the infinite expanse of the sea does not let us speak, but makes us sigh from time to time, as if words were unwanted in that paradise. Sometimes, involuntarily and almost by silent agreement our horses stop and holding our traveling companion's hand, it seems to us that no one can be unhappy in that country.[99]

The towns, the houses, and their magnificent gardens blended so harmoniously with the surrounding landscape that it is almost impossible to distinguish where nature ends and man's work begins: "plants and gardens happily surround the houses, and these only seem to have been built to embellish the landscape. In many places, one cannot find the classic architecture of streets, as houses, churches and gardens intertwine and merge in a thousand ways amid that eternal spring."[100]

The landscape of Tenerife does not overwhelm the visitor with its sublime beauty, as the ones that the Italian anthropologist experienced in South America. It is, in other words, a domesticated "second nature" where one may detect the gentle touch of human civilization, which has not defaced the original landscape but tried instead to live with it in the most harmonic way. When Mantegazza describes the terraces patiently constructed by the inhabitants to cultivate their grapes and the calm beauty of the ocean that seems "fratello d'un lago" (brother of a lake) one cannot help thinking of the landscape surrounding the village of San Terenzio in the Italian riviera, where the weary traveler built his final residence. Ultimately, Mantegazza seems to privilege the "unfinished" landscapes that encourage and almost invoke human intervention, as he glimpsed, or imagined, in the many "outlines of cities" he visited in the Rio de la Plata basin: an atmosphere that evoked an authentic "dawn of the world," where everything is barely sketched and awaits to be shaped. His concept of aesthetics, in other words, cannot be limited to pure contemplation of what is objectively sublime but requires an active participation:

> In front of perfection we are absorbed, and the mind cannot help but admire: our self-esteem is almost lost. Faced with sketched, incomplete beauty our thought becomes a living part of that picture, correcting and completing it in its own way. We voluptuously identify with nature, as if we wanted to steal a ray of the supreme pleasure of creation.[101]

Here lies the modernity—with all its contradictions—of Mantegazza's thought: on the one hand, he was deeply fascinated by the detached, superior calm of the "muddy" (fangosi) natives he encountered during his journeys through South America, but he cannot espouse their contemplative stillness, because it would preclude the creative act of poesis, which is essentially the act of bringing something into being that did not exist before.[102] Faced by the sublime beauty of American natural landscapes, the anthropologist-entrepreneur cannot let himself be totally absorbed by them: as his fictional hero Attilio, he must constantly dominate, control, and alter the landscapes and people he encounters. Nature must be transformed, domesticated, and turned into second nature, as the European migrants were doing in the *pampa gringa*, chasing away the "muddy" Native Americans and the proud *gauchos* of the interior, who had acquired many of their features and ended up embodying, according to Sarmiento, the "barbarism" that Argentina had to eradicate if it wanted to continue on its path to civilization. The Italian colony that Mantegazza tried to create by transplanting hard-working, "moral" Piedmontese and Lombard families into the remote province of Salta is not merely an economic enterprise, but also an aesthetic one, aimed at transforming the American uncontaminated landscape of the interior into a domesticated, agrarian one, which would become essentially a mirror image of Europe. When the Italian travel writer and journalist Edmondo De Amicis set foot in the rural colony of San Carlos almost forty years after Mantegazza, he was amazed to see how many Italian *contadini* (peasants) had settled in the area: even old native American women spoke the dialect of his native region of Piedmont, and Italian flags waved in the *pampero* wind above the rudimentary cabins built by his compatriots. The conquest of the interior that Mantegazza had dreamed of was finally accomplished, but the outcomes of the great modernizing effort envisioned by the Creole hegemonic classes were questionable, as they remained culturally and economically subaltern with respect to the imperialist model they so desperately tried to emulate. To paraphrase Mignolo's insightful words one last time, they had become internal colonizers but did not escape the logic of coloniality (see Mignolo, 86).

CHAPTER THREE

American Tears: Edmondo De Amicis and the Remaking of Italians in Argentina

Within the Italian borders, / Italians have been remade. /
Mussolini has remade them / For tomorrow's war, / For labor's
glory, / For peace and for the laurel, / For the shame of those /
Who repudiated our Fatherland.
　　　　—*Giovinezza*, official anthem of the Italian Fascist Party

Although Mantegazza in the introduction of *Rio de la Plata e Tenerife* claims that he did not want to write a panegyric of Italian emigration to Rio de la Plata, one may argue that the way he presented it to his readers may have enticed them to follow on his entrepreneurial path.[1] Even his fictional hero Attilio, despite the hardships he had to endure, is ultimately a conqueror, a successful businessman who finds in the new continent exactly what he was looking for: a meaningful and productive life and even a new ideal to which he can aspire. However, in the Italian imaginary at the time of the great migration, as reflected in literature and popular music, the figure of the emigrant was often portrayed in a completely different way. At the turn of the nineteenth century, the images that characterize the representations of emigrants are death, loss, sorrow, and nostalgia for their family members and the beautiful country left behind. The two short texts I will analyze in the following pages to illustrate this trend are a poem titled "Gli emigranti" published by Edmondo De Amicis in 1880, only a few years after Mantegazza's *Il Dio ignoto*,[2] and a popular Neapolitan song, "Lacreme napulitane," written by Libero Bovio in 1925, sung for the first time by Gennaro Pasquariello.[3]

In the first stanza of De Amicis's poem we notice a sudden overturning of imagery with respect to Mantegazza's and Virgilio's narratives, where migrating to America is presented as a rebirth and an escape from an apathetic life. In the poem, the emigrants climb onto the ship as if they are ascending on the executioner's block: "Ascendono la nave / Come s'ascende il palco della morte."[4] The ship becomes a monster that swallows in its huge belly hundreds of innocent human lives. The modern steamship literally devours the poor emigrants, as in Emile Zola's working class novel *Germinal,* where the coal mine pit is named *Le Voreux* (the Voracious), a monster that in order to keep going must phagocytize every day huge amounts of human flesh.[5] One may argue that the same phenomenon was taking place at the end of the nineteenth century in the port of Genoa, where brokerage companies, shipyards, and the entire naval industry relied heavily on emigrants to generate profit. In fact, the liberal economists and supporters of free emigration were closely connected to the industrial and commercial complex based in the Ligurian city.[6] Like the French miners in *Germinal,* the Italian emigrants line up to enter the bowels of the monster. Their cheeks are pale and hollow, the eyes lifeless. Men support their wives, broken and pasty, as they hold tightly the little ones to their chest. Everyone is terrified of the other monster they must face, the immense ocean, symbol of the unknown. The boarding of the ship also recalls the arrival of the lost souls in Dante's *Inferno,* when they are driven by the mythical *Caronte* across the river Acheron that will take them to hell. The scene is made more intense by the sharp contrast with the surrounding landscape. Although the boroughs of Sestri-Ponente and Sampierdarena near Genoa were at that time among of the most industrialized and heavily polluted areas in Europe (Sampierdarena was nicknamed "the Manchester of Italy"), with many steel plants that contributed to make the landscape quite "hellish," in the poet's words the city becomes a garden, even an earthly paradise. Genoa is "ricca e gentile," and the moribund emigrants stare at the surrounding mountains as they slowly disappear from the horizon.[7] The words and rhymes are carefully chosen to underline the dramatic effect: "the pupilla mesta" (sad) rhymes and contrasts with the city "in festa" (festive). The coastline of Liguria is a "vago lido" (beautiful shore) "che il tramonto indora" (gilded by the setting sun). On the ship and along the dock, a mournful choir emerges from the indistinct chaos of bodies, "ammonticchiati come giumenti" (piled up like animals). They migrate toward lands that are "inospiti e lontane" (unfriendly and distant); they were betrayed by a "mercante menzognero" (deceitful merchant) and they follow the same path taken by their friends and relatives, "in terre ove altra gente è morta" (in countries where other people had died). They are not, as in Mantegazza's account, people who seek new opportunities but quite simply "bestie da soma…carne da cimitero" (beasts of burden, flesh for the cemetery). In his analysis of the same poem, Luigi Cepparrone compares emigrants to the scapegoat, as theorized by René Girard in his famous work *Violence and the Sacred* (38). Emigration is an act of violence perpetrated by the Italian government, and the emigrants are the scapegoats, because by accepting to be exiled from their beloved country they will contribute to diminish the social tensions caused by unemployment and poverty. In De Amicis's words, the mother country becomes a ferocious father who devours his children. Nevertheless, they are incapable of hating their own fatherland, even if it rejects them: "L'amano ancora il maledetto suolo / Che i figli suoi divora, / Dove sudano in mille e campa uno solo" (And yet, they still love their damned country / who devours its children / Where a thousand people toil and only one prospers). After encouraging them to stick together and take care of each other in the difficult times, the author wishes that God may grant them a safe return to their beloved villages, where they will find their parents waiting for them. All of the emigrants, in fact, would abandon the ship immediately and return to their homes if they could: "E ognuno…Se lo potesse, tornerebbe al lido; / tornerebbe a morir sopra i nativi / Monti, nel triste nido / Dove piangono i suoi vecchi malvivi" (All of them, if they could, would go back to their native / mountains, to their sad nests / where their moribund parents are crying).[8] Cepparrone rightly notes that, although De Amicis in the poem strongly opposes emigration, his motivations differ from the landowners and their spokespersons, who usually depicted the emigrants as vengeful and ungrateful. Instead, he displays compassion for his fellow citizens and accuses the ruling classes of not being able to stop the hemorrhage of migration.

When the author traveled to Argentina and observed how the emigrants changed on the American soil, his view of emigration also changed quite radically, but the theme that remains constant is the attachment to the native country that both men and women preserve, despite their being ejected from it. Paradoxically, the sense of patriotism in the Italian "colonies" abroad is even stronger than among those who chose not to depart. Thus, as I will illustrate when analyzing the text *I nostri contadini in America,* the patriotic sentiments and behavior of Italian expatriates function as leverage to increase the sense of national belonging that Italians often lacked.

The same mechanism of nostalgia and attachment to one's country is at work in the song I am examining next, "Lacreme napulitane" (Neapolitan tears). The protagonist is a Neapolitan young man who is writing to his mother from America. It is the day before Christmas, and he evokes all the things that he misses the most: the fireworks, the bagpiper players, the nativity scenes, and, of course, his children whom he had to leave behind. While in De Amicis's poem the emigrants could find support in each other during their odyssey abroad, the protagonist of Bovio's song is alone, betrayed not only by his country but also by his own wife. Whereas in the poem emigrants may be interpreted as figurative scapegoat, in the song the protagonist becomes an authentic Christ figure, and the mother is turned into a Madonna who cries in front of the cross: "I dream every night of my home / and hear the voices of my children / but I dream of you as Mother Mary / with a sword in your chest, / before your son on the cross!"[9] Another important element that emerges in Bovio's lyrics is the nostalgia for the native landscape, a theme that one may find in the most famous Italian emigrant songs, like "Ma se ghe pensu" (But if I think about it), where an old Genoese man who had migrated to Argentina, where he had become successful, evokes the most important landmarks of the cityscape. In the Neapolitan song, the emigrant's plight is made even more unbearable for not being able to return home to his mother and children, because he has lost his honor. His economic situation is not as terrible, as in De Amicis's vision, in which emigrants have to beg from door to door for a piece of bread: the Neapolitan emigrant admits that he has enough food, but it tastes extremely bitter, and although he has money in his pocket, he has never felt so poor. In the text, we observe an interesting reversal: during the great migration, it was not uncommon for a young man to leave his wife and children behind, start a new family in America and never return. The so-called "vedove bianche" (white widows) were a common sight in Italian towns and villages at the turn of the century, but in Bovio's text the man makes the ultimate sacrifice and remains in exile, as he asks his mother to make "chella signora" (that lady) come back home and stay with the children, who are asking about her. He will continue to "work for everyone" and support his family, but since he has lost his honor, he won't be able to see his children ever again. Another element that the poem and the song share is the total dehumanization caused by the diaspora. For De Amicis, emigrants are "carne da cimitero," for Bovio "carne da macello" (flesh for the slaughterhouse). Once away from his country, the (male) migrant worker loses his identity as a human being: he is no longer a person but mere "flesh," a suffering body ready to be exploited, processed, and dissected—as a cow in a slaughterhouse—and eventually discarded in a cemetery. As Fernando Elisa Bravo Herrera writes in her important book on the representation of Italian emigration to Argentina, "the isotope of emigration in the anti-emigrationist texts is constructed in a space and in an itinerary filled with negative signs that include disaster, death, loss, betrayal, disillusion and exploitation."[10] All the elements listed by Herrera are present in the "anti-emigration" texts I briefly analyzed: failure, suffering, death, loss, betrayal, disillusion, and exploitation. Above all, what is missing in these narratives is a happy ending. As I will show, the themes listed by Herrera may be present in pro-emigration texts, because they contribute to building the pathos of the narrative and capture the reader's attention, but they are subsumed, retrospectively, into an overarching itinerary that leads either to integration in the host country or to a successful return to the motherland, as happens in *The Odyssey*, where the hero's original social status and personal identity are magically restored. The expression "nostalgia," which is a reoccurring theme in emigration narratives, is etymologically linked to the ancient Greek word *nostos*, which means "return home." The poem "Gli emigranti" ends with an invocation to God, who may let the condemned souls about to embark on the monster-ship cross the ocean again and go back to the "villaggi umili e cari" (dear and humble villages) and find again, on the threshold of the deserted houses, the old parents who stretch out their arms, eager to welcome back their lost children.

In an article titled "An Italian Hispanist of the Nineteenth Century," published in 1972 in *Hispania*, Edward Worthen writes that De Amicis's book *Cuore* (1886) was the most widely read literary work in the Hispanic nations except for *Don Quijote*.[11] He also recounts that the Italian novelist and journalist was so profoundly attached to Argentina that the last public speech he gave in 1907 was a celebration of the friendship between the two countries. His words echo the preface of Mantegazza's book I analyzed in the previous chapter: "I toast to your health and your fortune, brotherly citizens of two worlds; I toast to the prosperity and the industrious and fertile expansion of the immortal youth of Argentinian blood, of which I perceive the free and strong heartbeat, like a heart that beats inside our hearts."[12] One may be tempted to observe, reading these celebratory words, that Mantegazza's and Virgilio's dream of achieving a peaceful

brotherhood between the two people has been realized. The question that
needs to be answered is: how can we explain such a profound overturning
in De Amicis's perception of Italian emigration? The men and women to
whom he was speaking in 1907 were the same desperate people he saw (or
imagined) departing from the port of Genoa, leaving for hostile countries
where they would be begging for a piece of bread. How can we justify such
a profound transformation? To answer these questions, we need to examine the texts that De Amicis published after he traveled to South America
and observed Italian immigration in that country, to which, as Cepparrone
points out, he wanted to devote a book that he never managed to write.[13]

Although De Amicis's most critically acclaimed book about migration
is *Sull'oceano*, in which he narrates his journey from the port of Genoa to
Montevideo, in this chapter I will focus mostly on a lesser-known work,
published for the first time in 1897 under the title *In America*. The volume
consists of three different pieces: "Quadri della pampa," "I nostri contadini
in America," and "Nella Baia di Rio de Janeiro." As Maddalena Tirabassi
remarks, in 1884 the Italian author was invited by one of the most important newspapers of Buenos Aires, *El Nacional*, to give a series of conferences in Argentina.[14] In addition to the travel expenses, they offered him
40,000 lire (equivalent roughly to 200,000 euros). In April of the same
year, he boarded a ship called the *Nord America*, propelled both by steam
and sail, that carried 1,600 emigrants and about a hundred first- and
second-class passengers. The distinction is important. In a publication
dated 1898, the inspector Luigi Malnate, who was working in the port of
Genoa, distinguishes between *emigrante* and *passeggero*. The emigrant
goes to America "con il biglietto di terza classe" (with a third-class ticket),
either alone or with the family, to work for an unspecified amount of
time. The latter, on the other hand, possesses a second- or first-class ticket
(although he may occasionally travel third-class, if alone) and goes to
America "per diporto, o per concludere un affare determinato, ed anche
per esecitarvi la professione o mestiere, ma per un breve tempo presta-
bilito (for tourism or to pursue a business enterprise, and also to practice
a profession or craft, but only for a short and predetermined period of
time).[15] A total of 31,983 Italians arrived in Argentina in 1884, most of
whom came from the regions of northern Italy (see Tirabassi 11). Malnate
makes a further distinction and remarks that the "emigrante gratuito,"
whose ticket is entirely subsidized by an American government, must be
a "contadino" (a farmer) and not from any Italian region: northern Italian

farmers are preferred; southerners are merely tolerated. In *Sull'Oceano,* one may start noticing how De Amicis's representation of emigrants has changed: while in the poem I analyzed, "il suol che li rifiuta amano ancora" (they still love the country that rejected them), in the novel, the author's vision of emigrants is less idealized (Cepparrone, 54). An old man who is about to board the ship screams sarcastically: "Long life to Italy!" and shakes his fist toward the shore. Another one, who had fought in the Risorgimento, is leaving without regrets, because the outcome of the patriotic struggle had deeply disappointed him (Tirabassi, 13). The reality of emigration, as De Amicis gradually learned, is complex and cannot be easily summarized under the categories of victim and scapegoat. As Tirabassi underlines, the Italian government did very little to govern the massive exodus that affected Italy between 1870 and 1915. The shipping companies were transporting people in unsanitary conditions: in 1899, twenty-seven emigrants died of suffocation on a liner sailing to Brazil, and as De Amicis himself observed, an unbearable stench was rising from the hatchways where the third-class passengers were stowed literally like sardines: "In the hottest days, a pitiful stench rose from the hatches of the male sleeping quarters."[16]

The little volume *In America* does not describe the cities of Buenos Aires and Montevideo, as other Italian travel writers did. Instead, it opens with a narrative titled "Quadri della pampa," focusing not on emigration but the on landscape of the Argentinean interior, where the author observes the conflictual and yet harmonic relationship between men and nature. The spectacle that unfolds in front of him is almost impossible to grasp in its grandiosity. De Amicis, who had been a military man, compares the immense plain to "una piazza d'armi spianata per un milione di soldati" (a leveled parade ground suitable for one million soldiers) in the middle of which his carriage moves forward very slowly, like a sailboat in the ocean (29). The advancing herds, guided by skilled *gauchos* on their horses, gradually cover the entire plain and envelop the author and his fellow travelers in a fluctuating cloud of noises, smells, and colors that seems to swallow the carriage in which De Amicis is traveling. The scenery takes on an epic dimension, which is the genre that characterizes the entire narrative. The men on their horses are compared to "un antico popolo barbaro migrante alla conquista di un mondo" (an ancient barbarous people migrating to the conquest of a new world; 30). The sense of admiration for the people of the *pampa* emerges in almost every sentence.

The children, seven or eight years old, are "piantati, inchiodati sui cavalli in atteggiamenti superbi" (planted, nailed on their horses in superb poses; 31). The *gauchos* have "toraci enormi, figure strane e belle, che avean del guerriero e del pastore, del torero e del bandito...andavano e venivano... galoppando con l'alterezza di principi" (enormous chests, strange and beautiful figures, they resembled shepherds and warriors, bullfighters and bandits...they were galloping back and forth with the haughtiness of princes; 31). Most of all, De Amicis wants to give his readers the sense of grandiosity of South American nature. The Italian traveler is following a long and celebrated tradition dating back to Alexander von Humboldt, who had explored the continent at the turn of the eighteenth century, when Latin Americans were fighting for their independence. As Marie Louise Pratt writes in her seminal book *Imperial Eyes: Travel Writing and Transculturation,* the German explorer and naturalist "reinvented South America first and foremost as nature...a dramatic, extraordinary nature, a spectacle capable of overwhelming human knowledge and understanding."[17] There is, however, an important difference: whereas in Humboldt's descriptions "nature dwarfs humans, arouses their passions, defies their power of perception,"[18] in De Amicis the *gauchos* of the *pampas* are an essential component of nature and are almost indistinguishable from it. When he observes the struggle between the Latin American cowboys and the animals that inhabit the wilderness, he has the impression of assisting at "uno spettacolo grandioso e antico" (an ancient and grandiose spectacle; 31). All around him everything "was motion and strength, struggle, and courage; it was the fecundity, it was the abundance of flesh and blood, an immense quiver of life through the boundless plains, the feeling of a new world for me."[19] The inhabitants of the interior of Argentina seemed to him to be the heirs of the Spanish conquistadores who had children with indigenous women and now are fully integrated with nature: although they seem to dominate it, as the scene of the taming of the wild horse suggests, the dominion they create is almost diametrically opposed from the one that new European immigrants were about to establish. When the horsemen approach De Amicis's carriage bearing twisting armadillos they had just caught in the grass, armfuls of doves and partridges and ostriches captured with their *bolas*, they almost look like children exhibiting their spoils to the parents. The epic struggle between the man and the horse that occupies the central part of the narrative, although extremely violent and dangerous, is a game, an exercise that the people of the *pampas* perform almost daily through their entire life. The horseman is "un gaucho erculeo, dal gran busto patagonico, arcato di gambe e chiomato come un barbaro...il domatore aveva due speroni simili a due lame di pugnale" (a Herculean gaucho with a huge Patagonian bust, with arched legs and long-haired like a Barbarian...the tamer had two spurs sharp like the blades of a dagger; 33).

The mythical nature of the confrontation between man and horse is openly declared by De Amicis: "Mi parve allora di vedere il primo uomo domare il primo cavallo" (I thought I was watching the first man taming the first wild horse; 33). What the author is suggesting is that in the interior or Argentina one may witness the dawn of civilization: the gaucho still is intrinsically connected with the natural world; man and horse are situated at the same level, they fight with each other in a fair, equitable way. The systematic submission and exploitation of nature has not taken place yet because the technology used by the horseman is minimal: the metal spurs and a rope are the only tools used to tame the animal. The "civilized" onlookers are all rooting for the horse: "I understood for the first time the animal in all its beauty, in all its terrible strength, in the virginal pride of its race, born to be free, not yet contaminated by servitude."[20] But the outcome of the duel is contrary to their expectations, as the steel legs of the "aguzzino" (slave-driver) don't let go of the prey, and the other horses, saddled and tied to the surrounding trees, become restless, as if about to start a rebellion. Finally, the colt is vanquished: exhausted, covered with white foam, dripping sweat, his eyes lost and bloodshot, let go a last lamentable nigh and "dispare nel recinto dei servi, — e l'abominevole oltraggio è compiuto" (it disappears in the enclosure of the slaves — and the abominable outrage is accomplished; 35). After the taming of the horse, the narrator's gaze turns to the surrounding scenery and, as he describes the herds running through the plains, the military metaphor used at the beginning returns. The image of the "equine multitude" seems like a frightened army's retreat, chased by a superior enemy. What makes the passage even more intriguing is the comparison of the herd of wild horses with the indigenous population: "un esercito d'indiani della *pampa esteriore*, che si sentissero alle spalle il fragore incalzante delle artiglierie argentine" (an army of Indians of the exterior *pampa*, who heard behind them the insistent, deafening clamor of the Argentinean artillery; 35). What De Amicis evokes with this comparison is the famous "Conquista del desierto," a ruthless military campaign aimed at liberating the interior of the country from the "threat" that the indigenous people posed to European colonization. The campaign was headed by General Rosa, who had become a good friend of the Italian writer, as noted by Cepparone in his book (see Cepparone, 57–58).

The brave *gauchos* were repeatedly recruited to fight against the indigenous population, but they had grown so accustomed to living in the wilderness that they became the target of the new liberal hegemonic class, who saw them as an obstacle to the modernization of the country. From a Viconian perspective, the *gauchos* who fight against an uncontaminated nature, symbolized by the "Verginian" colt, exemplify the age of the heroes: the man on his horse, although living in primitive conditions, is a free man, and thus endowed with a nobility that new upcoming wave of European migrant workers—mostly peasants escaping from a long history of economic and social subjugation—did not possess.[21] Paradoxically, the *gauchos*, who had been instrumental in carrying out a first wave of "conquest," were being pushed aside and were eventually replaced by Italian peasants. Cepparone quotes a passage from an unpublished manuscript where De Amicis imagines "magnificent battles, invasions, and tremendous retreats of Indians...and on the other side the army of workers from every European nation, who will come to cultivate, to reap, to transform everything. And the ladies under the pergolas of hundreds of villas—and cities—and theaters."[22] Thus, in De Amicis's imagination, the European workers, instead of fighting against exploitation in their own countries, are partaking of an imperialistic conquest against the native people of Argentina, whose "wild" landscape is destined to be transformed, becoming the mirror image of a bourgeois fin-de-siècle countryside, with elegant ladies sitting under the pergolas of their villas, talking about the latest theater productions. In his writings, the two successive phases of the reconquest of America overlap: the "taming" of the wild horse is transfigured, as the herds led by the *gauchos* become a symbol of the fugitive Native Americans, retreating under the attack of the artillery. The arrival of the government troops, however, marks the decline and eventual disappearance of the "heroic" gaucho civilization that the author admired. The colonies created by the new immigrants that De Amicis visited and described so vividly in the second text contained in the volume *In America* do possess certain epic features, but it is a different type of "dawn of the world" that is taking place: from nomadic shepherds to farmers: from hunting and gathering to agriculture. *Trigo, trigo, trigo*: the Piedmontese women transplanted in the *pampa* who were interviewed by De Amicis confess that their men are so obsessed with wheat (*trigo*), that they cannot think about anything else. Wheat will cover the immense plains where the *gauchos* used to ride, free and unaware of the new world order that they had helped to create by fighting the natives. The Argentine artilleries will bring about not only the physical extermination of the indigenous population but also the extinction of their own "barbarian" culture, as defined by Sarmiento in the seminal book *Civilization and Barbarism* (1845), whose protagonist, Facundo, is a gaucho who exemplifies the primitive face of Argentina that needs to be erased.

In his reportage "I nostri contadini in America," the second text of *In America*, De Amicis states that the shape of the state of Santa Fe resembles the Italian peninsula: an enormous boot with its foot resting on the state of Buenos Aires and the top part bordering with the forests of Gran Chaco, still partially unexplored. Until just fifty years prior to his arrival, this region was a desert, where raids by native people arrived at few miles from the capital, the ancient and decadent city of Santa Fe. Now, it is an ocean of plowed fields covered with golden wheat. The author does not bother depicting the landscape, because it is irrelevant: an immense, monotonous plain crossed by many rivers that flow very slowly, allowing the water to penetrate the soil, thus making it extremely fertile. What made this region so rich and prosperous, however, is the hard work of the European immigrants: the same lost souls that De Amicis described while departing from the port of Genoa in the poem "Gli emigranti." "I think I saw a flag," exclaims one of his fellow voyagers as they are approaching the colony of San Carlos. "Lei è a casa sua," you are at home, are the first words pronounced by the leader of the group that came to welcome the illustrious guest. The colony is predominantly Piedmontese, and everyone speaks the regional dialect. Even an old Native American woman they encounter on the road, whose face is described as having the same color of the soil—the same muddy face we encountered in Mantegazza's narratives—and her smile that of a witch, replies in the same idiom when one of the colons asks her a question. It is a sign that the Native Americans have been totally assimilated. Some of the colons that De Amicis encounters were already there when the colony started, thirty years earlier. They fought with the indigenous people and the locusts for many years, but at the end they prevailed, and now most of them have reached a certain level of prosperity. When he describes the heart of the colony, De Amicis uses a military metaphor: it is like the headquarter of an invisible army, "disseminato in un gran numero di piccolissimi distaccamenti" (distributed through many tiny contigents; 42). It is as if an invading army were rapidly taking possession of the territory; it is the same army envisaged by the author in the preparatory notes mentioned earlier. The town is neither a town nor a village but the rushed sketch of a large city. It appears as a "una pagina d'appunti, con parole e frasi qua e là, separate da grandi lacune" (a notebook page, with sentences and words here and there, separated by vast gaps; 42). De Amicis is observing the birth of a new world, different from the one he described in the first text: the protagonists of this new and equally epic beginning are not the mythical heroes on their horses but an army of small ants who patiently plow the very same soil that the *gauchos* despised. Nevertheless, De Amicis notices "un non so che di giovanile e d'ardito, che parla di libertà e di speranza" (a certain something of young and daring, that speaks of freedom and hope; 42).

In the holidays, there is a "brulichio" (rolling swarm) of carriages along the road that stretches out to the distant horizon. It is like a slice of Piedmont transplanted onto the American soil: the author recognizes the same accents, clothes, and accessories. Some of the older colons show him the scars from the battles they fought for the unification of Italy and those, more recent, received while fighting the indigenous people of the *pampa*. The author does not seem to notice the contradiction that the same Italians who had risked their life to give their country an independent government were now fighting to deprive Native Americans of their own land. Even those who did not have many ambitions, once they settle in the new colonies, are caught in the spiraling desire of getting more and more land: they see those who came before and try to imitate them, "in una società impaziente di conquistatori, in una vasta libertà di spazio e di vita che rammenta l'infanzia del mondo" (in an impatient society of conquerors, in a vast freedom of space and life that seems like the dawn of the world; 47). The humble peasants, the spinners, the wet nurses from the poor countryside of northern Italy are suddenly transformed into entrepreneurs who discuss local politics and participate in the debates concerning the construction of new schools, public roads, and taxation. De Amicis is astonished by the metamorphosis. He no longer recognizes "his" peasants, once so respectful and almost afraid of those like him, who held a higher social position.

Used to hear their laments, their eternal discontent, always distrustful or falsely obsequious with the *signori*, with a certain something contracted and closed, unaware and indifferent toward anything that does not impinge on their immediate interest, I was surprised to see workers treat us as their equals, with a cheerful and courteous calmness, to hear them discuss politics and administration.[23]

If one recalls the "lost souls" that De Amicis portrayed as they were embarking on the monster-ship that was carrying them toward an almost certain death, it is not difficult to understand the author's astonishment. As noted by Giacomo Bove, who traveled back to Italy on the same ship with De Amicis, the author rejoiced when he saw the immigrants' regeneration, who were "instupiditi, macilenti, ignari del loro avvenire, ma pronti a qualunque lotta, corazzati contro qualunque sventura" (stupefied, emaciated, unaware of their destiny, but ready to any fight, armored against any catastrophe).[24] In the poem, the emigrants were the object of compassion, but once they settled in America, their metamorphosis is so complete that the bourgeois writer can no longer recognize them. Not only did they become financially successful, but they gained a self-confidence that in Italy they could never possess. One colon tells the prestigious guest: "Dica in Italia che vengano, che quello che ci manca qui son le braccia: le teste... ci sono!" (Tell everyone in Italy to come, because what we need here are hands. The brains...we got them!; 48).

The main objective of De Amicis's reportage, however, is to show the Italian readers that despite their being so far away, "his" peasants in America continue to remain attached to their mother country. Indeed, he remarks that while in Italy, where they felt the oppression of heavy taxation and mandatory draft, their "sentiment of the motherland" was either fading out or lost, but once they found themselves on American soil, it was reawakened, distilled and transformed into something new and more elevated: "They perceive the image of Italy in a new way, illuminated and speaking for the first time, and not under the form of their village or province, but the State. And as times passes that image becomes clearer and speaks louder."[25]

The text I am discussing was presented for the first time, in a slightly different format, in the cities of Trieste, Venice, and Turin between January and March 1887, shortly after the battle of Dogali, where an Italian battalion of over five hundred men had been wiped out by the Ethiopian army

(see Cepparone, 76). For the young Italian nation, it was a great humiliation, which was used by the conservative forces to attack the Socialists,
nicknamed the "internal enemy," because they opposed the military invasion of the horn of Africa.[26] The revenues generated by De Amicis's lecture
in Turin were donated to the families of the soldiers killed in the battle.
The choice of Trieste, which at that time belonged to Austria, was devised
to generate a patriotic reaction in the audience. The event was a success,
as the author himself stated in a letter to his publisher Emilio Treves
(Cepparone, 78). How could it have been otherwise? De Amicis addressed
the audience with these words: "Although almost all of them were forced
to leave their home, bringing with them only memories of struggles and
suffering, I never heard any of them, not a single one, pronounce a bitter
word against the motherland."[27] De Amicis's strategy is quite intelligent: by
showing the patriotism of Italians abroad, who should be resentful toward
their mother country that rejected them, he is making Italians at home feel
guilty for not showing enough love for their own nation. The same rhetoric
was used repeatedly throughout the twentieth century by Nationalist and
Fascist leaders. Several years ago, when I arrived in the city of Valparaiso,
in Chile, as I was walking out of the bus station, I noticed an unmistakable
Fascist building. It was the Scuola Italiana Arturo dell'Oro, named after a
young man from Valparaiso of Italian origins who served as a volunteer in
the Italian army during World War I and died heroically in the conflict.
The date on the building, in Roman numerals, is MCMXL (1940). The
school has become so successful that in 2003 another branch was created
in the nearby city of Viña del Mar. It is a "scuola paritaria," officially recognized by the Italian government: its graduates receive an Italian high
school diploma that gives them access the Italian universities.[28] In his book
Emigrant Nation: The Making of Italy Abroad, Mark Choate writes that
more than three hundred thousand reservists came back from abroad to
fight for Italy in World War I. Because of this massive counter-exodus,
Italy was the only combatant country in Europe to gain population during
the conflict, while all other European nations experienced a sharp demographic decline.[29]

During his visit to the San Carlos colony, De Amicis notices that, contrary to colons from other nations, Italian houses are bare and neglected,
as if Italians were trying to conceal their wealth. Although the sentiment
of "odio di classe" (class hatred) is not present in the colonies, because
the big landowners are so far removed, both physically and socially, the

less successful farmers are jealous of the more fortunate ones, which may explain their cagey social behavior. On the other hand, the author remarks that all the colons possess an admirable charitable spirit, which is not limited to citizens of their country but extends to all the members of the community. In his view, this global sentiment of human solidarity originates from the fact that everyone must confront "l'immensa natura" (the immense nature; 51), which is both generous and terrifying in its grandiosity.

De Amicis writes that Italian colons are often discriminated against and mistreated by the local authorities and law officers, despite their hard work and diligence, but he adds that the discrimination they face on a daily base is subtle and derives from the sense of superiority that native citizens feel toward new immigrants:

> The pride of the first lord of his land; He looks down on those poor folks who had to leave their homeland and make a living on that immense plain that he conquered and now he handed down to them. The vague fear of being surpassed by the immigrant population, often makes him feel the need to put his guest in their place with a haughty word.[30]

With these remarks De Amicis pinpoints one of the crucial conflicts that Italian migrants had to face: on the one hand, they were well aware of making a crucial contribution to the modernization of the host country and knew that they could rely on the support of the institutions, but even the poorest and most marginalized *gaucho* could look down on them with a sense of superiority, as the nomadic shepherd-warrior always does when forced to withdraw from his land by new settlers who are more focused on agriculture. Although one cannot deny that European immigrants were agents of progress, as Sarmiento and his liberal friends had foreseen, the natives, confronted by immigration that threatened to submerge them, often displayed a desperate arrogance, indicating a desire to reestablish a superiority that by then was irremediably lost. The Argentine ruling classes gradually abandoned the liberal doctrines that had inspired them, reclaiming the values of chivalry represented by the *gauchos*, who had become obsolete but continued to exercise a romantic appeal, precisely because they had been vanquished. It was a way to exorcise the demon of immigration, representing the newcomers as vulgar, cowardly, and overly attached to material possessions. No longer the nobility of the heroic man who fights alone against nature, as embodied in De Amicis's duel between the herdsman and the wild horse, but a new generation of "little ants" swarming through the uncontaminated plains of the interior, where horses, cows, and countless other animals had roamed free. The sense of precariousness that the dwellings built by the Italians in the San Carlos neighborhood is different from those built by the *gauchos*. The latter embraced the landscape of the *pampa* and became part of it; thus, his nomadic lifestyle was scarcely distinguishable from the Native Americans he despised. The houses of the Italian colons, instead, suggest that their objective was not to live with the land but to exploit it, to draw from it as much profit as possible. It is a "re-conquest" whose consequences on the environment will be more long-lasting and damaging than those of the first Spanish conquistadores. The metaphor more commonly used in those years by Argentine observers to describe the European immigration was "aluvión," a deluge. The mass migration, I would argue, would be better depicted as a drought, that in the long run would absorb and dry up the immense resources of the land. The "migratory chains" described by sociologists and historians of migration, featuring peasants constantly inviting their friends and relatives to follow in their footsteps, resulted in the "occupation" of the interior, to use a military metaphor, as De Amicis and other travelers often do in their travel narratives, which rapidly devoured the land and expanded the boundaries of "civilization." In a shorter version of the essay I am discussing, titled "Fra i nostri contadini in America," published in the journal *Fanfulla della Domenica*, De Amicis wrote that the immigrants from the regions of Piedmont and Lombardy were known as *comedores*, "land eaters," because "they rapidly plow, fertilize, and pass down to others their plots, and they go on plowing and fertilizing other lots, ignoring discomforts and dangers."[31]

Nevertheless, this new peaceful conquest, as it was depicted by contemporary observers, may be seen as a harbinger of a new and more devastating form of barbarism, which threatens to turn the fertile *pampa* into a no man's land where the pesticides produced by multinational corporations like Monsanto are destroying the natural environment and causing people to die of diseases that had never existed before, as vividly illustrated by Pablo Ernesto Piovano's prize-winning documentary *El costo humano de los agrotóxicos*.[32]

Dino Campana, one of greatest Italian modernist poets, visited Argentina at the beginning of the twentieth century, and he left a powerful representation of the Italian migrants' arrival in the port of Buenos Aires that strongly contrasts with the depiction given by De Amicis in the poem "Gli emigranti" discussed in the opening pages of the chapter. As the ship enters the Argentinian port, "sull'acqua gialla d'un mare fluviale" (on the yellow water of a fluvial sea) the Italians who are on the deck, "impazzano e inferociano accalcandosi / nell'aspra ebbrezza d'imminente lotta" (go crazy and turn ferocious as they throng / caught in the harsh euphoria of the impending fight).[33] In the next stanza, the poem introduces the innocent smile of a native boy who has come to the port to meet the newcomers: "leggerissimo / prole di libertà pronto allo slancio…accenna ad un saluto" (very light / child of freedom, ready to outburst, hints at a greeting). But the Italians are too absorbed by their dreams of conquest, and their response to the boy's timid greeting is a growl: "ringhiano gli italiani," Campana writes, which combined with the verb "inferociare" (to turn ferocious) gives an unexpected interpretation of the Italian migrant: no longer a victim, as in De Amicis's poem, but an aggressive individual who has come ready to fight and seize "his piece of America."

Indeed, the men and women that De Amicis met in the colony of San Carlos are very different from those he saw—or imagined—in the port of Genoa: most of them no longer dream about returning to Italy, although they still think about it with nostalgia. On Argentine soil, they take pride in their new status as small entrepreneurs. Those who had returned to Italy realized that they didn't fit any more: they can no longer accept the old condition of peasants, but at the same time they feel uneasy among the "signori," who possess higher levels of education and social distinction. Thus, De Amicis recounts, their stay in the mother country is usually short: they return and die in Argentina, a land they made their own, where their children were born: "conquistata dai nostri ospiti sopra la barbarie, fu riconquistata da noi sulla natura" (conquered by our hosts from barbarism, was reconquered by us from nature; 55). As the *gaucho* tamed the wild horses with his silver spurs, now the Italians are taming nature with the plow.

Despite the heated debates that involved nationalist supporters of colonialism and liberal intellectuals like Mantegazza, Virgilio, and De Amicis, who advocated free emigration, I would argue that there is a continuity between their politics, grounded in a common ideology based essentially on conquest. In De Amicis's reportage, the only ones who remain tena-ciously attached to the mother country are the women. He describes them as less inclined to accept the logic of profit embraced by their husbands; they miss their "bell'orto" (beautiful vegetable garden) where they used to grow their lettuce and radishes and the calm evening chats with their friends and relatives in the farmyard. In the *pampa*, they live far away from each other, and although their economic condition has improved, they don't understand their husbands' exclusive focus on "plata y trigo" (money and grain). In the new world, there is no space for "le cose dell'anima" (the things of the soul; 54), as the religious ceremonies are infrequent and the even the church buildings are neglected.

The author ends the reportage with another military metaphor: the farmers are soldiers who are called upon to carry on the incessant strug-gle against the "tyranny of nature." Paradoxically, once on American soil, the Italian peasants rediscover the original meaning of being a farmer, a noble profession "rifatta e nobilitata dalla fortuna" (remade and ennobled by fortune; 58). The sentiment of patriotism is ennobled too, as De Amicis observes a "povera contadina" (poor peasant) intent on carefully mend-ing her Italian flag, damaged by the strong winds of the *pampa*. Another woman sits in front of her "povera capanna" (poor shed) with a child in her arms; above her, another Italian flag flutters in the wind. Therefore, the poor migrant houses in the immense plain become "outposts"—another military metaphor—of Italian civilization. Defeated and humili-ated by the Ethiopian army at the Battle of Dogali, the Italian "patria" takes on a new, more authentic meaning, thus bringing back the impor-tance of patriotism for those working men and women who remained in the mother country:

And that poor peasant, seen from afar, with a child in her arms who was born on the Paraná river, and other children around her born in Italy, in front of that poor cabin above which the Italian national flag was waiving, in the middle of the immense American *pampa*, represented for us the love of one's country and the holiness of the family in the form most poeti-cally sweet, sad and solemn that a human mind may conceive.[34]

These words, pronounced in Trieste, a true "città-simbolo," situated on the contentious border with Austria, represent an admonishment for those men and women who were filling the Italian streets, calling for an end to the colonial war in Ethiopia, claiming that the "savages" in Africa and America were no different from the poor peasants in the southern Italian countryside who were being killed by soldiers carrying the same Italian flag when they revolted against their masters.

CHAPTER FOUR

From Free Emigration to Imperialism: The Debunking of the Argentine Myth

> *The great Proletarian has risen.*
> —Giovanni Pascoli, *La grande Proletaria si è mossa,* 1911

The Universal Exhibition that took place in Turin in 1898 drew eight thousand exhibitors and 3.5 million visitors and included one division devoted to "Italians Abroad" (Italiani all'Estero). Its objective was to celebrate the fiftieth anniversary of the Albertine Statute, the constitution of the newly unified kingdom—which would remain in force until the fall of Fascism—while showcasing the progress being made by the Italian nation. In his critically acclaimed book *Un principe mercante: Studio sulla espansione italiana,* published in 1901 by Fratelli Bocca Editori, Luigi Einaudi, a professor of political economy at the University of Turin, who became the first elected president of the Italian Republic in 1948, admits that the "Italians Abroad" section of the World's Fair was one of the least visited at the exhibition but argues that nowhere else a visitor could capture the accomplishments of the Italian people during the previous thirty years. Einaudi understood that many Italian emigrants and their children rapidly lose their *italianità,* as they are absorbed by the dominant destination culture. This process, however, can be avoided by encouraging Italians to migrate toward those countries where their compatriots already have formed a solid and respected nucleus, where they "find a similar and not numerically preponderant race, where the future may allow for a slow fusion instead of a lethal absorption."[1] There is an important difference between the two terms "fusione" and "assorbimento." The former indicates an active and mutual interaction, while the latter implies a passive subjection and a fatal vanishing. Einaudi writes that about one-fourth of the Argentinian population is Italian, and in Buenos Aires, the percentage of Italian residents is almost one-third.[2] The Italian "colonization" may be favorably compared with the one accomplished by the Anglo-Saxon "race" in North America: "Argentina would still be a desert, her cities a jumble of straw and mud without the persevering work, without the colonizing courage, without the entrepreneurial spirit of Italians."[3] The main tenet of Einaudi's book is to show that the famous British imperialist slogan "The trade follows the flag," implying that commerce is based on colonial expansionism, can sometimes be deceptive, as other Italian liberal economists, like Jacopo Virgilio, had claimed.[4] Einaudi shows, through a detailed analysis of an Italian "prince-entrepreneur," Enrico Dell'Acqua, that commerce must follow migration: "free colonies, not the official ones, must attract the merchants eager to create an outlet for the industrial products of the motherland."[5] Dell'Acqua was a small industrialist from Busto Arsizio, a town near Milan, who developed a wide commercial network for Italian textile products throughout Latin America. He did not focus on luxury products but on objects that could be purchased by as many consumers as possible. The metaphors used by Einaudi to describe the marketing strategies developed by Dell'Acqua are military, as in De Amicis's portrayal of the Italian "colons" in the Argentinian pampa. The Italian entrepreneur focused his attention on South America, the way "a general chooses on the map the best place to engage battle, or the fortress, whose fall will mark the conquest of a vast region."[6]

Einaudi dismisses the arguments of those who interpreted the Argentinian crisis of 1891 as an indication of a structural problem in its economy: the disaster is compared to a brief thunderstorm ("un temporale d'estate"), after which the skies once again became clear and tranquil. For a while, European emigrants turned to Brazil, but only for a short period, because they realized that the vast and fertile plains of the Rio de la Plata region offered greater opportunities. The author provides a graph that illustrates how Italian migration to Argentina was temporarily affected by natural and man-made events. The diagram shows an irresistible growth: the small torrent of 1857 has become a large river that does not seem to slow down.

A positive consequence of the economic crisis was that it put an end to "the idle and ostentatious reign of Argentinians, replaced by the patient and tireless work of French and English capitalists and Italian workers."[7] The rhetorical strategy adopted by Italian observers remained largely unchanged from Mantegazza to Einaudi: the Spaniards managed to conquer South America and subdue the native population but did not implement a real transformation, as in the United States. To accomplish that, the tenacious work ethic of northern European capitalists was required. How Italians fit into the picture is not entirely clear, because in the theories developed by the rising discipline of anthropology they belonged to the same "Mediterranean race" as the Spaniards. However, social scientists like Alfredo Niceforo, whose work I briefly discussed in the previous chapter, argued that northern Italians belonged to the same "Aryan race" as the Germans and Celtic populations, who had settled in the Po Valley in ancient times. Indeed, the emigrants who created the first colonies in the *pampa gringa* were for the most part from Piedmont and other northern Italian regions. The racist distinctions presented by Niceforo in *L'Italia Barbara contemporanea* (1898) and *Italiani del Nord e Italiani del Sud* (1901) were transplanted into American soil, seized by local social scientists, and broadcasted through newspapers and magazines, becoming part of what Antonio Gramsci would later call "senso comune," or common knowledge.

Although Einaudi based his volume on a careful analysis of a textile entrepreneur from Lombardy, the book covers a wide range of professions, thus offering the reader a broader view of the Italian epic "conquest" of Argentina. The first category he examines is "Il Marinaio" (the sailor), symbolizing the thousands of Ligurian merchants and sailors who settled by the small river Riachuelo, creating a "colony" called La Boca, now a neighborhood of Buenos Aires, where the main language spoken was the Genoese dialect. The port consisted of a wooded wharf, about two kilometers long, where all kinds of vessels were docked.

> It is true that the children of those sailors, who grew up in the new environment, partially modified the harshness of their idiom, but they have not canceled, nor will they be able to remove from that place—now transformed as if by magic into a populous and almost clean suburb— that peculiar character that makes those who visit it believe they are in a Ligurian port. Warehouses, taverns, trading posts, theaters, food stores, goods depots, workshops of every quality belong for the most part to the Genoese or their descendants.[8]

Einaudi continues by saying that the transformation of La Boca was miraculous: when the first Ligurians arrived, it looked like a primitive encampment surrounded by water; the houses were woodsheds built on stilts with makeshift bridges between them; the streets were muddy and dirty and the carriages that transported the merchandise had huge wheels to prevent them from sinking in the mud, where the horses almost drowned.

Later, other Italians and Europeans arrived, until a young man from Dalmatia, an area on the Adriatic Sea that for over five hundred years had been Venetian, gained control over the entire sector. Nicola Mihanovich is another example of a "principe-mercante" who started with a small boat, towing ships into the port of Buenos Aires. After a few years, his fleet included over 125 vessels, for a total of over forty thousand tons. Now, his ships are sailing all over South America, and he even created a rural colony in Chaco, one of the least-developed areas in northern Argentina, called "Dalmatia," that supplies the lumber for his shipyards. As Einaudi puts it, "such is the role of great men, of the rich entrepreneurs of new countries: to take the risk of starting new colonies, plow the deserts and fall the forests."[9]

The second category is "Il Colono," embodied by the thousands of Italian peasants who settled in the *pampa gringa*. Before their arrival, Argentina had to import most of its cereals and other primary necessities from over-seas, while today it rivals the United States and Russia on the international market. Italians have realized "un'opera colonizzatrice la quale non impallidisce dinanzi ai risultati della colonizzazione anglo-sassone nel Far-west americano" (a colonizing enterprise that does not pale in comparison to the results of the Anglo-Saxon colonization of the North American Far West; 43). In the interior of Argentina, Italians found over 4 million hectares of fertile soil, which required a very small investment to cultivate and were made available to them almost for free. Einaudi concludes with a polemical note: "È questo il motivo per cui il contadino italiano ha sempre preferito le pianure americane alla chimerica colonizzazione interna" (this is the reason why the Italian peasant always preferred the American plains instead of the chimeric internal colonization; 45). The transformation of the submissive Italian peasant into a courageous entrepreneur outlined by Einaudi echoes De Amicis's remarks in his reportage *I nostri contadini in America*: "The northern Italian day laborer and the southern peasant disappeared, replaced by the dynamic colon, self-confident and owner of his own land, improved Italian reproduction of those millions of farmers who constitute the backbone of the Northern American Union."[10]

Einaudi adds that more than half of the rural population in Argentina is Italian: southerners prefer to settle in the cities and towns, Ligurians took over vegetable gardens and fruit orchards, while Piedmontese are mostly found in the open field where they grow wheat, linen, and corn. Whereas they all started as day laborers or sharecroppers, many immigrants now own their own land, and a small number have accumulated huge fortunes, like Giuseppe Guazzone, another *principe mercante* who was nicknamed *el rey del trigo*, the Argentinian king of wheat, who in one year was able to sow 27,000 hectares of grain. When describing the harvest operations of La Empresa Agricola Pastoril, directed by an Italian lawyer, Enrico Nolasco, Einaudi again uses military metaphors:

> In the harvesting season, squadrons of horse artillery seem to be traversing the fields. It's a true army that maneuvers under the command of experienced officers. However, they do not sever human lives, but slender plants…that will come to Europe to compete with the products of our farmers who, lazy and slow in accepting modern technical innovations, continue to scythe, rake and stack hay by hand.[11]

Einaudi uses the Argentinian model of agriculture to criticize the lack of investment and modernization of Italian landowners, which makes their products less competitive on the national and international markets. The solution they used was to raise the custom duties on imported goods, a strategy that Einaudi, a traditional liberalist, strongly opposes. In his book, he also touches briefly on the wine industry, especially in the regions of Mendoza and San Juan, where Italian entrepreneurs like Antonio Tomba became international leaders in grape and wine production, with over ten square kilometers of vineyards that "sembrano città verdi divise in quartieri e regioni da ampie e dritte vie" (resemble green cities divided into neighborhoods and regions by wide and straight roads; 54).

Italians had been successful in many other areas: countless were the humble smiths who started their own metallurgy companies and are now sending their children to Italy to acquire the scientific and technical knowledge to manage their companies. More recently, an increasing number of Italian engineers had been going to Argentina to oversee established factories and create new ones. Italy, however, cannot compete for large government contracts with more industrialized European countries like England because Italian entrepreneurs, although very capable, do not have the capital necessary to invest in big projects that developing countries like Argentina need to build their infrastructure:

> Railroads, canals, and ports require the intervention of capitals from old nations, which may go to supply with confidence the new nations with those fundamental infrastructures without which colonization may not expand, population will not increase, and industries will not flourish. The capital necessary for these enterprises did not come from Italy; and thus, Italians in America had to be content with achieving the leadership in the projects of slow formation.[12]

When a public contract for a new railroad, canal, or port becomes available, the Italian industrialists cannot compete with Great Britain, whose banks could afford to put in enormous sums of money on long-term projects that may not deliver an immediate return on the investments. Thus, Italian companies are for the most part excluded from lucrative government contracts. Furthermore, Einaudi admits that English engineering firms prefer to hire their own managers and specialized personnel, letting Italians play a more subordinate role: "La mano d'opera italiana esegue ciò che il capitale e l'intelligenza inglesi comandano" (Italian labor executes what English capital and intelligence command; 73). As I am going to discuss later in the chapter, the dominant role played by English capitalism in the Argentinian economy will be one of the main arguments used by critics like Luigi Barzini, Enrico Corradini, and Giovanni Bevione, all of whom are associated with Italian Nationalism, to undermine the myth of a greater Italy in South America and push instead for a military expansion in other areas, like Libya and the Horn of Africa, where Italian workers would no longer be "enslaved" to foreign capitalists but rather become free citizens on newly acquired Italian soil.

Einaudi's book should be interpreted as an incitement addressed to both the Italian bourgeoise and the government to pursue more aggressive and less protectionist politics. In the conclusion, the author addresses explicitly that sector of the Italian bourgeoisie "adoratrice reverente del quattro per cento dei titoli di rendita pubblica, la classe media burocratica, militaresca e clericale" (who faithfully worships the 4 percent government bonds interest, the bureaucratic, military, and clerical middle class). Fortunately, that parasitical class does not represent all of Italy. In Lombardy, Piedmont, and Liguria there is already a class of merchants and industrialists and a mass of resourceful, dynamic workers, who managed to perform miracles despite the "cappa di piombo tributaria" (oppressive tax lead mantle) under which they are forced to operate. Those men and women, when they find themselves in a young society that encourages entrepreneurship, show the world the treasures of energy and obstinate industriousness deeply hidden within the "Italian race." Those individuals, had they remained in Italy, would have sought a position in public administration, enlarging even further the masses who worship the "quattrini pochi ma sicuri" (small but guaranteed income) represented by government jobs (160–61). Einaudi wants the Italian bourgeois class to follow the example of the Italian merchants in the Middle Ages and the Renaissance who established an unparalleled commercial network across Europe. The "modern prince" he envisions is someone who manages to conquer the global markets, thus contributing to the creation of a greater Italy beyond its national borders.

The danger that Italian emigrants may rapidly lose their *italianità* is real, and the Italian economist calls upon the Italian authorities to work closely with South American governments, drawing up commercial treaties that would facilitate the flow of Italian goods across the two continents. Italian authorities must be very careful not to upset the patriotic sentiments of young nations like Argentina, which may feel threatened by the massive flow of Italian emigrants into their territory. The preservation of the Italian language and culture is an objective that must be pursued with great diplomacy by subsidizing the already existing Italian schools abroad and working to convince the Argentinian government to recognize and accept Italian diplomas and university degrees. Einaudi even envisioned the creation of an Italian university in Argentina "la quale sia un centro ed un faro luminoso della cultura e della civiltà nostra in mezzo alla popolazione di origine italiana" (that will be a center and a bright lighthouse among our population of Italian origins).

In his book *Emigrant Nation*, Mark Choate writes that Einaudi "replaced the image of ancient imperial Rome with the mythic wealth of medieval Italy, replicated in Latin America."[13] The concepts of "emigration colonialism" and military imperialism advocated by Italian Nationalists and later by Mussolini, however, shared a similar military perspective, based on conquest and expansionism. In the frontispiece of Einaudi's volume, the places where Dell'Acqua's company established commercial branches are marked by little flags, as on a military map, showing the power of Italian capitalism, whose "captains" of industry symbolize the officers that will direct the emigrant invasion of the South American continent. In this process, the Italian men and women who were leaving Italy to put an end to brutal centuries-old exploitation are recruited as "soldiers" of an imaginary Italian army. From the point of view of Italian emigrants, remaining under the protective umbrella of Italian government and its much-publicized *italianità* often meant renouncing the many opportunities that the new country had to offer and establishing connections with workers from other countries who shared the same needs and hopes: national pride should replace international solidarity. Indeed, although Dell'Acqua's commercial "empire" collapsed a few years after the publication of Einaudi's book and his accomplishments were rapidly forgotten, the expansionist values that he embodied were appropriated by Fascism.

In 1929, the same year in which the Pope and Mussolini signed the Lateran Treaty fortifying the Fascist dictatorship, a bronze statue celebrating Dell'Acqua was erected in Busto Arsizio's main square, inaugurated by Giuseppe Bottai, minister of Fascist corporations. The monument includes several figures. Hermes, the Greek god of commerce, holds a caduceus in his right hand, followed by a young man who carries in his arms a heavy bundle of fabrics. On the opposite side are a young boy and a woman with a spindle, a traditional female profession in the pre-industrial era. Above them stands a man on horseback, allegorical representation of Enrico himself: as a captain of industry, he occupies a higher position, looking toward the future, in the same direction indicated by Hermes. Working men and women (and children) are relegated to an inferior position, embodying the "infantry" of industrial expansion.

Luigi Barzini and the Deconstruction of the Argentine Myth

Luigi Barzini's book, titled *L'Argentina vista come è*, published in 1902 by the *Corriere della sera,* is a collection of articles, or dispatches, that the young journalist wrote between November 1901 and September 1902 for the prestigious Milanese newspaper. I interpret the contribution of Barzini, who was about the same age as Einaudi when he traveled to Argentina, as a polemical response to the economist's celebration of Italian emigration to the Rio de la Plata region. But before looking at the differences between the style and content of the two texts, however, I would like to emphasize an important similarity: the use of military metaphors. Both authors perceive emigration in terms of conquest and colonial expansion, but whereas Einaudi celebrated the many accomplishments of Italians abroad as evidence of what Mark Choate calls "emigration colonialism," Barzini was much more skeptical about the feasibility of a peaceful colonization process. In a chapter titled "Errors and Defects of Italian Emigration," Barzini writes:

> The intellectuals in the masses are like officers in the army, a small minority that guides, at least with their exemplary behavior, that unites them in a common action. Remove the officers from an army of heroes and you will have the most shameful retreat. The army of our emigrants lacks officers, and they stray and surrender bit by bit, often giving in to that powerful weapon called "national dignity."[14]

In the same text, the author seems to implicitly address Einaudi when he remarks that for many years, Italian politicians and economists had focused almost exclusively on material wealth, like the remittances that Italians workers were sending back to their mother country and the Italian products that many of them continued to purchase while living abroad,[15] while no one worried about the price being paid for these material progresses: "we did not see the fallen soldiers in our immense army, who crossed the Atlantic in large squadrons, to fight in silence, under another flag, the most desperate battle."[16]

   Throughout his book, Barzini's intention is to dismantle the liberal emigration narrative, and he does so eloquently by quoting extensively from local newspapers. Although he does not say it explicitly, by deconstructing the Argentine myth, he opens the path for the nationalist movement that was developing in Italy during the same period, which was extremely critical of both liberalism and emigration. Contrary to Einaudi, who opposed Mussolini's politics, Barzini joined the Fascist Party from the beginning and signed the Manifesto of Fascist Intellectuals in 1925. Some of the rhetorical strategies used by Barzini to condemn emigration, however, are not very different from those adopted by De Amicis in his early works, especially in the poem *"Gli emigranti"* previously examined.

   The first chapter of Barzini's book is titled "L'Addio" (The Farewell), and it employs the same images found in De Amicis's poem. The setting is the Gulf of Genoa, portrayed as a paradise lost, with a gentle breeze from the hills bringing the perfumes of the Mediterranean vegetation. A series of personifications make the passage more poignant. On the ship, the author contemplates the statue of Neptune, an allegorical representation of Andrea Doria, the great Genoese admiral, who seems to be whispering the words: "Qui, qui si sta bene!" (Here, here we live well!; 2). As the ship liner leaves the harbor, the city of Genoa appears to be smiling in the sun, protected by its fortresses, and exhibiting its enchanting beauty. As in De Amicis's poem, the emigrants' departure is compared to death:

> Indeed, the emigrant's departure for a distant country is a little like a death. He dies to his habitual life. He dies to his loved ones, dies to his own country, he disappears in the unknown. Perhaps, he vaguely hopes to return, it's true; his death contains the hope of resurrection. But in the moment of separation the whirlwind of sorrows dissipates every dream. He has the lost gaze and the desolate expression of those who face the unfathomable abyss of another life.[17]

As the ship sails on, the beautiful face of the motherland fades away in the distance (la faccia della Patria impallidisce lontano), thus reinforcing the parallel between one's country and the mother. Contrary to Einaudi and other pro-emigration authors, the only possible way for the emigrant to come back to life is to return to Italy. The idea of building a new life away from the mother country, while maintaining one's *italianità*, as many Italians were doing at that time, is not contemplated. The reason is simple: from a nationalist perspective, every Italian citizen who does not return home is irretrievably lost: his or her children will become Argentinian, and Italy will have lost precious national assets that no longer belong to the mother country.

Barzini starts by examining one of the many "Emigrants Guides" that were being published at that time. But the one he discusses claims to be profoundly different. The author is Giuseppe Ceppi, a journalist who, according to the Guide's preface, had been writing for fifteen years for the most prestigious Argentinian newspaper, La Nación. Like Barzini, the author wants to tell the truth about his adopted country, instead of writing another panegyric of emigration that indiscriminately encourages the arrival of people who may not find suitable occupation in Argentina. In the opening pages, Ceppi claims that "Non esiste nessun paese nel mondo dove gli italiani possan stare meglio che nella Repubblica Argentina"

(There is no country in the world where Italians can live better than in the Argentine Republic; 10). In the capital, there are over three hundred thousand Italians, more than in most Italian cities. On the buses, in the theaters, and everywhere across the city, one can hear all Italian dialects being spoken; the climate is temperate, like southern Italy; the language is very similar to Italian and can be learned in just a few months. The current president, "Giulio" Argentino Roca, the military commander of the famous "Conquista del Desierto" that represented the final defeat of the Native Americans, is a strong supporter of Italian immigration; upon their arrival, emigrants are housed and fed at no charge in the Hotel de Immigrantes for several days while they look for a job; once they find one they like, they are transported, always free of charge, to the location of their choice. Farm workers are always in high demand, especially during the harvest season, which may last up to four months, and so are domestic workers, especially women. Those who arrive in Buenos Aires must be prepared to live separately from their spouses, at least initially, because men find more jobs in the countryside, while women are easily employed in the bourgeois homes of the big cities.[18] The *Guida* warns the readers that the occupations they will find may be "forse più pesanti dei lavori che si fanno in Italia" (perhaps even harder than those they were doing in Italy; 18). Thus, "Solo devono emigrare i lavoratori forti, robusti, avvezzi alle fatiche. Quelli che sono deboli e delicati faranno bene a non muoversi" (Only strong workers, used to hard labor, should emigrate. Those who are weak and delicate should not depart; 23). When they arrive in Buenos Aires, immigrants should be willing to move out of the city right away, because rent is extremely high and jobs scarce. Although Argentina offers many opportunities to start one's own business, emigrants "si devono rassegnare alle contrarietà dei primi tempi, vivendo male, adattandosi a qualunque lavoro, senza debolezze né abbattimenti" (must endure the initial setbacks, living badly, accepting any employment, without weaknesses and depressions; 31).

The *Guida* makes it clear that some people should not migrate to Argentina: in addition to those who are either sick or too old,[19] "Those who have studied and have received a specialized education must not emigrate. They would form what could be called the epidemic of emigration, due to the damage they cause to those who emigrate and to the Argentine Republic that receives them."[20] These people include misfits ("spostati"), lawyers without clients, doctors with no patients, white-collar workers without a permanent position, and in general young individuals with neither a profession nor a trade, who have received enough education to develop a sense of entitlement. These people would end up being unhappy and cursing the country that welcomed them. Nevertheless, the author observes that Italian workers are usually very well regarded in Argentina, as they constitute the foundation of the country's prosperity. Although Italian capitalists are quite rare, there are some large companies and a great many small ones that were created and continued to be owned by Italians.

Barzini's reaction to the advice offered by the *Guida* is predictable: the mythical America that many Italian emigrants had dreamed of never existed, and it is time to break the magical spell in the minds of Italian people: "America is a country where people suffer, where they cry and where they perish, like everywhere else. Over there, the struggle for life is less disciplined and consequently violent, terrible".[21] Battle-hardened and fierce "mastiffs" come from all over the world to participate in the great *curée*, but Italians are not equipped to succeed in the mad rush. The term *la curée* was used by the French Naturalist novelist Émile Zola in the eponymous novel to symbolize the feverish financial speculations that characterized France during the Second Empire, leading to the Franco-Prussian War and the fall of the French Empire in 1871. The Italian author believes that Argentina is experiencing a similar, artificial growth: using a metaphor from our own time, one may say that the national economy is like a "bubble" ready to explode. Furthermore, Argentina no longer needs professors for its universities, nor doctors for its new hospitals, as it did in the 1860s, when the newly graduated doctor Mantegazza landed there in search of opportunities. Italian emigration has become, as Barzini puts it, an "emigration of muscles." And he wonders: "Isn't it painful and humiliating? This constant subtraction of our vital forces, this transfusion of our blood for the regeneration of distant nations, product for the most part of the ignorance of our masses, isn't it a very sad thing?"[22] The tables are turning in Barzini's narrative: Argentina is no longer the promised land described by Einaudi and his liberal friends, but a cruel monster that devours innocent victims.

Upon his arrival, Buenos Aires appears to the Italian journalist as a monument to bad taste, a poor imitation of Europe: "La più grande caratteristica di Buenos Aires è quella di non avere nessuna caratteristica" (The most distinct characteristic of Buenos Aires is its absence of character; 14). Everything is vulgar, inauthentic, an endless series of samples of European architecture randomly scattered throughout the urban landscape. Even the May Pyramid in the Plaza de la Victoria, erected to commemorate national independence, is made of stucco; Barzini is surprised that it is still standing after ninety years. Like most iconic buildings in the city, it comes wrapped with black pipes containing electric lights, another vulgar symbol of modernity used profusely throughout Argentina. The two European nations that dominate the collective imaginary are France and England: "Parigi è nella loro mente il compendio di tutto il bello e di tutto il buono che possegga l'Europa" (In their minds, Paris is the compendium of everything good and beautiful that Europe possesses; 19). Thus, the upper classes try to imitate Parisian design, fashion, and way of life. Every evening, the local high society gathers in Palermo's beautiful parks, where women display the latest models imported from France. The financial district, instead, is entirely British, and so are the names of the banks and the language spoken in the streets and commercial offices. "The British are the true proprietors of Argentina; they own all the railroads, the port, the colossal aqueduct infrastructure, the tramways and all the main companies" (17).[23] The British colony lives totally separate from the rest of the population: at the end of the day, bankers and businessmen get on the train at the Retiro central station and return to the exclusive neighborhoods of Flores and Belgrano, in their villas surrounded by greenery. One may wonder why Italian neighborhoods are absent from Barzini's description of Buenos Aires. Nevertheless, Italians are everywhere: the street vendors who drag their miserable life along the streets; those who dig the ditches for the sewage system; the bricklayers hanging from the scaffolds on high rise buildings. All are Italian; every single stone in the city was laid by Italian laborers. The only Italian district depicted by Barzini is La Boca, and it is not a pretty sight:

> The elegant people never go to the other side of the city. There is the *Boca del Riachuelo*, a strange district, almost a village, with small wooden houses made with zinc-coated iron, and crates of oil, sometimes even bricks. From the dirt roads, on which the wind raises dust into tornadoes, you can see small enclosures full of garbage…broken pieces of furniture, rags, and all sorts of things certainly collected on the street for reasons we do not know, perhaps because of that strange obsession with collection that sometimes accompanies poverty. In some courtyards at the foot of stunted trees burned by the sun, tomatoes and weeds grow among which

the chickens rummage. In some places the ground is swampy; the streets lead to real marshes. Here the houses are built on palisades, like those of lakeside villages; the water rots around the houses, all covered in green mold. In some less inhabited streets oxen graze freely, throwing their lamenting mooing to the wind. Everywhere there are small dark shops where everything is sold; poor dusty displays covered with flies; taverns from which the warm stench of wine emerges as if from the mouth of a drunkard; shady cafés where you don't drink coffee.[24]

In an enlightening essay on the history and identity of the neighborhood, Vanni Blengino remarks that it was nicknamed "La Boca del Demonio" (The Devil's Mouth) because of the strong anticlerical sentiments of its residents, which date back to the Risorgimento, when many of the inhabitants were Italian political exiles. In 1904, the population of La Boca elected the first Socialist congressman in the American continent, Alfredo Palacios, a professor of law who helped create legal protections against sexual exploitation, child and women labor, and excessive working hours.[25] When the first Salesian missionaries arrived in Argentina to convert the "savages" of Patagonia, they realized that there was "another Patagonia" that needed to be evangelized: "There is another Patagonia, metropolitan, to be evangelized in Argentina: it consists of Italian, Spaniard, French people barricaded in a peripheral neighborhood, a territory governed by Satan, La Boca del Demonio."[26] Although originally founded by Ligurian sailors, La Boca had become a multiethnic community where, in the disreputable bars and restaurants that travelers like Barzini did not dare to go, new art forms that would become quintessentially Argentinian were being developed, like the tango and the sainete, the famous Argentinian popular theater whose protagonists usually spoke cocoliche, a mix of Spanish and various Italian dialects.[27]

For Barzini, Italians are victims of a hallucination—Gli allucinati is the title of one of his first dispatches, dated January 13, 1902. While previous observers praised the hospitality system established by the Argentinian government,[28] for the Italian journalist the Hotel de Immigrantes where emigrants were housed and fed for several days, is a filthy lazarette of poverty, where Italians "sono accampati come un'armata alla vigilia della battaglia" (are camped like an army the day before a battle; 24). After they arrive in Argentina, emigrants are no longer human beings but objects: "gli uomini diventano cose, macchine che non costano nulla e che arrivano in abbondanza" (men become things, machines that cost nothing and keep arriving in abundance; 24). Indeed, goods receive better treatment, housed in well-ventilated, dry brick buildings equipped with elevators, whereas the "Hotel" is a "grande baracca di legno cadente e infetta, nella quale vengono condotti come mandrie all'ovile da inurbani impiegati" (a huge woodshed, crumbling and infected, where [Italians] are led by rude officers, like a flock to the sheep pen; 26). Originally built in 1883 to house up to four thousand people, the following year the facility was expanded to accommodate twice as many guests.[29] Around the building, there is a sort of no-man's land ("indefinable, irregular, muddy, which lies between the turbid and stormy Rio de la Plata and the city, a strip of land that seems to be a neutral zone between the realm of water and that of men").[30] The circular structure of the hotel evokes a panopticon, the mechanism designed by Jeremy Bentham in the eighteenth century and made famous by Michel Foucault's studies on disciplinary societies,[31] with a central post where the guards are housed, surrounded by the dormitories that resemble spokes on a wheel:

> In the middle of the main building, resembling a gasometer, there is a circular, dark, and damp courtyard, a kind of well, on which the doors of the dormitories open…The pungent smell of carbolic acid cannot overcome the nauseating stench that comes from the dirty and slimy floor, and which emanates from the old wooden walls and from the open doors; a smell of piled up humanity, of poverty.[32]

For the bourgeois Italian traveler, the concentration of extreme human poverty, which certainly existed in Italy too, is both striking and humiliating: he sees his fellow citizens crammed with hundreds of men and women from other nations, awaiting an unlikely redemption that their native countries could not offer. Furthermore, the racial element plays an important role in Barzini's narrative, adding to the sense of humiliation: the night guardian who oversees the dormitory is an old Native American, who now embodies the "executive power." When an Italian man pulls out his accordion and timidly starts playing a song, the overseer stops him immediately. The night rapidly falls on this sad place of suffering, while outside, in the nearby city center, Argentinians get ready to go out to restaurants and theaters, and the air reverberates with electric lights. Italian emigrants are excluded from the cheerful, Carnival-esque atmosphere that characterized Argentina during that period, because they represent the despised, ignored forces that make possible the luxurious lifestyle of the metropolitan capital.

Contrary to Einaudi, who interpreted the Argentinian financial crisis of 1891 as a tragic but temporary accident from which the country quickly recovered, Barzini believes that its roots are much deeper, and the ruling classes refused to address them. The metaphor employed to describe the disproportionate resources squandered every day in the capital is of a monster with a huge head sitting on a small and fragile body. The population of Buenos Aires is eight hundred thousand, almost one-fourth of Argentina. Most of the nation's wealth comes from the provinces, but it is entirely absorbed by the capital, where everyone seems to live in a state of "collective delirium." The national debt continues to increase, and yet nothing is done to stop it: the government has difficulties paying its creditors and the salaries of public employees, who often go for months without their stipend. For Barzini, the elegant boulevards with their stylish restaurants and theaters and the crumbling buildings where the immigrants are housed are two sides of the same coin: the opulence displayed every evening in the parks of the Palermo district conceals the extreme poverty of the working classes, which for the most part are foreigners. Rent in the city is extremely expensive and when immigrants move out of the Hotel de Immigrantes, they often end up in *conventillos*, the miserable, overcrowded tenements that house the foreign population.

Barzini writes that when the Bank of Buenos Aires collapsed in 1891, it was the third-largest credit institution in the world. The government should have invested in building a solid transportation infrastructure, which would have lowered the market price of wheat, corn, and linen coming from the interior. Instead, farmers are often forced to let their products rot because they cannot compete on the global markets: wines from Mendoza are more expensive than the ones imported from Europe, and construction lumber is imported from North America because there is no practical way to transport it from the forests of the Chaco to the major cities. Barzini writes that Argentina is "come un albero, ricco di frutti splendidi ma posti troppo in alto per arrivarvi con le mani. E mancano le scale" (like a tree, rich in splendid fruits but placed too high to reach with your hands. And there are no ladders; 36).

The problem of transportation is connected with the hegemony of English capitalism: the most valuable *estancias* located close to the railroads are in the hands of British companies, which can export their products at a competitive price. The railway industry is solidly in the hands of British investors, and the Argentine government cannot do anything to modify the tariffs because of the deep debts owed to English banks. But the main problem, in Barzini's view, is that the ruling classes have formed a sort of "oligarchy" that is profoundly corrupted and exerts total control over the political system. Although Argentina has a very progressive constitution, the elections are often a farce, characterized by open intimidation and violence:

> The oligarchy that drains the forces of Argentina and exhausts its promising energies is based on these elections. From the elections the octopus-like government is born, and vice versa: like the story of the chicken and the egg. It is a closed circle, whose anachronistic existence is explained by the exclusion from political life of that large part of the population that works, produces, and pays the most, and which would have precisely the greatest interest in honest politics: I am referring to the foreigners. With this extraordinary organization, electoral control of the people is completely lost in the complex governing body. A machine without regulation.[33]

The judicial system and the police force are corrupt as well, always favoring "il figlio del paese," the native son. Barzini quotes the German chancellor Bismarck, who once said that if the Argentinian government does not solve the problem of justice the country will have no future (75). Justice is especially important in a young country like Argentina, where the memory of the abuses of power that occurred during the brutal dictatorship of General Rosas and his *caudillos* are still very fresh. The Italian journalist utilizes the usual racial stereotypes to explain the spread of violence in the country: the Spanish colonizers, who lived for centuries side by side with Native Americans, are notoriously hot-blooded and more prone to violence than other Europeans: "And so the Argentinian blood is Andalusian with a pinch of Indian blood, and thus the Argentine is courteous, chivalrous, perhaps even generous, but oftentimes impetuous and violent as well. The revolver and the dagger are endemic, and people kill for no reason, as the *criollo* custom establishes. Pistols are in everyone's pockets."[34]

As Eugenia Scarzanella shows in her book *Italiani malagente*, the arguments presented by Barzini to characterize Argentinians of Spanish descent were derived from contemporary Italian anthropology, which was eventually used against Italians, who supposedly shared with Spaniards

the same "Mediterranean" racial and psychological features.[35] When looking at a photograph portraying police officers in the Province of Santa Fe,
the Italian journalist has no hesitations recognizing the moral character
through their physiognomy:

> I threw a glance at their physiognomies; a collection of resolute types, proud
> eyes, mustaches and strangely cut beards, and here and there hooked noses,
> prominent cheekbones and wide mouths cut as if with an axe's swing, all
> undoubtedly characteristics of a mixed race. There was also a Negro.[36]

It turns out that all of them were assassins, hired by the Governor precisely because he could easily blackmail and send them back to prison if
needed: "Io conosco la storia di tutta questa gente, li ho tutti nel pugno"
(I know the history of all these people, I have them all in my fist; 86), he
exclaimed with a certain pride. Instead of being the instrument of justice, as in any civilized country, the police force becomes enslaved to politics: policemen do not defend society at large but rather the interests of the
dominant political party: "Formano dei piccoli eserciti pretoriani sempre
pronti all'arbitrio ed alla violenza partigiana, a portare nella lotta politica
l'influenza decisiva della forza brutale contro il diritto" (They form small,
Praetorian armies always ready for arbitrary acts and partisan violence,
to bring into the political struggle the decisive influence of brutal force
against the law; 87). Foreigners are the most common targets of police violence, and the Italian journalist presents several instances in which Italians
were incarcerated, beaten, and even killed by the police for no reason.

It is not surprising that the local media reacted with indignation to the
publication of Barzini's letters. In one of the dispatches, the author openly
addresses their criticisms but did not stop his investigations, whose find-
ings were defended by many independent newspapers that recognized his
courage and integrity. *El Municipio*, an important Argentinian newspaper quoted by Barzini, wrote: "Malgrado gli attacchi anche grossolani, dei
quali è oggetto il menzionato corrispondente, dichiariamo che il Barzini
merita il nostro più alto concetto di considerazione e stima, per la sua
autorità, per la sua franchezza, per la sua indipendenza" (Despite the vulgar attacks, of which the aforementioned correspondent is the object, we
declare that Barzini deserves our highest consideration and esteem, for his
authority, for his candor, for his independence; 49). *The Standard*, which
represented the interests of the English colony, commented:

These correspondences may be more beneficial than the unhealthy mass of other publications whose disgusting flattery generates suspicions. Since the country is commercially, politically, and socially ill, Barzini is right to say so, dispelling such misunderstandings and illusions. We do not believe that he has exaggerated the social ills, since they grow instead of diminishing; the incautious emigrant who believes he can find integrity of government and justice is warned. By getting rid of false ideas, he is doing us a good service. Our best friends are not the ones who flatter us, and the indigenous press should bear this in mind when weighing the value of Barzini's opinions.[37]

The corruption, in Barzini's view, does not spare the Argentinian army: while in Europe there is a considerable military tradition of which citizens are proud, in Argentina the army is traditionally composed of people who are at the margins of society: whoever can avoid the military service does so, without being ashamed of it. The author quotes Argentinian sources claiming that the army has way too many officers, in average one for every five soldiers. Argentinians are courageous fighters but do not know much about military science; there are also too many indigenous and "meticci" (mixed-breed) in the army, who are not disciplined. Women often live with their husbands and follow them everywhere on the battlefields, just like the Native Americans. Moreover, soldiers are poorly trained, and the government spends too much money for the service they provide to the country. The only exception is the Navy, where there is less political interference and consequently corruption is less common.

With all the great resources that Argentina has at its disposal, it would not be difficult to balance the budget and get the economy on the right track, but that cannot be achieved because the ruling classes' bad habits have spread throughout society. Argentinians inherited from Spaniards a love for luxury and unnecessary expense, which is not limited to the elites but extends to every social class. People usually do not carry a wallet but keep the money haphazardly in their pockets, as if they despised it:

The Argentine carries his paper money bagged in the pockets of his pants. Any sum is carried like that, like a handkerchief. To pay, he pulls out a handful of bills, throws one all crumpled up at the seller with a unique air of disdain, and casually puts the rest back into his usual pocket.[38]

People tend to be careless about money, even when they don't have much of it. Both family and government budgets are out of control because at every level of society everyone wants to make a good impression, indulging in expenditures they cannot afford:

> Luxury overruns all fields, like a splendid nettle, and even grows inside Buenos Aires' financial budgets....Absolutely useless boulevards are built because Paris has them too. It is the sterile luxury of those who spend for the sake of spending, to "show off," of those who know little about the value of money.[39]

Consequently, there is a great waste of resources, weakening the "moral resistance" of society: everyone spends huge sums on fashion, festivities, and decorations that are neither necessary nor sustainable. When the funds are not available, it is almost unavoidable to borrow money at very high interest rates or to turn to gambling, a national obsession that finds its most astonishing manifestation in the Stock Exchange.

> Little by little everything tends to become a game, from business to politics; work is increasingly avoided to achieve wealth and prosperity, because it is too long and harsh and difficult compared to other ways. Since people spend money incessantly, it is necessary for them to earn it quickly. The result is an imbalance in all aspects of social life. The moral structure of society is weakening, and disgrace will befall when conscience, that powerful regulator of human actions, loosens or ceases to function![40]

Barzini is concerned because those who pay the price for the enormous squandering of resources are the immigrants, who in large part are Italian. Instead of trying to control expenses, the government's answer to the financial crisis is to increase production through immigration. Nevertheless, in Barzini's view, more and more immigrants have been leaving Argentina because unemployment is on the rise, the cost of living is unsustainable, and workers are literally starving. He quotes a passage from *La Prensa*, one of the major Argentinian newspapers, saying: "The most resourceful and capable men do not find a field in which to apply their initiatives; it would seem that Argentina, vigorous and full of energy, was transformed into an exhausted, drained country, having just enough life to provide the scarce daily bread."[41]

Barzini, like other Italian travelers, observes that the *pampas* of the interior were desolate until European colonizers made them fertile. He does not mention, however, the contributions of immigrants from other nations. According to him, Italian labor accounts for 96 percent of what is produced in Argentina. From the docks of Buenos Aires to the granite quarries of Tandil; from the wheat fields of Santa Fe and Cordoba to the metallurgic plants where steel is forged and transformed, it is the Italians who are responsible:

> We Italians are the worker bees of that great hive; Argentina only exists and grows by virtue of Italian labor. Without us, it would have no production, nor would it have agriculture, nor industry, it would have no theaters, palaces, ports, railways. It is the labor of our compatriots that has truly created the Argentina of today, and without that labor it would have no economic power, like any Guatemala or Bolivia.[42]

Italians are especially successful in reutilizing materials that Argentinians discard, but Barzini argues that most enterprises that liberal economists would call "Italian" actually are not, because "è il capitale che dà la nazionalità all'impresa" (it is the capital that gives a nationality to the enterprise), and in all the companies being created, administered, and staffed by Italians, the character of *italianità* disappears after just one generation. "A poco a poco, per cessione o per eredità, passano *tutte* in mani straniere—che spessissimo sono quelle dei figli—e di nostro non resta che la mano d'opera, la forza motrice. È poco" (Little by little, through a sale or the death of a family member, *all* companies end up in the hands of foreigners—most of the time the children—and nothing truly Italian remains, except the labor, the power that propels them. It is not enough; 155). All the contributions made by Italian scientists to the creation of Argentinian higher education are forgotten. In their eyes, Italians are the thousands of uneducated, starving individuals who humbly accept any occupation, and make incredible sacrifices to elevate their position. In a society so devoted to luxury and wasteful expenditures, Italians are often ridiculed and disparaged, as Vanni Blengino shows in his analysis of the Italian immigrant in Argentinian literature.[43] The immigrants who are subjected to discrimination realize that to succeed and to grant their children a better future they must abandon their *italianità*. Thus, they often change their last name, and if they do not, their children will, to escape the negative stereotypes that are associated with Italian immigrants. Barzini writes that the term *gringo,* commonly used to identify Italians, is derogative, although its origins are uncertain: "Until a few years ago, it represented a mortal offense, but then the *gringos* increased so much in number that the word lost much of its original meaning, becoming a simple derogatory expression."[44] Another, even more insulting term is *tano,* which derives from *napolitano,* originally used to identify southern Italians.[45]

Despite the enormous progress that Italians made in Argentina, Barzini observes that they continue to be ridiculed:

> Since the poor southern emigrants, Calabrian, Abruzzese, Neapolitan, Sicilian, are the most impoverished and uncultured, the word *tano* has gradually come to designate the lowest step of human degradation. Saying *tano* is like saying "miserable!" The irritated Argentine calls you gringo to your face; when angry, he shouts *tano.* This means that the words equivalent to *italiano* and *napoletano* occupy a place in the vocabulary of insults. And our pride cannot be flattered.[46]

In Argentine popular theater, the "tano" becomes a mask like *Arlecchino* of the traditional *commedia dell'arte,* embodying an illiterate young man from the countryside whose manners are in stark contrast with the more educated townsfolk. The *tano,* Barzini writes, "is mocked by everyone and speaks in blunders; he is a bit like the 'foolish servant' of the classic Italian comedies, but more servant and more foolish, and what's more he is a thief and is beaten."[47] Italians in Argentina are transformed into *commedia dell'arte* characters who perform the most humiliating jobs without complaining. They are expected to show gratitude because if they had remained in Italy they would be starving. In Barzini's view, the native thinks of himself in these terms: "tutta questa gente moriva di fame nel suo paese, è venuta qua, ed io non la scaccio; come sono buono, generoso, ospitale!" (all these people were dying of hunger in their country, came here, and I do not drive them away; how good, generous, and hospitable I am!; 165). The Italian government does very little to change this dominant mentality because of the precious remittances that Italians abroad keep sending back home. Any restrictions on Italian immigration to the Rio de la Plata would cause great losses for the Italian economy. Despite the enormous number of Italians living in Argentina, their voices are not heard because they lack the cohesion that only a strong, unified central government can provide. While other observers viewed the presence of many different mutual aid societies as indications of the strength of the Italian community in Argentina, Barzini interprets this internal diversity as a weakness: "Gl'italiani al Plata sono riuniti in circa trecento associazioni diverse: il che significa che sono perfettamente disuniti" (The Italians in the Plata are organized in around three hundred different associations: which means that they are perfectly fragmented; 168). The most eminent historian of Italian emigration to Argentina, Fernando J. Devoto, devoted the longest chapter of his book *Storia degli italiani in Argentina* to these associations, which found no comparison to other Italian communities abroad. At the end of the nineteenth century, mutual aid societies were the emblem of Italians abroad.[48] There were over one thousand mutual aid societies spread all over the world, from Cairo to Melbourne. The main characteristic of those in Argentina was their wealth: almost ten million liras. By comparison, in the United States during the same period there were 437 Italian societies, but their available capital was only 2.4 million. According to Devoto, mutual aid societies in Argentina were much less fragmented. Although regional associations existed in the Rio de la Plata, they were a minority. This is because many societies were started by patriots during the Risorgimento, when Italy had not yet been unified. Conflicts did exist, especially between republicans and monarchists, but the differences did not prevent their members from realizing important projects, like the Italian hospitals that were built in several major Argentinian cities. Barzini acknowledges that the Italian Hospital in Buenos Aires had welcomed over forty thousand patients in the last twenty-five years and that the newly built facility "non ha nulla da invidiare alle migliori cliniche" (compares favorably to even the best clinics; 171), but he does not explain how a disaffected Italian community in the Argentine capital could have raised over 3 million liras for the project. Devoto remarks that the presence of a powerful Italian bourgeoisie in Argentina accounted for the formation of selective Italian clubs, like the *Circolo Italiano* in Buenos Aires, established in 1873, whose honorary members usually included the President of Argentina and other eminent politicians. The Argentinian historian remarks, however, that most twentieth-century Italian governments looked at Italian private associations "con un misto di sufficienza e disinteresse" (with a mixture of conceit and indifference). While Einaudi saw "transnational" entrepreneurs like Enrico Dell'Acqua as models to be imitated, for most politicians "l'Italia fuori d'Italia" (Italy outside Italy) represented something to be disregarded and forgotten.[49] From a nationalist standpoint, the presence of many different associations, oftentimes conflicting with each other, may have been perceived as problematic, but their presence and proliferation on foreign soil was a sign of the nature of Italian national identity, which has been constructed, since the Middle Ages, as a conglomeration of many independent city-states. When Italians migrated to the Americas, they took with them these regional differences and formed associations that brought together people from the same area, sometimes from the same town, but that did not prevent the formation of a strong national identity.[50]

In the chapter "I figli degli italiani," Barzini addresses the question of assimilation. Italians abroad had gained the reputation of integrating faster than any other group. While some may consider it a great quality, for him it is a sign of weakness, because "assimilarsi vuol dire finire di essere italiani" (assimilating means to stop being Italian; 174). For the most part, the children of Italian immigrants do not maintain any connection with the culture of their parents. The main reason has to do with the language: most parents do not speak Italian but a regional dialect. Moreover, parents are uneducated and thus unfamiliar with the great accomplishments of Italian civilization and cannot pass on to their children the sense of national pride that could motivate them to learn more about Italy. Italian culture is perceived almost as a stigma of social inferiority, and when kids start going to school, they try to sever any ties with the culture of their parents, who usually acquiesce to their desire because, even for them, their native country is connected to memories of humiliation and sacrifice; therefore, it is normal, as Barzini puts it, that they "vogliono renderli uguali agli *altri* più che sia possible" (they want to make them like the *others* as much as possible; 177). Finally, Italian emigration was for the most part male. The small percentage of Italian women in the Italian communities abroad explains the disaffection toward Italian culture:

> A large part of our emigrants dispersed throughout the Argentine Republic marry women of the country, *criollas*, often brown *chinitas*, daughters of the Pampa, wretched and proud as the thistles of their plains. There is no Italian in the house, and the children grow up ignorant, if not disdainful, of their father's homeland.[51]

When men depart Italy, leaving behind their women, they renounce their ancient beliefs, traditions, and domestic affects that women traditionally cultivate: "Every woman that emigrates brings with her a little strip of the homeland closed in her heart. She will always tell her children about it; she will teach them the prayers that she learned there; she will recount the legends that she learned there; she will make them love it, because she loves it"[52] (178). Barzini realizes that Argentina needs to make every possible effort to assimilate the new masses and instill in them a profound love for the country; he does not oppose it, but he is saddened by how quickly the new generations lose any affection toward their parents' homeland, as if ashamed of it.

In Vanni Blengino's book mentioned above, *La Babele nella pampa*, the author explains that in the first Argentine naturalist novels, inspired by Émile Zola's famous narrative cycle *Les Rougon-Macquart*, the notions of "blood" and "race" play a dominant role. The children of Italian immigrants are depicted as morally and physically degenerate, unable to conceal the features inherited from their parents. The protagonist of Eugenio Cambaceres's novel *En el sangre*, published in 1887, has "la testa grande, i lineamenti camusi" (a huge head, a snubbed nose) and "l'espressione maligna dei suoi occhi infossati" (a malignant expression in his sunken eyes), the unmistakable signs of an inferior, dangerous race (64). When they become economically successful, children of immigrants are often criticized for their excessive greed and lack of compassion. In Juan Antonio Argerich's *Innocentes o culpables* (1884), the author writes in the introduction: "¿Cómo, pues, de padres mal conformados y de frente deprimida, puede surgir una generación inteligente y apta para la libertad?" (How is it possible that an intelligent generation suitable to freedom, may be born from parents so deformed, with a sunken forehead?).[53]

That was the reaction of the native ruling class—an oligarchy, as it was defined—whose power was rapidly slipping away. In Buenos Aires and other major cities, Italians were forming their own exclusive clubs, and even though a traditional Spanish *appellido*, or last name, still carried high-class connotations, the sons and daughters of immigrants were enrolling in the most prestigious universities, "invading" spaces that traditionally belonged to the native upper classes. The second-generation Italians constituted a threat, "la minaccia che milioni di uomini poveri, ma ansiosi di ricchezza, possono costituire nel futuro per la classe dirigente" (the threat that millions of poor people, but eager to become rich, constituted for the future of the ruling class).[54]

During the same period, two other writers of Italian descent, both physicians, used the same "medical" arguments to express diametrically different opinions about the new immigrants. Francisco Sicardi, in his narrative cycle titled *Libro estraño* (1894), argues that the *gauchos*, although respected for their heroic contributions, are bound to disappear: impoverished and unable to adjust to modernization, they sell their properties, waste their money in gambling, and consequently their "race" gets weakened, ready to be replaced by a new one, willing to work hard and suffer to construct a better future for their children. Their simple and austere brick farms are like temples of a new religion of work, erected in the middle of the desert: "Si formano fattorie, lontani e piccoli villaggi...che troviamo piazzati come fortezze gigantesche, costruite dalla forza della nuova razza, segno indelebile dello sforzo titanico della virtù e del lavoro"[55] (They form farms, distant and small villages...which we find placed like gigantic fortresses, built by the strength of the new race, an indelible sign of the titanic effort of virtue and work). Sicardi was a philanthropist and a doctor who rejected socialism and anarchism, which were becoming increasingly popular in Argentina. In his novel *Hacia la justicia*, the main protagonist is Desiderio, a psychopath who embraces Socialism, the "virus" that came from Europe. In his works, Sicardio called for a collaboration between different classes, since all problems can be solved with hard work and sacrifice. The protagonist of Manuel T. Podestà's novel *Irresponsible* (1889), by another writer and doctor of Italian descent, is a sickly young man, with whom the author juxtaposes the healthy immigrants, bearers of a prosperous future for the nation: with their physical strength and good mental health they will mix easily with the native population and workers from other nations, thus giving birth to a stronger Argentina.

In the agricultural colonies that were being created in the regions of Santa Fe, Cordoba, and Entre Rios, Italians worked side by side with men and women from many other nationalities. When De Amicis visited the area, he noticed that colons of different countries helped each other against natural calamities and corrupt government policies. He was impressed by their attachment to the motherland, symbolized by the Italian flags that he saw hanging from the simple farmhouses and the carriages that came to welcome him. He also witnessed how the colons would continue to speak their native dialect (especially Piedmontese) and remarked that the immigrants often hired Italian teachers so that their children would not forget the language. When Barzini visited the same area in 1901, he painted a much gloomier picture of the very same people. The term he uses to define them is *peon*.

The *peon*—Italianized into *peone*—is the humblest being that exists. He is something less than a man: he is a work machine with the strength of a man. The *peone* does everything: he is a porter, laborer, street sweeper. He lives for the daily wage, today he transports the stones to the construction site, tomorrow he brings the sheaves of wheat to the fields. He wanders around always in search of work; he passes from colony to colony, from province to province, very happy when a long occupation allows him to remain somewhere. He almost always travels on foot like the Wandering Jew, but without the legendary shoes, because his are worn out.[56]

The food that *peones* receive in exchange for their labor is always horrible; they drink warm, muddy water, sometimes mixed with a spirit extracted from sugar cane; their work is terrible, always under a torrid sun; their pay is minimal, from half a peso to two pesos a day; when the harvest is bad, or even a complete loss, the compensation is limited to food and permission to sleep at the *estancia*. The lucky ones are those who find a permanent position, usually for 15 or 20 pesos a month. But they still live like animals, many in the same room; if they get sick, they call a *curandera*, who administers them the most extravagant potions until they die in their bed. If the *peon* has a wife, they often live separately, because it is easier for women to find a job as a domestic worker in the city. Barzini is convinced that if Italian emigrants were to devote the same amount of work to their land back home, Italy would be the richest country in the world. Every *peon*'s dream is to become a *mediero*. The *mediero* rents a piece of land, builds a miserable shed made of sun-dried bricks, and covers it either with a straw or a tin roof. The rent conditions are so difficult for the farmers that they are forced to get more land than they can possibly care for. Usually, a family gets one hundred hectares, but they do not have enough time and resources to manage it properly. The land is not fertilized, the weeds thrive, and after a few years the plot is so impoverished that it must be abandoned: the desert will invade it once again. The author of the *Guida dell'Emigrante,* discussed earlier in the chapter, however, viewed things differently: he blamed the Italian colons for their failures. In a chapter titled "Sentimentalismi e realtà," he remarks that some immigrants "si lasciano dominare dai ricordi nativi" (they let themselves be dominated by native memories; 43). As a result, they are always thinking about returning, thus remaining restless and uncertain. Unfortunately, many Italians do not care for the land they are assigned, do not plant trees, and create gardens to embellish their properties. Thus, the countryside acquires a squalid and monotonous aspect that generates melancholy. The Argentinian government would like immigrants to become citizens and develop a sense of belonging, but unfortunately "they only want to get the highest possible profit from the land, sowing either linen or corn year after year, leaving it impoverished after a few years."[57]

Barzini claims that he met many sharecroppers who had become starving day laborers and were traveling around the province of Santa Fe looking for work. When he arrives in Argentina, the emigrant usually has no capital, so he must purchase everything on credit: the seeds, the machinery, the material to build the house, and even the food. If something goes wrong, because of a drought or a swarm of locusts, the creditors come down on him like vultures and seize everything he owns. Moreover, emigrants focus exclusively on cash crops—wheat, linen, and corn—while the rest of their property is neglected, because it would take time away from their main goal. Barzini argues that this way of life has a negative impact on the emigrant's character, because after he is done plowing the land, he lives for many months doing nothing, waiting passively for the time of harvest. As a result, he turns into a "half gaucho," apathetic and indifferent: "senza il sollievo ed il conforto di una vita civile ha perduto la grande forza della volontà, si arrende alla sciagura, cede, è vinto" (without the relief and comfort of a civilized life he has lost the great strength of willpower, he surrenders to misfortune, he gives in and is defeated by it; 193). Fortunately, Barzini admits, not all the landowners are so exploitative: some provide seeds, machinery, a good shelter, and rent the land at a fair price, thus allowing farmers to save some money and eventually to buy their own. Ideally, the Argentinian government would like all emigrants to turn into colons, because they develop an attachment to their property and the country, but the process is not easy because the land distribution system is faulty. Even the author of *La Guida dell'Emigrante* admits that the national and local governments made the mistake of "non ritenere le terre meglio situate e distribuirle ai coloni che vogliano coltivarle, pagandole in parecchi anni" (not retaining the better situated plots and distributing them to the settlers who want to cultivate them, letting them pay for them over several years; 63).

In Argentina there is still an enormous amount of good land that only needs to be made productive: that is the mirage that attracts many emigrants, but the reality is that most of it is already in the hands of great *latifondisti*, landholders who usually obtained it in exchange for their military service. The land still available is located far from the railroads, which makes it very difficult to transport and sell the crops and ship them overseas. Barzini claims that colons are usually swindled by the large landowners and their agents, who advertise the land in misleading *réclames*, which carry descriptions that somehow never correspond to the real situation. Sometimes, the agents give a parcel of land they are having trouble selling an Italian name, like *Nuova Torino* or *Margherita*, to attract Italian emigrants. Other times, landowners sell properties for which they do not have the legal documentation. Farmers purchase them anyway and then later become dispossessed. They can either buy the land a second time at a higher price or leave it—after having worked for years to make it more productive.

In the chapter "Nelle colonie argentine: I coloni," the Italian reporter quotes *La Patria degli Italiani*, the most important Italian newspaper in Argentina, stating: "Tutto il meccanismo dell'economia rurale non ha che uno scopo solo: impinguare la scarsella ai latifondisti ed alle imprese di colonizzazione" (The entire rural economic system has only one objective: making the large landowners and the colonizing enterprises richer; 203). In Barzini's view, the Argentinian government must assign the land directly to the farmers, without intermediaries, otherwise they will start leaving the fields, as is already happening all over the country, where the unemployed number over two hundred thousand, many of whom used to be agricultural workers. For that to happen, the Italian authorities should be more proactive and exert pressure on the Argentine government, instead of considering emigrants as a "zavorra," deadweight to be discarded. The multitude of workers who leave Italy every year constitute a precious resource for the host countries, and the Italian government must protect them from the abuses that are taking place in Argentina on a daily basis. Barzini also criticizes the way the consulates are managed: the personnel do not remain in the same location for more than two or three years, so they do not have enough time to get to know the local culture and the Italian communities who live there. England, on the contrary, selects its diplomats very carefully: they are fluent in the language and have a thorough knowledge of the local politics. Argentinians respect British citizens because they know that if something happens to one of them, there will be immediate repercussions. "E noi? Ah! quanto lunga, dolorosa, raccapricciante sarebbe la storia dei delitti impuniti nei quali la vittima è stata italiana" (And us? Ah, how long, painful, horrifying would be the chronicle of the unpunished crimes whose victims are Italian; 215).

In conclusion, many of the Italian journalist's observations were very well known in Argentina: "For sure, I was not revealing any secrets: those who live and have lived in Argentina are aware of it, unfortunately. It's a situation that millions of people know well, widely reported by local newspapers and debated by polticians."[58] As a diligent reporter, Barzini traveled through the country, interviewing people and consulting the local press. As opposed to De Amicis, whose trip was sponsored by the Argentinian press and whose main interlocutors were Argentinian politicians who favored immigration and wanted him to offer a positive image of their country, Barzini quickly became persona non grata because of his own writings. He hoped, however, that his critical articles may benefit not only Italy but also Argentina. The local political class, he writes, is extremely concerned about their international image. When an authoritative English newspaper criticizes any aspect of their government, it originates an internal debate on the necessity of reforms: "Perhaps, the reforms will not come, but they are discussed, and this for Argentina already is a great result, caused by the control exercised by the foreign press, which for Argentineans is something both new and fastidious."[59] The Italian journalist is pessimistic about the outcome of his investigations because it is easier for Argentina to keep expanding its internal frontiers and invite more and more foreign workers, as was already happening in the southern part of the country, instead of addressing the structural problems. Italian emigrants have the right to be informed, however, about the real state of the economy and the Italian authority must do more to protect the rights of its citizens.

Ultimately, Barzini perceived immigration in Argentina as a military enterprise that the Italian state should direct and control, very much like an army. In the book's introduction, he writes that Italian public opinion has the right to know "what happens to this *army* of our workers that abandons the motherland and gives its immense power to another nation."[60] In addition, his militaristic conception is connected to an idealized view of the Italian armed forces that does not take into account the profound class conflicts that were unfolding at the time: "The military profession has always been perceived as one of the noblest, and later the army became the object of great honor and love when all the people were called upon to fight the holiest battles; the army has become one thing, one flesh with the people."[61] The idea of the army becoming "the flesh of the people" and the object of everyone's love is very questionable, especially in the light of the protests against the disastrous Ethiopian campaign that took place all over Italy. The famous saying, "O brigante o emigrante," either brigand or emigrant, which is commonly used to describe the condition of southern peasants after the Risorgimento, shows that emigration was often perceived as a silent protest against the Italian government and its army, and the "holiest battles" were the ones that southern peasants fought against the Piedmontese.

Giuseppe Bevione in Argentina and the Emergence of the Nationalist Movement

In the same period that Barzini visited Argentina, there was an impressive wave of social protests in Buenos Aires, Rosario, and other major cities in the Rio de la Plata region, whose initiators were often Italian political activists who escaped political persecutions. Nevertheless, neither Barzini nor Giuseppe Bevione, who was sent to Argentina by the Italian newspaper *La Stampa* in 1910 to report on the celebrations for the one hundredth anniversary of Argentina's May Revolution, mention these political unrests and the role played by Italian immigrants in the labor movement. The first decade of the twentieth century in Argentina was characterized by political repression: two important laws were promulgated restricting the freedom of expression and the rights of foreigners. The 1902 Law of Residence targeted the leaders of the working-class movements, and the 1910 Law of Social Defense made possible the deportation of political activists deemed to be a threat to the political establishment.[62]

Bevione arrived in Buenos Aires in 1910 as an ambitious reporter who was only six years younger than Barzini and had just completed an important assignment in London. After his stay in Argentina, in 1911 Bevione was assigned by *La Stampa* to cover the Italian invasion of Libya, which he enthusiastically supported. In his reportages, Tripoli is described as "la Terra Promessa, che dobbiamo conquistare prosperando, o perdere spargendoci pel mondo a servire e soffrire" (the Promised Land that we must conquer while prospering or lose by scattering ourselves through the world to serve and suffer).[63] Thus, the reader should not be surprised that his book *L'Argentina*, published in 1911 by Fratelli Bocca in Turin, follows the same path traced by Barzini a decade earlier.

When Bevione arrives in Buenos Aires the city has reached over 1.3 million residents and the streets are characterized by intense traffic. Nevertheless, the atmosphere is different from London, where people are constantly busy, absorbed in their own tasks (18). The mild climate and the clear skies inspire everyone to spend time outside. The author has the sensation of living in an opulent society, a rich pasture where the struggle for life does not cause any anxieties, because tomorrow will be a better day. Bevione writes that Argentina was nicknamed "el pays de mañana," because everything is postponed until the next day. The society is pervaded by a sense of optimism that derives from a combination of self-confidence, well-being, and good nourishment (19). While other Italian observers were fascinated by Argentinian women, Bevione thinks that the sense of abundance and leisure that dominates society tend to make women lazy and overweight.[64] While Mantegazza portrayed the *porteña* woman as an allegory of the youth, energy, and unlimited potential of the nation, in Bevione she is emblematic of its decadence. Her eyes are magnificent, profound, and voluptuous but often short-sighted, requiring glasses (*pince-nez*), suggesting an inability to clearly distinguish remote objects. Similar to Argentinian society, Buenos Aires women travel comfortably immersed in their luxurious carriages and do not see the crisis that is looming at the horizon. Her beauty is "flaccid," indicating a society that is overindulging in its affluence. In fact, the ostentation ultimately undermines her elegance, grace, and harmony.

Decadence is the main theme that characterizes Bevione's narrative. Argentina has all the bad features of a "vecchia razza in decadenza" (old and decaying race; 114). The abundance of natural resources seems to increase the general tendency to relax and enjoy life effortlessly. "La terra è così friabile e dolce, che il vomero può incidere per chilometri il suo solco, senza che l'aratore lo debba una sola volta squassare" (The soil is so crumbly and soft, that the plow can carve its furrow for kilometers, without the plowman having to exert himself even once; 27). Gradually, the strong, healthy Italian immigration, composed for the most part of farmers, who contributed to modify the landscape of the interior making it more productive, is being replaced by an "immigrazione spagnuola, debole, pigra e cittadinesca" (Spanish immigration, weak, lazy, and city-like; 28). In Bevione's opinion, Spaniards came in great numbers, "but the desert frightened them, and the hard work of the first sowings was greater than their hearts: they stayed in the populous cities to await the flow of wealth, hoping to bring a little stream into their *almacenes* and into their *boliches*."[65] Italians, on the contrary, were not intimidated by the immensity of the task they were facing and managed to accomplish what no one else before them had done: "costituire gli elementi essenziali di una nuova civiltà" (build the essential elements of a new civilization; 87). As Bevione travels through the province of Santa Fe, he is overwhelmed by the spectacle of the countryside:

> I felt my soul swell up with enthusiasm at the thought that those who had plowed and given that immense region to civilization were children of Italy. It filled me with pride knowing that the great green oasis that extends into the Argentine desert would still be three-quarters wild and uncultivated pampa if the Italians had not come, and if in fifty years of courageous work they had not created a garden from it. When people doubt the qualities of our race, they are unaware of its offshoots into the world. When people say that we bear the burden of too many centuries and civilizations in our blood, they do not see what our decrepit and rotten race has managed to do in South America.[66]

Unfortunately, the efforts of so many Italian emigrants did not bear the expected fruits because, as Barzini already explained, most of the fertile lots located close to the railroads remained in the hands of a small group of landowners. Bevione visited a colony called Pilar, where his hosts are an Italian-Swiss family called Vionnet. Interestingly, they are not farmers; instead, they own a *tienda*, or *almancen*, where they sell everything on credit, since their customers can only pay for the merchandise after the harvest. For Bevione, their presence is a blessing, because otherwise the farmers would not be able to survive. The Vionnets reside in Esperanza, the first formally organized agricultural colony in Argentina, but they have two branches in other locations. Every year they sell over five million units of merchandise and buy grain and other products for over four million. The land in Esperanza and the nearby towns are thoroughly cultivated by the colons who began to settle there in 1856. Normally, a concession was 33 hectares, but at least four concessions are needed for a family to survive. Bevione and his friends also visited a farmer whose last name is Oliva and owns 2,500 hectares of land. Now he and his family live in a beautiful house, with elegant furniture purchased in Buenos Aires, including a pool table, but when he arrived in 1866 with his brother, they had nothing. Currently, he owns around eighty concessions, which he rents to sharecroppers. Bevione celebrates Signor Oliva's success but claims that his two sons, who both speak Italian, are "perduti alla patria" ("lost to the fatherland"; 94), a term frequently used by Nationalist authors.

The reason why children of emigrants are so rapidly integrated into Argentinian society and "lost" to their parents' culture is political. Bevione remarks that there is only one area where the Argentine government has excelled: the creation of a strong national consciousness. The state understood very well that in a country with such a high percentage of immigrants the main problem was how to transform them into loyal Argentinian citizens, and they succeeded in "bollandoli a fuoco dello stemma repubblicano" (branding them with the republican emblem; 97). Although all the economic sectors are dominated by foreigners, the natives retain control of the political system. Bevione writes that when King Umberto I was killed in 1900,[67] many balconies throughout the country exhibited Italian flags, since so many Argentinians are of Italian origin. In 1911, this display of Italian patriotism would not be possible, because whenever a foreign flag appears, the Argentinian flag has to be displayed too.

Every individual born on Argentinian soil is automatically a citizen. European nations tried to oppose this law, which was based on the *jus soli* principle, but even a progressive political figure like Bartolomé Mitre, who adored Italy and even translated Dante's *Divine Comedy*, did not budge on the issue. The school is the main channel used to inculcate a sense of national belonging. In the school curriculum, the generals who fought for the country are transformed into national heroes: "The vital question was and is not to remain submerged under the cataracts of foreigners arriving by the million from the civilized countries of Europe, but to make them harmless to the established race, indeed to absorb them in the shortest amount of time possible."[68] The objective of the school system is to make every young man and woman proud of being an Argentinian. Bevione quotes extensively from the textbook used in elementary schools, called *Catecismo de la Doctrina Civica*, authored by Enrique Vedia and adopted in 1909, and makes fun of the propagandistic language adopted by the author. Interestingly, the epigraph of the volume

I consulted, also available online, is "Votar es Gobernar" (to vote is to govern), which reads like a response to Juan Bautista Alberdi's famous motto "Gobernar es poblar" (to govern is to populate). Indeed, populating Argentina through immigration was an important task, but convincing newcomers to actively participate in political life was equally important for the new republic. Bevione writes that in the presidential elections of March 13, 1909, in Buenos Aires, only twenty-five thousand people voted. Foreigners are not interested in politics and get involved only when their immediate interests are endangered. Consequently, politics remains the domain of a restricted set of families. "La politica resta così l'affare particolare di un numero molto limitato di persone, tutte quante del paese. Ci son famiglie provinciali estesissime, che da anni vivono e prosperano facendo politica, e trasmettendosi i seggi elettivi e gli impieghi migliori" (Politics thus remains the particular business of a very limited number of people, all of them from the country. There are extensive provincial families, which for years have lived and prospered in politics by passing on electoral seats and the best posts; 57–58).

The Italian government should do more to contrast the Argentinian assimilationist politics, protect its citizens, and preserve their *italianità*, as Barzini and others observed. Bevione, however, believes that it is the lack of solidarity among Italians abroad that undermines the success of the community:

> Our compatriots who work in the Republic represent myriads of isolated and dispersed monads, who ignore one another, and do not make the slightest effort to get to know each other, understand each other, organize themselves, and create, by the fusion of collectivity, the specific force that must defend them. The Italian who goes to America slips into blind and ferocious selfishness. He works with tremendous energy, from dawn to dusk, to conquer fortune as quickly as possible: but he immediately loses passion and interest with anything that has no direct or visible relationship with wealth. The Italian, even of a good race, as long as he is in America, is a citizen on leave, a resignee of all citizenship and obligation. He cares little about what happens in the fatherland and nothing of what happens around him, in the country that hosts him.[69]

I argue that Bevione's critique of the corrupt Argentinian political system and his characterization of Italian avarice are valid, but instead of looking beyond the Italian diaspora community abroad, as many Italian migrants and political activists were doing when they united with workers from all over the world and organized the first strikes in Argentina, he calls upon the Italian authorities to organize and direct them, as if they were soldiers of an immense army in desperate need of stronger leadership. Paradoxically, Bevione, recognizing that Argentinian production is in the hands of the workers, writes that if they were to go on strike, they could shut down the entire economy: "Essi son tutto. Senza di essi l'Argentina soffrirebbe la fame e l'onta di non poter far fronte ai suoi impegni con l'estero. Se gli Italiani dell'Argentina incrociassero le braccia per una sola settimana, la vita della Repubblica si arresterebbe per incanto" (They are everything. Without them Argentina would suffer from hunger and the shame of not being able to meet its commitments in foreign trade. If the Italians in Argentina crossed their arms for just one week, the life of the Republic would come to a halt as if by magic; 136). Yet, because of his nationalist ideology, he cannot envision an actual general strike that would involve workers of all countries, including Argentinians. He ignores the emergence of a transnational workers' movement that was unfolding in Argentina in the very same period he was writing. Instead, he modifies the Marxist concept of an international proletariat and deprives it of its revolutionary content by describing Italy as a "proletarian nation," a concept that would be developed further by the founder of Italian Nationalism, Enrico Corradini, and expressed even more eloquently in Giovanni Pascoli's famous speech La Grande proletaria si è mossa," which he delivered on November 26, 1911, to honor the first Italian soldiers killed in the invasion of Libya.[70]

Bevione points to Japanese emigration policy as a model the Italian government should follow: like Italy, Japan is a rising military and imperialist power with limited economic resources and an abundant population. Bevione quotes a speech given to Argentinian authorities in which the Japanese ambassador openly rejects emigration: "Nell'eccesso di popolazione noi non vediamo una maledizione, anzi l'amiamo, e ci adoperiamo per tenerla vicina ai suoi focolari" (We do not see a curse in the surplus of population; instead, we love it, and we strive to keep our people close to their homeland; 159). The only place where Japan is willing to send its people is Manchuria, a region that the Japanese Empire eventually invaded in 1931. For the imperialist Japanese government, emigration is "evil." And Bevione totally agrees with the position:

Like all great social phenomena, emigration is interwoven with advantages and damages, but the damages are preponderant, and moreover of a permanent nature; they violate the invaluable common good, meanwhile the advantages are transitory, and concentrate on conquests, which are possible to achieve in another way.[71]

Emigration may have been a necessity in the recent past, when Italy was still undeveloped, but now that it is becoming industrialized, it can easily absorb all the young people who continue to leave the country. Furthermore, the Italian government must realize that emigrants are precious "commodities" that Argentina cannot do without and leverage that powerful argument to secure better treatment for its emigrants abroad.

Despite his powerful criticism, Bevione ends the book on a positive note: he believes that Argentina will succeed in overcoming the political problems that hinder its economic development. But to achieve that objective, the government must implement a courageous campaign of land redistribution that seems Socialist:

The grave problem of land, which is at the root of all the Republic's problems, cannot be solved except through an energetic and, if necessary, autocratic policy of forced expropriations, through the restitution of the purchase price by the state and a scrupulous reassignment of the land to small settlers.[72]

In other words, the *latifondisti,* who received the land from the government for almost nothing, should return it to the state, which will redistribute it to the farmers. Only if the government has the courage to give the land to those who work it will the Argentinian society and economy find a new balance and manage to get rid of the huge debts that are strangling its finances. The country has been squandering its enormous natural and human resources, but this process cannot continue for too long, or it will perish:

The country must triumph or die; Argentina must elevate itself to the group of free and dominant states or fall irreparably into the flock of exploited and enslaved nations. Now I have the absolute conviction that nature will win, that the fertile soil will shape man in its image and likeness and that Argentina, along with Canada and Australia, will play a critical role in the future history of humankind.[73]

Enrico Corradini and the (Im)possible Return to the Homeland

Although Bevione advocates for a redistribution of the land to those who work it and recognizes the disruptive power of a general strike, which would show the Argentinian elites how essential Italian migrant workers are for the economy of Argentina, he does not present the political struggle that was unfolding in the lands where Italians were migrating. To get more a fully developed representation of the ideologies that inspired Nationalist authors like Bevione, one must turn to fiction. In the last part of the chapter, I would like to examine two novels that Enrico Corradini, the founder and leading figure of Italian Nationalism, published shortly after his voyage to South America, *La Patria lontana* (1910) and *La Guerra lontana* (1911). In *La Patria lontana,* the struggle between the three main ideologies of the time, Nationalism, Liberalism and Socialism, is enacted in an allegorical fashion.[74] The main hero of the novel is Piero Buondelmonti, whose last name means literally "The Good Man from the Mountains." Piero comes from Tuscany, a region where the rural economy was based on sharecropping, and he possesses the manners and sentiments of the traditional Tuscan landowners: he likes to fraternize with the workers and knows how to gain their trust. During the trip from Genoa to Brazil, he shows empathy for third-class passengers, "perché egli era veramente un giovane di gran cuore, sentiva pietà per quelli che soffrono e nutriva simpatia per il popolo, per I forti lavoratori" (because he was truly a young man with a big heart, he felt compassion for those who suffer and harbored sympathy for the people, for the strong workers).[75] As all allegorical figures, however, he is endowed with a double nature, and when he writes about politics, "egli era semplicemente l'apostolo dell'eroico nazionale...la romanità era diventata sangue del suo sangue e carne della sua carne, come espressione della più vigorosa volontà collettiva di vastità, d'unità e dipotenza" (he was simply the apostle of the national heroic...the Roman spirit had become the blood of his blood and flesh of his flesh, as an expression of the most vigorous collective will of vastness, unity, and power; 23–24). While the other first-class passengers watch the migrants from the upper deck with a mix of nausea and disgust at the "carnaio umano che traversava l'oceano insieme a loro" (human carnage that was crossing the ocean with them; 14), Buondelmonti listens to their concerns and talks to them, almost like a Christ figure. This is how the narrator describes the emigrants on the deck of the ship:

There was the refusal of the scum of the cities, hunted by the greed of adventure, there was the refusal of the poverty of the countryside, hunted by hunger; (...) sailing toward the unknown New World...at night they descended into the holds and formed a purulent, fermenting mass of human flesh...then, once on the American shores they would disperse, out of the unknown and then right back into it.[76]

Signora Axerio, who later becomes Piero's lover, encourages her dandy, nihilist friend Filippo Porrena to obseve the scene: "Look at him, look how he talks to everyone and everyone talks to him! They are his new friends. He makes them recount their lives, their plans for the unknown future, gives them advice, he sees in everyone, amid all their vileness, a noble force to be lifted up and directed toward an objective....They are rushing from all sides! It's a mob!"[77] (18). The novel starts in media res, with an animated conversation among first-class passengers, all businessmen from Uruguay, Argentina, and Brazil and all equally proud of their *italianità*.[78] Giovanna Axerio's husband Jacopo, an illustrious surgeon who has been invited to lecture to medical students in various Brazilian universities, agrees with them: patriotism is a sentiment; therefore these gentlemen should be considered Italian if they feel that way. Buondelmonti strongly disagrees; patriotism for him is an economic relationship, not merely a sentiment. Since they are operating on foreign soil, these businessmen no longer belong to the Italian nation as they have situated themselves outside *italianità* "For them to remain Italian, nationally speaking, the land where they work and enrich themselves would need to become Italian; 7).[79] For Buondelmonti, who is the spokesperson for Corradini's ideas throughout the novel, the nation is a "concentration camp," and the only way to avoid being enclosed within its narrow boundaries is through imperialism: "Il solo modo di essere nazionalisti, scusino, patriotti, è di essere nazionalisti" (The only way to be a nationalist, excuse me, a patriot, is by being nationalist; 8). Jacopo Axerio tries to reject Buondelmonti's thesis, claiming that the world is moving rapidly toward universal brotherhood. As a doctor, he maintains that human life is sacred and should not be crushed in battlefields. During the trip, the doctor displays his surgical skills by performing a complex surgery on an emigrant who has been injured in a fight. Even his rival, Piero, publicly acknowledges his talent, but there is a strong contrast between the empathy that Buondelmonti shows when he interacts with the poor migrants and the complete detachment exhibited by Jacopo while operating on the man, who is in front of him naked, tied to the bed and unconscious. The narrator writes that the doctor "aveva un fremito di gioia dentro la barba mentre si metteva il grembiale bianco e i guanti bianchi" (had a quiver of joy inside his beard as he put on his white apron and white gloves; 20).

Buondelmonti is a well-known writer traveling to South America to investigate the conditions of Italian emigrants, just as Corradini did in 1908. When he arrives in Rio de Janeiro, he is welcomed by the leaders of the Italian community who invite him to present his ideas, thus exacerbating the conflict with Axerio, who fears that Piero's popularity may obscure his own. As the novel unfolds, the reader discovers that Doctor Axerio is not as progressive as he likes to portray himself. Although he publicly supports feminism, his relationship with his wife Giovanna is based on brutal possession, and when Giovanna finally opens up to Piero, she realizes that she can no longer submit to his desires and decides to flee the house with her new lover. When Jacopo finds her gone, his only concern is his own reputation in the Italian community, not his wife's well-being. In a previous discussion with Buondelmonti, Jacopo had claimed that everyone must fight "quella parte animalesca con cui l'uomo ha avuto origine" (that animal part with which man originated; 157) and cultivate reason, compassion, and love. Instead, when his wife abandons him, the "beast within" gets the upper hand, and the two rivals find themselves fighting "la lotta per la ragione più feroce, la donna" (the struggle for the fiercest reason, the woman; 166). Jacopo, who has confronted Piero with a handgun, tries to shoot Giovanna but instead hits Piero, who has thrown himself in front of her. Giovanna falls on Piero's agonizing body, crying, and her husband shoots her several times in the back.

Piero is seriously injured, but a young member of the Italian community in Rio de Janeiro remains by his side until he recovers. Giacomo Rummo is a dedicated Socialist leader, born in the mountains of Abruzzi and the director of the local Italian radical newspaper. Since the first encounter, Rummo and Buondelmonti show respect for each other despite their ideological differences because they share a common loathing for the bourgeoisie. Buondelmonti appreciates Giacomo's sincerity and passion, two qualities that are not common in liberal elites, as exemplified by Axerio. The narrator comments: "gl'ispirava simpatia e voleva addomesticarlo" (he had sympathy for him and wanted to tame him; 45). During Piero's convalescence, the Socialist activist shows a profound devotion for the Nationalist leader. The way he greets the visitors to the hospital room, arranges the flowers they bring to him, talks to the doctors and nurses, and constantly remains by his side, "assorto nell'ufficio amoroso" (absorbed in the loving office), suggests a certain feminization, signaled also by his "voce stridula di propagandista" (shrill propagandist's voice; 172). Corradini writes that the Socialist activist "aveva nel fondo del cuore un bisogno di affetti mai soddisfatto" (had deep in his heart a need for affection that was never satisfied; 170). In fact, Rummo lost his mother and father when he was very young and later fell in love with a woman who rejected him. The narrator remarks that his Socialist faith filled the void that he had inside, although the memory of a real love that he never experienced remains hidden in a part of his inner being where his thoughts rarely venture. Like Buondelmonti, Rummo also has an allegorical double nature. As Corradini explains it, he transferred his frustrations and his "feroci cupidigie in un cuore più vasto, nella lotta delle classi. Era anch'egli l'individuo tragicamente collettivo" (fierce greed into a vaster heart, in the class struggle. He also was a tragically collective individual; 212). Rummo tries to transcend his personal conflicts through a superior ideal, but as the events in the novel illustrate, his total dedication to the working class conceals a hatred that is devouring him from within.

The narrative develops on two different levels: as a political allegory and as a romantic love story. The turning point of the romance between Piero and Giovanna comes when Axerio assassinates his wife, Giovanna; at the political level, the crucial moment is the upcoming war back home. Although the author does not give any clear indications, one may assume that he refers to the conflict with the Ottoman Empire, which led to the Italian invasion of Libya. Corradini repeatedly mentions that Giuseppe Garibaldi's son is already recruiting volunteers and that Buondelmonti is eager to join him.[80] Upon learning about the imminent war, Buondelmonti immediately writes to Garibaldi's son and collects funds from the local Italian community. One of the main supporters is Lorenzo Berènga, a successful Italian entrepreneur who bears on his cheek the scars from a wound he received during Italy's war against the armies of Menelik II, emperor of Ethiopia, which culminated in 1896 with the Battle of Adwa. For Lorenzo, as well as Corradini, a war against Libya represents an opportunity to avenge that humiliating defeat and reclaim an international position of leadership for Italy.

Buondelmonti is a minor but important character in another nationalist novel that Corradini published in 1911, titled *La Guerra lontana*. It is necessary to look at it because Corradini's Nationalist ideology and his hatred for Socialism are rooted in the tragic events narrated in that novel. The protagonist of *La Guerra lontana* is Ercole Gola, a journalist who runs a newspaper called *Il Giornale di Roma*. Like Buondelmonti, Ercole is a tall and strong man born in the mountains of Lazio; he is nicknamed *Il Buttero*, "The Herdsman," and has abandoned his ideals and wasted his great literary talent for the sake of popularity and economic success. Throughout the novel, he rediscovers his passion for Nationalism, and when the Italian troops are defeated at Aduwa and Italian public opinion, instigated by the Socialist and Liberal press, turns against the Prime Minister Francesco Crispi, Gola's newspaper is the only one that remains faithful to Crispi. In the middle of the crisis, when everyone is abandoning Ercole and his newspaper is in serious financial trouble, a young man shows up at his office, offering his services because he wants to contribute to the fight that Gola is waging against a system they both perceive as corrupt. At first, Ercole hesitates, but as he starts talking to him, he realizes that the young Piero embodies the ideals of his youth that he had forsaken: "Il Gola lo fissò e si ricordò di se stesso quand'aveva la stessa età, gli parve d'avere dinanzi agli occhi il suo ritratto d'allora" (Gola stared at him and remembered himself when he was the same age, it seemed to him as if his own portrait were before his eyes; 169). Piero becomes for Ercole the son he never had, tells him of the corruption that is afflicting the capital, and warns him to not make the same mistakes he did when he arrived in Rome. After Ercole kills in a duel a young and popular congressman who was strongly opposed to Crispi's imperialist politics, and all his friends abandon him, Piero remains faithfully by his side. Finally, Ercole decides to leave Rome and migrates to San Paolo, Brazil, with his mother, where he is offered the editorship of a newspaper. Piero accompanies him to the port of Genoa, where they see all the migrants. Ercole hugs him and repeats the same words that his *maestro*, the poet Giosuè Carducci, had told him, to keep loving his country with all his heart and never stop fighting "per la resurrezione e la grandezza della patria" (for the resurrection and the greatness of the fatherland; 273).

Piero followed his spiritual father's advice, and now he can finally use his rhetorical abilities to convince the Italian community in Brazil that the approaching war represents a unique opportunity to make Italy great again. Everyone will be gathering the next day to listen to Buondelmonti's speech, which is also a fundraiser for the war. The only one who openly opposes the conflict is Giacomo, although he starts having doubts, realizing that the Socialist ideal that he pursued is being replaced by the "guerra della nazioni" (war of the nations; 213). Isolated from the Italian community, stuck in a squalid room filled with political pamphlets, the night before Buondelmonti's talk, the Socialist leader experiences an existential crisis. He hears a voice from within saying: "Tu ti sei messo l'odio nel cuore come se ti fossi messo unserpente nel seno e con questo ti sei dato a lottare per i lavoratori" (You put hatred in your heart as if you had put a snake in your soul and with this you set out to fight for the workers; 217). Rummo, remembering the workers that the very same day had come out of the factories shouting their love for the "distant homeland," wonders how he can reconcile that vivid memory with the political principles that he has repeated to himself so many times: "Non esiste la patria! Esistono i lavoratori di tutto il mondo!" (The homeland does not exist! Only the workers of the world do!; 218). During the night, a personification of his "patria" comes close to him and whispers: "Why did you betray me? Why did you act against me?" The following morning, however, he decides to stick to his anti-militarist principles and begins contacting his comrades, inviting them to come protest the imminent conflict. While the Nationalist leader is speaking, a telegram arrives, announcing that Italy has declared war. Piero realizes that the emigrants sitting in front of him, rejected from their mother country, could be turned into intrepid fighters for their distant homeland. Thus, he asks who in the audience will go back to Italy with him. Giacomo, who was listening in silence, bursts into tears, screaming: "Evviva la patria! Evviva la patria!" (Long live the homeland! Long live the homeland!) and falls on the floor, "atterrato dall'invisibile nemico, la patria trionfante" (crushed by the invisible enemy, the triumphant fatherland; 227). The novel ends with the image of the ship, loaded with over four hundred emigrants going back to Italy with Buondelmonti. They are from every region of Italy, most of them simple workers, who suddenly, "vivevano come nella poesia" (were living as if in a poem; 242). For Corradini's hero, this fatal moment represents the triumph of the theories that he had been developing in his book *L'elogio della Guerra*, arguing that war destroys inferior races and makes powerful ones emerge and prosper. He had compared war to the labor pains that women experience when giving birth. War also is the channel through which the individual is subsumed into something superior that transcends him: "like music, art, religion, war is a human effort to emerge from the individual sphere and expand through time and space."[81] Thus, his life, like those of the other returning migrants, has become "lyrical," as in poetry and art. Giacomo, the Socialist pacifist converted into a Nationalist warrior, states: "We must die to ourselves to live again in a greater life. Christians say to live again in Christ, we say for the fatherland."[82] When the ship is about to enter the Mediterranean with its load of emigrants magically turned into soldiers, which Piero calls "the Roman lake," he delivers his final speech, explaining to his fellow volunteers that, if they prevail, they will no longer need to migrate to foreign lands, because they will be able to go to territories that Italy has conquered: "Allora l'Italia non sarà soltanto dov'oggi è Italia, ma sarà dovunque saranno gli italiani" (Then Italy will not only be where Italy is today, but everywhere there are Italians; 255), and they will not be forced to speak the language of their master but their own language. Then, the people all over the world will respect and fear the name of Italy just as they do for England, the imperial power that Italian Nationalists have always wanted to emulate.

In both Mantegazza's novel *Il Dio ignoto*, analyzed in a previous chapter, and Corradini's fictional texts, the ideological positions of the authors are unashamedly displayed, culminating in a delirium of power. The cultural critic Terry Eagleton wrote that the novel is not only a *product* but a *necessity* of ideology, because the imaginary nature of the fictional text endows it with a freedom that would be unthinkable in a political essay or in real life.[83] The protagonist of Mantegazza's novel becomes the chief of an indigenous confederation and is magically endowed with the power to control and subdue the most "ferocious" Native Americans. A similar dream of power and control is realized in Corradini's narrative, in which the subjugation of Native Americans is replaced with the conquest of Giovanna Axerio, the wife of a prestigious representative of the liberal bourgeoisie, and the Socialist leader Franco Rummo, who is feminized and ultimately subjugated by Piero Buondelmonti's hypermasculinity. Barzini's dream of transforming the Italian migrants into an organized army guided by leader-entrepreneurs who will function as military officers is miraculously realized in the epilogue of *La Patria lontana*, when the migrant workers no longer exist as individuals, subsumed into the deadly embrace of the nation that leads them to war: "Laguerra è il sacro supremo atto dell'incarnazione nazionale, mentre le esistenze individuali muoiono" (War is the sacred supreme act of the national incarnation, while individual existences die; 244).

CHAPTER FIVE

The Whole World Is Our Homeland: Italian Transnational Anarchism in Argentina

> *The landowners and the governments own the material "homeland," the soil, the capital, everything; the worker is driven away from the land that saw him being born. He has nothing to defend, nothing that he may call "his property" and thus he has no "homeland." The landowner and ruler are his enemies, while beyond the national borders all those who work and suffer like him are his brothers.*
> —Almanaque Popular de La Questione Sociale, 1895

> *What damage would we suffer if the landowners were to disappear? It would be as if the locusts had disappeared.*
> —Errico Malatesta, *Fra contadini*

The texts I have analyzed thus far do not touch upon the question of class conflict in the Rio de la Plata region, almost as if it did not exist. The only exception is Enrico Corradini's *La Guerra lontana*, which culminates in the triumph of Nationalism and the annihilation of Socialism. Nevertheless, at the turn of the nineteenth century, both Socialism and Anarchism were an important presence in the Americas, and Italian activists played a major role is the development of working-class movements, both in North and South America. As recent studies have convincingly argued, Italian Anarchism was a transnational movement that developed through a global network, as militants often followed the same routes of Italian emigration.[1]

Anarchists believed in the abolition of private property and the establishment of a classless society, but whereas Marxists maintained that a centralized state is necessary, at least initially, to create a successful transition to communism, Anarchists were fiercely opposed to any form of hierarchical organization, because it would limit individual freedom and hinder the revolutionary process. Militants often differed in the philosophical principles and methodologies, but the most influential group in Argentina during the period examined in this chapter was represented by Anarcho-communists, who held that some degree of organization was necessary to bring about an effective change and rejected the solitary acts of violence advocated by their individualist comrades. The two main Italian representatives of anarcho-communism in Argentina at the turn of the nineteenth century were Errico Malatesta and Pietro Gori, who both resided for several years in the region, where they strongly influenced the workers' movement.[2] Although they shared similar views, their methods greatly differed: Malatesta rarely used emotional body language and adopted instead a model that could be defined as Socratic, while Gori addressed his audiences in artistic ways, using a language rich with religious overtones.[3] Malatesta's most famous political pamphlet, *Fra Contadini* (Between farmers), which was published in 1884, is structured as a conversation between two peasants—Berto and George—one younger and more politicized, the other older and initially skeptical about his friends' revolutionary ideas. The latter's advice is "leave politics to the gentry who have nothing to do and think about getting on in life....There have always been rich and poor, and we who were born to work should be content with what God gives us."[4] Throughout the dialogue, Berto explains to his friend why he decided to join the Anarchist movement. The language used by Malatesta is clear and simple but never condescending. Berto manages to convince his friend why it is necessary to seize the land from the landowners and make it available to everyone: "it's wrong that some people find every comfort at birth and others find hunger and want" (23). George, the older peasant, continually questions his friend's assertion, who always responds in a placated manner. He argues that Socialism has lost most of its initial revolutionary potential: once it was enough to say that one was a Socialist to be persecuted by the police and landlords, while today many Socialists only want to be nominated members of Parliament and no longer adhere to the founding revolutionary principles (62). Thus, Berto warns his friend: "When someone tells you he is a Socialist, ask him to take the property from those who have it, to put it in common for all. If the answer is yes, embrace him as a brother, if it is no, be careful, because you have an enemy in front of you" (61). When asked, George states that he is a communist but points out that the essential thing is that "no one starts ordering others about" (68), because "for people to become educated to freedom and the management of their own interests, they must be left to act for themselves, to feel responsibility for their own actions in the good or bad which comes from them" (53). The opinion of the minority needs to be respected, since, as George puts it, "where truth and justice are concerned numbers don't count, and often one person alone can be right against one hundred or a hundred thousand" (72). However, just as minorities have the right of insurrection, so the majority have the right to defend themselves and eventually expel from the community those who refuse to collaborate and do their share.

Malatesta continued to articulate his ideas in the journal *La Questione Sociale*, the first serious Anarchist newspaper to be published in Italy. When he fled to South America, he resumed its publication in Buenos Aires, between 1885 and 1886. The journal contained articles authored by the most important Anarchist thinkers of the time. An accomplished theoretician and political activist, Malatesta became instrumental in the creation of the first anti-capitalist unions in Argentina. The Argentine historian Osvaldo Bayer remarks that

> without the long stays of Malatesta (1885–1889) and Pietro Gori (1898–1902) in Argentina it's quite possible that the movement would not have grown so quickly nor would it have coalesced as it did; instead, more likely it would have fallen into the divisive and destructive arguments typical of libertarian socialist movements worldwide. (22)

Malatesta was a great organizer; upon his arrival in Buenos Aires he immediately established contacts with Spanish and Argentine comrades, instead of remaining confined within the Italian diasporic community. He reached out to workers, spreading the principles of Anarchism and drafting the charter of the bakers' organization, which was profoundly cosmopolitan and very different from the other mutualist societies already present in Argentina. Gori, who was younger than Malatesta, continued his comrade's work and helped in the creation of the first national labor union, the Federacíon Obrera Argentina (FOA; Argentine Workers Federation), whose Inaugural Congress took place in 1901 at Ligure Hall, in the Genoese neighborhood of La Boca. Most of the delegates were Italian. Both Malatesta and Gori belonged to the organizational wing of the Anarchist movement and opposed the individualist tendencies, represented by the periodical *El Perseguido*, published between 1890 and 1896, that were partially responsible for the debacle of Anarchism in the first half of the twentieth century.

In this chapter I will focus mostly on Pietro Gori (1865–1911), a lawyer, activist, and scholar who devoted his entire adult life to spreading Anarchist ideals both in Italy and the other countries where he lived, including Switzerland, England, the United States, and Argentina. Gori came from an upper-class background: his father was the officer in charge of the military fortress in Messina, Sicily, and the mother belonged to an aristocratic family from Rosignano Marittimo, in Tuscany. Very early in his life Pietro embraced libertarian ideas, expressed for the first time in a small volume titled *Pensieri ribelli* (Rebellious thoughts). He studied law at the University of Pisa, where he graduated in 1889 with a specialization in criminal sociology, a discipline that he continued to pursue while in exile. The title of his dissertation was *La miseria e il delitto* (On crime and poverty). Because of his political activism, he was repeatedly imprisoned and forced into exile, first in Switzerland, where he composed the famous song "Addio, Lugano bella" (Farewell, beautiful Lugano) that became the most iconic text of Italian Anarchism. After graduating, he started working as an attorney and often represented Anarchists in court. Many people came to listen to his closing statements, which were carefully crafted to provoke an emotional response in the audience. As his comrade Luigi Fabbri wrote, "He spoke very well, but he spoke the language of the people. And the people flocked in when his name was announced for a rally or a conference."[5] He briefly worked with Filippo Turati, an attorney and one of the main leaders of the Italian Socialist Party, but unfortunately their ideas could not be reconciled. Gori embraced Marxist and Socialist principles and even translated (badly, according to Turati) Karl Marx's *Communist Manifesto*. Due to his belief that the state is an oppressive institution, however, he could not accept the principles on which the Socialist Party was being developed. On the other end, he also criticized the individualist position of the Anarchists who advocated individual acts of violence—the so-called propaganda by the deed—and rejected any form of organization. Like his comrade Malatesta, he tried to bring together Socialism and Anarchy by reaching out to wide audiences and collaborating in the formation of labor unions and organizing strikes. What makes Gori so intriguing is his charismatic personality and his ability to manipulate a variety of genres, including popular music, and connect with his audiences at an emotional level, turning politics into a "spectacle," as Emanuela Minuto showed in an insightful essay.[6] The Anarchist leader managed to raise political awareness by using rhetorical strategies from literature, popular theater, and religion. Furthermore, Gori was a skilled musician and a great performer. During his stay in the United States, where he toured extensively, giving hundreds of talks, he often accompanied himself with his guitar, using modalities borrowed from the gospel tradition. The trials against Anarchists were another "stage" through which Gori displayed his rhetorical skills. People flocked to the hearings to listen to him; the Italian authorities responded by requiring that he hold them behind closed doors.[7] In his *Prison Notebooks*, the philosopher and founder of the Italian Communist Party Antonio Gramsci strongly criticized Gori's "melodramatic" style, "che sente di sacrestia e di eroismo di cartone" (that reminds of sacristies and cartoon heroism).[8] In his opinion, Gori's popularity among the working classes would have contributed to a passion for melodrama that in the long run would be detrimental to the formation of an authentically modern class consciousness. Nevertheless, since the Italian proletariat was for the most part illiterate and profoundly influenced by religious imagery and rituals, Gori's strategy of using the stories from the New Testament and endowing them with a modern revolutionary meaning proved successful. He compared the "prophets" of Anarchism, who often sacrificed their lives to achieve a society with liberty and justice for all, to the apostles of Christianity, and Gori himself, who spent many years in exile persecuted by police, was described as a prophet, an apostle, and a martyr.[9] As the hero of Corradini's novel, Gori was seen as a Christ figure who spoke the language of the people and fought for their redemption. However, whereas for Corradini redemption may only occur when the workers embrace the nationalist credo and identify themselves entirely with the mother-nation, Gori's utopia, as outlined in one of his most important essays, strongly rejects the State: "Lo Stato, nella esperienza millenaria, ha sempre più dimostrato...la sua inettitudine di mettersi alla testa del movimento progressivo dell'umanità" (The State, during its millenary existence, always demonstrated...its inability to lead the progress of humankind).[10] The rejection of the motherland's myth resonated with Italian immigrants, who were forced to seek a more dignified life abroad, away from their native land. Gori argued that the democratic ideals of Risorgimento had been betrayed and the bourgeois state became the new oppressor. Instead of rallying around the national flag, immigrants should consider all fellow workers their brothers and sisters, regardless of their nationality. At the turn of the nineteenth century, it was becoming increasingly clear that the promised land did not exist, as workers were faced with discrimination, poverty, and exploitation even on the shores of Rio de la Plata. Instead of embracing Nationalism, Gori and his comrades advocated a new kind of cosmopolitanism and encouraged workers not to see "foreigners" as their enemies but as precious allies in the struggle for a new world order based on human solidarity. *Senza Patria,* without a homeland, is the title of a short play written by Gori and performed innumerable times in Italy and abroad. One of the protagonists, a peasant from Tuscany, fought in the Risorgimento but was forced to leave Italy, just like the Anarchists who were being treated as criminals, obliged to wander from one country to another, as Gori writes in his famous song *Addio Lugano.*

In the pamphlet *La nostra utopia,* Gori tells the story of a "conversion" he performed in Missouri, in a small Italian community inhabited by miners. He recounts that the individuals he met were totally unaware of their rights. They did not show any solidarity toward their fellow American workers and constantly competed with them by accepting lower wages, thus favoring capitalism. Gori told them that, because of their behavior, they were called "Chinesi d'Europa" (41). He was expecting a violent reaction, but instead they listened to him and invited him to remain in their community for several days and share his ideas with them. When Gori returned to Missouri on his way back from the West Coast, he saw that they had completely changed their lifestyle: "Non erano più macchine da produzione quelle. Erano uomini affacciati sugli orizzonti d'una vita nuova" (They were no longer production machines. They were men looking out toward the horizons of a new life; 42). They no longer spent all their money in the local taverns fighting against each other, but they formed a small union, ordered Socialist and libertarian books and periodicals, became more educated, and developed a sense of solidarity they did not possess before. The bar owners, hating the conversion, called them "senza-patria," a term used by the reactionary Italian prime minister Francesco Crispi, because they no longer spent their free time getting drunk in their premises, but the Italian immigrants had gained something more precious: a sense of dignity and a new political awareness.

After his stay in the United States, the Italian activist briefly returned to Europe but was forced to leave again, this time for South America, where his friends and comrades had repeatedly invited him. Gori arrived in Argentina in June 1898. Disguised as an English tourist, he crossed the French border, arrived in Marseille, and got on a ship to Brazil.[11] He departed shortly after the protests that took place in Milan and other Italian cities, leading to the death of hundreds of workers. In that instance, the Italian government had used the artillery against the strikers and instituted military tribunals that sentenced to prison over 1,500 people, including Filippo Turati, the leader of the reformist Socialist Party, who had spoken out against any form of violence. Gori gave a speech prior to the riots, comparing the uprise with those that had taken place exactly fifty years earlier against the Austrians. Consequently, he was targeted as one of the main instigators of the protests and condemned for subversive activities.

On June 26, 1898, the most important Anarchist periodical in Argentina, *La Protesta Humana,* welcomed to Buenos Aires "el compañero abogado Pedro Gori," who had to leave Italy because of the "feroz persecution de las autoridades" (the ferocious persecution of the authorities).[12] The journal, available in digital format, is a great source of information about Gori's activities in Argentina, and shows how the lawyer rapidly integrated into the Anarchist transnational community.[13]

On July 10, the front page of *La Protesta Humana* announced that Gori would give a talk at the *Teatro Doria,* one of the most noteworthy venues for the Italian community of Buenos Aires, situated at 2230 Calle Rivadavia. Before being rebuilt in 1903 and renamed the Teatro Marconi, it was a simple "baracón de madeira," a large wooden construction.[14] The ticket for the conference, titled "Provocatori e sobillatori nei recenti moti d'Italia," was fifty centavos, and the event constituted a fundraiser to benefit the families of the workers killed and imprisoned by the Italian authorities. On the same front page, the journal announced another conference, with the title "La función histórica del periodismo en la sociedad moderna," to be given at the prestigious *Circulo de la Prensa,* where the public consisted of journalists and potential "adversarios." The periodical offered a detailed summary of Gori's "brillantisima" lecture, in which the Italian lawyer criticized "el mercantilismo" of the bourgeois media, typical of North America, that featured sensational news just to gain more readers, whereas the true mission of a modern democratic press should be to educate and elevate people. The conference was such a success that the room turned out to be too small and many were left out, unable to attend. On page 4 of the same issue, another announcement addressed to "Los compañeros de Sud America" stated that Gori had accepted an invitation to give a series of conferences throughout the nation. The editors encouraged comrades from other cities to contact the three main Anarchist periodicals of the capital if they wished to have Gori talk in their area: *La Protesta Humana*, *L'Avvenire*, and *Ciencia Social*. On the same page, the periodical published a list of those who had contributed to the fundraisers for the victims of police repression in Italy. Most donations are very small: 50 *centavos* and even less, but it is interesting to notice that the last names of the donors were for the most part Spanish, from cities as far away as Chivilcoy and Tucumán, thus showing that the network of workers solidarity transcended the ethnic boundaries and was not limited to the Argentine capital. The total amount raised by the subscription exceeded 1,250 pesos, to be sent to "Enrique" Ferri, a famous criminologist like Gori, congressman, and director of the Socialist newspaper *Avanti!* He also presided over the committee created to help the victims of police brutality. Ferri's role shows that the international solidarity network included other leftist political leaders who did not fully agree with the ideas professed by the editors of *La Protesta*.

On July 24, the summary of Gori's conference at Teatro Doria took up three full columns of the front page of the journal. In his speech, the Italian orator spoke out against the recent laws issued by the Italian government, in particular the infamous Article 248 that allowed the authorities to imprison anyone who professed ideas that were considered subversive.[15] Gori wondered how Italian political leaders, many of whom had fought against foreign oppression during the Risorgimento, could turn against their own people demanding social justice. He directly addressed his audience, composed for the most part of emigrants who had come to America to escape poverty and pellagra, a disease caused by a poor diet based almost exclusively on corn: protesters assaulted bakeries in Milan because they were hungry, and the army responded with extreme ferocity, by killing women and children. The reviewer, of whom only the initial "M." is recorded, remarked that Gori was interrupted multiple times by the enthusiastic audience, which included a lot of women, an indication that the so-called sexo débil was beginning to play a more active role in the movement.

Both Gori and Malatesta were strong supporters of women's emancipation. In the previously discussed pamphlet *Fra contadini*, the author explains: "For us, woman must be equal to man, and when we say man, we mean human being, without distinction of sex" (24). The relationship between feminist militants and the Anarchist movement, however, was complex and often controversial. On January 8, 1897, the new feminist *Periódico Comunista-Anarquico* saw the light in Buenos Aires, titled *La Voz de la Mujer*, whose motto was: "Ni, Dio, Ni Patrón, Ni Marido" (No god, no master, no husband). In the first issue, all the articles were in Spanish, except a long one dedicated to "La donna nella società attuale," authored by "una stiratrice," an iron lady, who pointed out that women are the victims of the tyranny of men, both inside and outside the house. The "woman question" was an important one for the Anarchist movement, because their activists were often accused of destroying the moral foundations of society by preaching free love. "El amor libre" is the title of another long essay authored by Carmen Lareva that appeared in the first issue of *La Voz*.[16] Gori discussed the subject of women emancipation in a conference given on November 25, 1900, in Buenos Aires.[17] The orator starts by comparing himself to a medieval knight, fighting his battle in the field of ideas, "nella giostra del pensiero" (in the tournament of thought; 168). He hopes to receive as a prize for his endeavors a smile from the "cortesissime donne e fanciulle di Buenos Aires" (very courteous ladies and girls of Buenos Aires; 169). He encourages women to be actively involved in the epic battle for the establishment of a more just society and refers to Brandimarte and Clorinda, the two female warriors in Ludovico Ariosto's and Torquato Tasso's Italian renaissance epic poems. As mothers, women should reject the myth of patriotism and refuse to send their sons to war. To those who order women to sacrifice their children for the nation, they should respond that in other countries there are also women and mothers just like them. Instead, they should unite and fight in the name of "la patria unica degli oppressi" (the sole motherland of the oppressed; 171). The orator acknowledges that women are the victims of male tyranny and have to fight for their own emancipation, but their struggle must take into consideration the "social question" as well, without which "il femminismo sarebbe vana accademia di poche pettegole ambiziose" (feminism would be a vain academy of few ambitious gossipers; 172). Unfortunately, many workers do not care about the emancipation of their female companions, and as a result, women often end up being subjected to the hegemony of the Church. Many comrades tend to exclude their female companions from the social struggle, as if politics did not concern them. They say, "Senti cara, tu va nell'altra stanza, queste sono uerrae non ti interessano" (Listen, honey, go to the other room, these things do not interest you; 173). Conversely, many women perceive politics as a fight for power and are eager to participate "alle lotte poco decorose del potere" (in the undignified power struggles; 173), thus becoming part of the oppressive and enslaving mechanism created by bourgeois governments. Gori is convinced that women will not achieve a true emancipation as long as economic inequalities continue to exist. He goes on condemning, on the one hand, the hypocrisy of bourgeois marriage, which amounts to a form of legalized prostitution. The unity of the proletarian family, on the other hand, is constantly threatened by the lack of economic opportunities and political oppression. Proletarian young men and women are forced to migrate, leaving behind their spouses and elderly parents. Contrary to what bourgeois journalists and politicians affirm, it is the capitalist system that is destroying the family. Anarchists, instead, want to "purify love" by liberating it from the tyranny of capital and the hypocrisy of bourgeois morality. Love, however, cannot be free until the "antisocial egoism" that is generated by private property is eliminated. At present, the two most essential human instincts, procreation and conservation, are continually violated by the monstruous capitalist system: workers cannot marry the women they love and start a family because they will not have the economic means to support them. Thus, only by freeing the worker from his present condition can the relations between men and women start again on an equal basis, and the legal and religious rituals that characterize marriage will automatically disappear: "La famiglia libera dell'avvenire...avrà per soli vincoli l'affetto, la stima e la simpatia" (the free family of the future will have as only bonds affection, esteem, and fondness; 181). Gori concludes his lecture with a long quotation from Mario Rapisardi's poem "hymn to free love" and beseeches women in the audience to help him and his comrades in their crusade against political oppression: "Aiutateci voi, o donne, nella uerra terribile e santa" (Help us, ladies, in the terrible and holy crusade; 183).

Reading the text of Gori's conference, one cannot avoid wondering how Italian immigrant women at the turn of the twentieth century understood literary references to Renaissance authors and appreciated the bookish language used by Rapisardi. For the most part, immigrant women in Buenos Aires worked as domestic servants, seamstresses, cooks, teachers, and nurses, and they suffered systematic discrimination, low pay, and long hours.[18] Among developing countries, Argentina's sexual disparity in education was admirably low, but immigrant women were nevertheless often trapped, as feminist critic Maxine Molyneux comments, "within their communal cultures in sexual and family matters" (126) and thus most likely unable to fully understand Gori's sophisticated language. It is undisputable that the Italian lawyer supported women's rights: the periodical *La Questione Sociale,* founded by his comrade Malatesta in 1883, dedicated several essays to women's issues, but Molyneux remarks that the "apparent sympathy for feminism in principle within the Anarchist ranks was matched by substantial opposition in practice" (127). Indeed, in his lecture, the Italian orator seems to relegate women to a secondary role in the revolutionary process: not as active, autonomous subjects, but rather as "helpers" and "comforters" to their male companions. This paternalistic view of women was typical in Anarchist circles; according to Molyneux, Gori asserted that women should be prohibited from working in areas that could be dangerous to maternity and could undermine their morals (129). Molyneux, who exhaustively studied the feminist journal *La voz de la mujer,* notices that the editors, most of whom were women, never took up the topic of domestic work and never proposed in their articles that men should do their fair share of this labor in the household. Despite the theoretical discussions on free love, which the periodical keenly supported, traditional notions concerning the division of labor still prevailed in the Anarchist community. Overall, there was a disconnect between the lofty utopian *pronunciamentos* of Anarchist male leaders and the lived needs and expectations of poor immigrant women. As Molyneux remarks, migrant women may have viewed the family as a site of oppression, but it was also a place of relative security. For this reason, most of them were not ready to dismiss it altogether, as the abolition of marriage would leave them more exposed (142).

The Anarchist movement was especially committed to advancing workers' rights in Argentina, and Gori and Malatesta were successful in communicating with them and organizing their struggles. *La Protesta* published a summary of a conference that Gori gave on Sunday, July 17, 1898, organized by construction workers—"los albañiles"—titled "Los derechos de los trabajadores y la cuestión social." Toward the end of the talk, Gori called upon workers to form labor unions and get organized, because if they remained isolated, they would have no power. This call to organizing provoked the immediate reaction of the so-called "individualistas" Anarchists who assaulted the stage and tried to attack the speaker with words that were considered "inappropriate" by the editors of *La protesta.* The Italian activist, however, remained calm and invited his

opponents to continue the discussion in a public debate at a date and location to be decided. The editors of *La Protesta* shared with Gori the notion
that Anarchists needed to join the unions and change them from within,
as Malatesta had done when he helped write the statute of the bakers'
union a few years earlier. In fact, on the same page, right after the review
of Gori's speech, there is an article titled "A propósito de organización"
whose implied readers may have been those comrades who had contested
Gori at the end of his talk.

On the third page of the same issue, the editors announced a "Meeting
Popular," scheduled to take place on July 24 in a public square, to pro-
test the repressive measures implemented by the Italian government. The
program would include Anarchist, Socialist, and Republican speakers.
Among them, once again, "el abogado Pedro Gori" was featured. On the
same page, they also announced the publication of Gori's dramatic text
Proximus tuus, included in the anthology *Teatro del Pueblo,* available in
Spanish at the *Libreria Sociológica* for forty centavos.

On August 7 of the same year, the front page of *La protesta* featured
a large advertisement for a festive event known as a *Gran Velada Popular*
that was to take place the same day at the *Teatro Olimpo.* Tickets sold from
fifty centavos to five pesos and benefited the *Circulo Internacionale de
Studios Sociales,* an institution founded by Errico Malatesta in the 1880s
to advance workers' education and promote their emancipation. The soi-
rée was articulated into nine different parts and included music, theatrical
performances, lectures, and even a raffle. Once again, Gori was called to
play a major role in the event: his choral performance, titled *I profughi
d'Italia,* kicked the evening. off, followed by his "drama simbolico-social"
Primo Maggio, whose prologue was recited by the author himself. After a
"mandolinata" by a group of music students, Gori gave a talk on the theme
"L'Arte Social." In addition, on the following page, the journal offered a
summary of two other conferences by the Italian lawyer, one in the popular
Barracas neighborhood, and the other in the town of Lujan. In Barracas,
Gori was applauded "frenetically" by the audience, while the conference in
Lujan, attended by around five hundred businessmen, industrialists, and
workers, was so "splendid" that at the end the speaker and his friends were
invited to a "fraternal dinner."

During his initial months in Argentina, Gori was presenting all
over Buenos Aires and the surrounding areas. On August 7 at 9 p.m. he
gave a lecture for the Sociedad de Obreros Panaderos, one of the first

revolutionary trade unions in Argentina, founded by Ettore Mattei and Errico Malatesta, whose original name was Sociedad Cosmopolita de Resistencia y Colocación de Obreros Panaderos. The first article of the statute illustrates the union's objective: "Lograr el mejoramiento intelectual, moral y físico del obrero y su emancipación de las garras del capitalismo" (to seek the physical, moral, and intellectual betterment of the workers and liberate them from the claws of capitalism).[19] The union, celebrating its eleventh anniversary, invited all the workers and their associations to participate. After the political speeches, a typical Argentine dish of *asado con cuero*, consisting of an entire calf barbecued with its skin on, was served.

The Anarchist movement was an important presence in the capital and especially within the Italian community. Their activities were not limited to politics, but they created opportunities for socializing, with music, art, theater, and of course good food. One short note in the same issue draws attention to the conflicts that existed within the Italian community in Buenos Aires: the *Meeting Popular* that had been scheduled on July 24 to protest the Italian authorities' repressive measures was prohibited, and the editors suggested that the decision may have been influenced by the "so-called representatives" of the Italian community in Argentina, who did not want any bad publicity in the capital about police repression.

On August 21, *La Protesta* announced that on the same day Gori would be giving another presentation in the Barracas del Norte district on the importance of solidarity in class struggle and society. The editors invited the "bourgeois individualists" and the "so-called Anarchist individualists" to participate and discuss their ideas with the speaker. The lead article, on the front page, deals with a related topic: the difference between solidarity and charity. The author, an important Spanish anarchist named Alselmo Lorenzo, concludes with the following statement: "Charity is unjust and reactionary. Solidarity is just and progressive."

In the meantime, the Italian lawyer was working on a more academically oriented project: Criminology. On page 2 of the same issue the editors announced that Gori would give a lecture at the Law School of the University of Buenos Aires on "The Evolution of Criminal Sociology." A critical review of the speech would be published in the monthly *Ciencia Social*, an academic Anarchist periodical. Founded in 1897, *Ciencia Social* featured essays by some of the most important intellectuals of the time, from William Morris to Octave Mirbeau and Miguel Unamuno.

La Protesta Humana continued to advertise Gori's conferences. On September 18, the lawyer spoke at the Union Liberal about war, both as a manifestation of militarism and as part of the struggle for liberation. On August 28 he was in Barracas del Norte to discuss the differences between Socialism and Anarchism, where he was confronted by José Ingenieros, a leading Argentine Socialist intellectual at the turn of the century. The editors remarked that the discussion was "borrascosa" (stormy) because the Socialist leader used sarcasm and offensive words, which provoked a strong reaction from the public. At one point, Gori refused to continue debating, since "frente a adversarios semejantes se rehusaba a la polémica en cualquier terreno, ya fuera la tribuna o la prensa" (confronted by such adversaries, he refused the polemical topics in any area, including the stage and the press). Despite this tense encounter, Ingenieros and Gori became friends and collaborated on various scholarly and political projects. When the University of Buenos Aires decided to discontinue Gori's university lectures on criminal sociology, he strongly criticized the decision in the pages of the Socialist periodical *La Vanguardia*, which usually opposed Anarchist initiatives.[20] On October 9, *La Protesta* announced that Gori's course at the university had been reinstituted. At that time, the Anarchist lawyer was in the process of founding his own academic journal, *Criminalogía Moderna*, whose first issue was published on November 20, 1898. The Editorial Board included university professors from various Argentine law schools, several judges and congressmen, the assistant director of the Buenos Aires Psychiatric Hospital, and even Manuel Mujica Faria, secretary of the Buenos Aires Police Department. The international contributors hailed from several European countries, the United States, and Australia. Among the Italian experts were Cesare Lombroso, Napoleone Colajanni, Arturo Labriola, Paolo Mantegazza and other prestigious scholars.[21]

In the opening article, titled "Guerra al Delito!," the author acknowledges that Argentina has to protect itself from immigrants with criminal tendencies who are constantly arriving in the country but points out that social reforms are equally important to prevent the spread of violent crimes.[22] On the last page of each issue, the "Guia professional" features an advertisement for the "Consultorio Jurídico" directed by Pedro Gori and Arturo Riva, a member of the periodical's editorial board, dealing with "Asuntos commerciales, civiles y penales," assisting clients in the American continent and Europe. Their main office was located at the same address as the direction of the periodical, with a secondary branch in La Boca. The Latin motto of the journal, "Contra Violentiam Ratio," shows the Positivist belief shared by Gori and his collaborators: only reason may defeat social violence.

In her book *Italiani malagente,* Eugenia Scarzanella argued that both Italian Positivism and Cesare Lomboso's criminal anthropology had a lasting impact in Latin America.[23] The Italian historian notices a strange paradox: the instruments used by Argentine government to denounce the supposedly degenerative and atavistic features of southern European immigrants were based on Italian criminal anthropology. Although initially "scientific" racial theories were used to justify the repression and extermination of the native population, during the period of mass migration Lomboso's "scientific" classifications were turned against Italians, who became "malagente," bad people, as the title of Scarzanella's book suggests. According to Lombroso and his followers, the so-called Latin race had a greater tendency to commit violent crimes, lending the stereotypes against southern Italians already present in European culture since the Enlightenment scientific validation. The migratory "flood" carried, in addition to the fertile loam, a quantity of residual scum that could be harmful to society. Cornelio Moyano Giacitúa, professor of law at the University of Cordoba, remarked that "junto con el carácter emprendedor, inteligente, desperdido, inventivo y artístico de los italianos, viene el residuo de su alta criminalidad de sangre" (together with the entrepreneurial, intelligent, inventive, artistic character of Italians, comes the residue of its high violent criminality).[24]

The attention of several Italian observers focused on the Argentine penitentiary institutions, which enacted a system of "penal welfare" that implemented many of the theories developed by Lombroso, considered one of the most advanced in Latin America. The Penitenciaría Nacional, originally built in 1877, under the direction of Antonio Ballvé took a new direction, based on the same disciplinary principles that had been pioneered in the penitentiary facility of Elmira in the state of New York. Ballvé, who knew well the Elmira prison, called on Ingenieros to direct an office inside the facility whose objective was to "study" the new inmates and prepare a detailed profile of their personality.[25] Recent historical research has shown that prisons became "sites for the observation, classification and normalization of subaltern groups, not only the so-called criminal class."[26] In the modern penal institutions, strong emphasis was being placed on the redemptive power of compulsory work. Statistics showed that most inmates had no stable occupation; government officers thus concluded that Argentina was missing a disciplined, specialized, and productive working class that would identify with their job. Consequently, prisons turned into a place where workers would be disciplined and learn to become productive members of society.

Gori's position with respect to the question of crime and penal institutions is ambivalent and seems to contradict his revolutionary ideology, which preached the destruction of the bourgeois state and the emancipation of the working classes. Whereas in Italy he was constantly criticizing the bourgeois state apparatus and was repeatedly imprisoned for his political activism, in Argentina he took on a different persona: although he continued his proselytism among immigrant workers and helped them organize, he also collaborated with the police and the judiciary system, showing that he agreed with the disciplinary approaches that were being employed. Most of the Italian scholarly articles on Gori I consulted, focus almost exclusively on his political activities, but they neglect the scholarly work he pursued while in Argentina. When one analyzes his writings for *Criminalogía Moderna,* it becomes clear that, despite all his good intentions and his criticisms of Lombroso, traces of his racist ideas remained embedded in Gori's thought, especially when he describes the inmates in the penal colony of Sierra Chica, located south of Buenos Aires. As I will show in the following chapter, Gori's observations are similar to those of Gina Lombroso, daughter of the famous criminologist, who visited South America and published a book titled *Nell'America Meridionale (Brasile— Uruguay—Argentina), Note e impressioni.*

During his visit to Sierra Chica, Gori was accompanied by Juan Vugetich, an anthropologist and photographer who became famous for his system of identification through fingerprinting. In a three-part essay devoted to the penitentiary, Gori writes that there are 387 inmates in the facility, of which sixty-five are Italian; sixty-seven are illiterate, and they would remain so because the penitentiary does not have a school. In one of the very few essays devoted to Gori's work as a criminologist in Argentina, Martín Albernoz remarks that while the Anarchist condemned certain disciplinary techniques used in Sierra Chica, as the red cap that prisoners were required to wear and the habit of placing the inmates in solitary confinement on the anniversary of their crime, his impressions about the penal colony and its director, Miguel Costa, were overall positive. Gori

especially appreciated the usage of coercive labor as an instrument to reha-
bilitate the prisoners, a practice that legal scholars have consistently criticized for its negative impact on salaries, creating an unfair competition on
the labor market.[27] The Italian lawyer thought that solitary confinement
activates the most degrading and "perverse" impulses, including homo-
sexuality. He commends Costa for his excellent work, despite the lack of
support from the local government. Thanks to his progressive approach,
some prisoners may move freely around the premises without having to be
contained. He observes the inmates in the various shops and is surprised
by the calm and precision with which they perform their tasks. It is as if
meaningful work gave them a new life.

Not all inmates, however, are depicted in such positive terms.
Albornoz shows that Gori characterized some of them as similar to mon-
keys: "Uno de ellos llamó la atención de Gori: era un "curioso tipo de
semi-salvaje," "al que casi se le podría tomar por una especie de mono"
(one of them captured Gori's attention: he was a curious quasi-savage
individual who could be almost compared to a species of monkey; 40).
Despite the overall positive assessment of the facility, the "descent" into
the penitentiary evokes comparisons with Dante's *Inferno*, where some
of the prisoners are described as monsters, as in the case of inmate no. 91,
who had been previously featured by Alberto Ghiraldo in a volume titled
Sangre y oro, published in 1897.[28] Gori's depiction of the prisoner and his
emphasis on degeneration shows that he was employing the same theories of Lombroso:

> The very harsh features of his physiognomy created a more ferocious
> look: the enormous jaws resembled those of carnivorous beasts, the prom-
> inent cheeks, the asymmetric ears shaped like a handle, the exaggerated
> arched bones above the eyes, summarized, in a more noticeable form, all
> the degenerative characters.[29]

The concept of degeneration is connected with the theory of atavism
advocated by Lombroso, who claimed that criminals embodied a regres-
sion to prior stages of human evolution.[30] Albornoz points out that in his
investigative essay Gori described the so-called *gaucho malo*, who had
been portrayed most famously by Faustino Sarmiento in his seminal book
Facundo: "The bad gaucho was the environmental derivation of the likable
'beduin of the pampa,' who could suddenly become a ferocious beast under

the influence of alcohol. The prisoner number 218's luck was to become the typical incarnation of that Sarmentian type."[31]

Needless to say, the individualist wing of the Anarchist movement was extremely critical of Gori's endeavor, and also *La Protesta Humana*, which until then had been very supportive of his work, began issuing disclaimers about the possible contamination with Lomborso's ideas of the "born criminal." Instead of declaring "a war on crime," as the lead article in the first issue of *Criminalogía Moderna* stated, the editors thought that one should reach out to "criminals" and try to understand their motivations. Moreover, the editors saw the danger inherent in Gori's scholarly inititiative:

> A small group of intellectuals and scholars who could produce a progressive discussion, unchained the most reactionary behaviors in the "generality of the social masses," so that when they hear yelling: "War on Crime!" they jump on the first shabby or degenerate worker, on the first slacker or life survivor, and help the cops put him in chains or beat him up.[32]

In the meantime, Gori's reputation in Latin America continued to rise, also outside Anarchist circles. In 1901 he traveled to Chile, where he visited Santiago and Valparaiso and contributed to the growth and consolidation of Anarchism in that country. His conferences constituted, as Angiolo Tommasi writes, "una revolucíon en los cerebros de muchos" (a revolution in many people's brains).[33] Although the trip was sponsored by the Sociedad Cientifica Argentina, Gori took advantage of the opportunity to reach out to workers and militants in the area who had read the Argentine journal *La Protesta Humana*. By reaching out to a variety of audiences and presenting himself as a moderate, peaceful person, he showed people that Anarchism was a not a violent organization as the bourgeois media often portrayed it. According to Albernoz, Gori modified the perceptions that Argentine people had about Anarchists: "Gori llegó incluso a ser considerado un 'anarquista transformado' y un buen amigo de la policía" (Gori even arrived at being considered a "transformed Anarchist" and a good friend of the police; 42). When President William McKinley was killed in 1901 by a Polish anarchist in Buffalo, New York, *La Protesta Humana* celebrated the event, while the Argentine mainstream newspaper *La Prensa* remarked that Gori would not have approved of it, because it was the act of an angry man. Gori gave his last lecture in Buenos Aires in January

1902; the most important mainstream newspapers commented very favorably on the event and praised his ability to communicate to large audiences, although he was speaking in Italian. The Socialist newspaper *La Vanguardia,* on the other hand, commented sarcastically about Gori's departure:

> The Anarchist Gori, before leaving (luckily for us) our Anarchized republic, went to bid farewell to the Anarchist Roca and Mitre. Anarchically, they gave him two Anarchist autographs that Gori will show at Anarchist conventions as the most evident testimony of the apotheosis of Anarchism of the greatest Anarchists in Latin America.[34]

The Italian press in Buenos Aires was not very appreciative of Gori's stay. Upon his return to Italy, Gori sued the Italian-Argentine newspaper *L'Italiano* for the editorials they published against him. When the infamous law against "dangerous" immigrants was passed the following year, both *La Prensa* and *La Nación* interviewed Gori, who strongly criticized it, as he had done in the past, because it did not reflect the liberal principles on which the Argentine Republic had been founded. Both newspapers opposed the law as well.

Most historians of the labor movement in Latin America give a positive assessment of Gori's political work in the region. After the fall of the authoritarian and repressive regimes in Eastern Europe starting in 1989, scholars have begun to reassess the philosophy of Gori, Malatesta, and their comrades. Davide Turcato, who has written extensively on Anarchism, observes that the transnational nature of the anarchist movement was unique, because "their ideology was not nationalist, but anti-nationalist, and their project was not to uphold or build the nation-state, but to abolish it."[35] The transnational and cosmopolitan features of the movement distinguished it from Socialism and resonate with the revolutionary slogan of *The Communist Manifesto*: "Proletarians of the World, Unite!" Anarchists were fiercely opposed to nationalism, an ideology that provided the foundation for the development of Fascism. As Gori writes in an essay titled "La base sociologica dell'anarchia," "La religione antiumana del patriotismo sarà vinta dalla fede grandiosa nella solidarietà di tutti gli uomini e di tutti i popoli" (The anti-human religion of patriotism will be defeated by the great faith in the solidarity of all humas and all peoples; 63). Both Malatesta and Gori always stated that there should be no conflict between

Socialism and Anarchism since they both fight for the emancipation of the working class, but their relationship was very conflictual. In one of his theoretical texts, Gori makes an important remark: Socialism must be superseded to achieve what he calls "la libertà delle libertà," the freedom of freedoms. In other words, the objective is to end exploitation but also any form of "coazione," or coercion. Socialism, he asserts, is "ricchezza social-izzata" (socialized wealth) while anarchism is "libera associazione delle sovranità individuali" (free association of individual sovereignties; 76). Another important element of Gori's thought is the role that he assigned to emotions: the first form of rebellion, in his opinion, comes from the heart (75); only later is it rationalized. The theory, therefore, represents a "trans-figuration" of the sentiment. This statement explains why in his political speeches and creative works he always aimed at producing an emotional response, a strategy that caused Marxist and Socialist critics like Gramsci to dismiss Gori's approach and Anarchism in general as irrational and politically counterproductive.

Unfortunately, the Anarchist movement in Argentina and Uruguay was discredited by the hegemonic narrative constructed by the Socialist Party as an element of confusion and disorder that turned workers away from their legitimate objectives. It was described as an incoherent, naïve, and utopian ideology. Most recently, this narrative has been deconstructed by the Argentine Communist Party, according to which,

> Socialists, by accepting a parliamentary game that was distorted in advance, became accomplices of the ruling class; the only alternative, at the end of the nineteenth century, in a context of fraudulent democracy, was the total refusal of the system.[36]

Argentine parliamentary democracy was a mere illusion, with very lim-ited participation: the hegemonic classes had total control over politics, and immigrants were excluded. Furthermore, many of them had come to Argentina with the dream of "fare l'America" and were less likely to develop a strong class consciousness. They usually joined mutual aid soci-eties and clubs that focused on patriotism and national or regional cohesion unity instead of transnational class solidarity. The organizational branch of Anarchism, to which Gori and Malatesta belonged, had to fight on sev-eral opposing fronts: against the local authorities and capitalists who tried to keep workers divided, representing Anarchists as dangerous criminals;

against the individualist component of the Anarchist movement,[37] whose individual acts of violence generated police repression. Finally, they had to respond to the attacks of the Socialist Party that, as a means of gaining control of the labor movement, depicted Anarchism as an enemy to be eliminated.

Despite the Socialists' repeated attempts to keep Anarchists out of workers' organizations, in many of them the two components coexisted, reaching important results.[38] Gori was instrumental in overcoming internal division, which led to the creation of the FOA in 1901. Their founders saw the federation not merely as an instrument for class struggle but as the embryo of a democratic society, where members collectively and responsibly could exercise their rights. The following year, however, the FOA, in which Anarchists were the majority, split again, and Socialists created their own organization. The schism coincided with Gori's departure from Buenos Aires, and the Anarchist movement became once again hegemonized by the violent individualist groups, which led to the deportation of many activists. The following years also coincided with the growth of the Argentine Socialist Party, whose founder, Juan B. Justo, was a strong critic of Anarchism. It is unfortunate that Socialists and Anarchists in the Rio de la Plata could not reconcile their differences and continue fighting together beyond national boundaries. The upcoming first global conflict of the twentieth century would enhance the sentiments of patriotism among immigrant communities. Over three hundred thousand Italian citizens volunteered and returned home to fight in World War I.[39] The great revolutionary slogan "La nostra patria è il mondo intero" remained a utopian dream, as multitudes of young proletarians were sent to die in one of the most horrific human carnages that history had ever experienced. The gospel of Enrico Corradini and his proto-Fascist friends who preached the religion of the fatherland prevailed, isolating even more the *senza-patria* (stateless) from the rest of the community. Anarchists became the "internal enemies" to be hunted down and exterminated, while Socialists lost almost entirely their revolutionary potential, caught in the power games of bourgeois institutions, just as the Anarchists had predicted.

A few years after Pietro Gori's departure from Buenos Aires, Gina Lombroso and her husband Guglielmo Ferrero toured Argentina and Brazil, invited by the highest political and cultural authorities.[40] Lombroso's daughter was especially interested in the Argentine prison system and mental institutions, where her father's teachings had been well received, in some instances by the same scientists who had collaborated with Gori. In her accounts, however, his desire of "going to the people" to emancipate and instill in them the seeds of rebellion, is missing. Criminology became thoroughly "medicalized," and offenders were studied to be disciplined so that they would better conform to the requirements of modern forms of labor organization.

CHAPTER SIX

In the Shadow of "Great Men": Gina Lombroso's Travels to South America

Here is a voice out of Italy that is still innocently attuned to the Middle Ages!

—Mary Siegrist's review of Gina Lombroso's book
The Soul of Woman, The New York Times,
July 29, 1923

Gina Lombroso, daughter of Cesare, the internationally known anthropologist and founder of modern criminology, was a gifted and intellectually accomplished woman who had been educated to the highest standards, receiving a university degree in literature and philosophy in 1897, at the age of twenty-five, and a few years later, in 1901, in medicine. At a very early age, Gina began helping her father in his research projects, and soon after she was editing essays for the scholarly journal he directed, *Archivio di Psichiatria*, where she also published several book reviews. Gina and her sister Paola were strongly influenced by Anna Kuliscioff, a native of Russia who had escaped political persecution and settled with her Anarchist partner Andrea Costa in Italy, where she became one of the leaders of the Socialist movement. Kuliscioff had a degree in medicine and edited *Critica Sociale*, the most prestigious Marxist journal at the turn of the nineteenth century, founded by Filippo Turati. Kulischioff often visited Cesare Lombroso's house, and her Socialist ideas had an impact on Gina, who became interested in social and political issues and decided to undertake sociological research on the factory workers of Turin and their families.[1] Despite her early exposure to progressive ideas, however, Lombroso maintained throughout her life a rather conservative view about the role of women in society, which often put her in conflict with the rising feminist movement. Her positions reflected in part the theories of her father Cesare, who argued that women were biologically destined to play a subaltern role with respect to men, although he recognized and welcomed their scientific contributions. Gina's ideas on women were fully developed and presented in a book published in 1920, titled *L'anima della donna,* but they also emerge in the travel book she wrote after visiting Brazil, Uruguay, and Argentina.[2] The young scholar and social activist always saw herself as a supporter and adviser of other dominant male figures: first her father Cesare, who constantly relied on her advice, then her husband, Guglielmo Ferrero, a leading representative of Italian Positivism and a favorite pupil of Cesare's, with whom he wrote a book titled *La donna delinquente* (The criminal woman), published in 1893. Gina married Guglielmo in 1901, but it was a difficult relationship: she had hoped to collaborate with Guglielmo as she had with her father, but that turned out to be impossible because of her husband's individualist personality. Nevertheless, she endured, and her altruistic attitude led her to give up her passion for medicine and dedicate herself to her family. Thus, despite her undoubted talents, she continued to live and work in the shadow of the strong male figures with whom she was associated.

In 1906, following the publication of a ponderous and controversial six-volume work on the history of ancient Rome, Gina's husband was invited to lecture at the prestigious Collège de France, where he met Bartolomé Mitre, statesman and owner of the newspaper *La Nación,* who invited him to Argentina to give a series of lectures related to his research.[3] He also received a generous offer from the Academia Brasileira de Letras to present in Rio de Janeiro and other Brazilian cities. In one of the few scholarly articles devoted to Ferrero's travels to South America, Livio Sansone writes that Guglielmo Ferrero's journey contributed to enhance the reputation of Cesare Lombroso's theories in the Southern Cone, where the questions of degeneration and the decadence of the so-called Latin race were intensely debated.[4] Gina Lombroso's travel book, however, is much more insightful than her husband's fictional/philosophical work *Fra i due mondi,* published in 1913, also based on their journey to Argentina.

Lombroso's text, *Nell'America meridionale* (1908), is dedicated to the Italians of America that she met during her journeys, who continued to remain attached to their homeland, although they "transplanted their seeds overseas," where they created "new Italies" whose future—she hopes—will be as glorious at the one of their homeland.[5] Although her declared intention is to offer a portrait of the Italians of America and their new lands, the description of Italian diasporic communities, especially in the in the first sections of the book, is rather limited. Instead, Lombroso seems more interested in the landscape of Brazil, the first nation she visited. The architect Antonio Januzzi, who designed many of the modern buildings by the sea promenade, is the only Italian mentioned in the chapter on Rio de Janeiro. What makes the iconic Brazilian city unique, in the author's view, is how it coexisted with the surrounding natural landscape, which always seemed on the verge of submerging it: a city scattered among a multitude of picturesque islands, clinging to vertical cliffs, emerging in the middle of a virgin forest.

As she was heading by train toward San Paolo, the most Italian of Brazil's cities, Lombroso observed the great spectacle of the tropical forests, which both fascinated and frightened her: "When in a restricted space life accumulates, overlaps so furiously, as in a tropical forest, it is no longer the sense of infinite that penetrates within, but solitude and discouragement."[6] Interestingly, she compares the discouragement one experiences in the jungle to the feeling of solitude and powerlessness in the modern city, where the swarming crowds are totally indifferent to one's needs and desires: "In front, behind, above, underneath, creepers, birds, flowers, trees that live for themselves and among themselves, that don't call you, that don't invite you, that reject you as an intruder."[7] No sensory Symbolic "correspondances" in the Brazilian forests: nature does not communicate to the poet/observer; it remains silent and hostile.[8] The author observes that one may understand, after having traveled for many hours amid the jungle, the sense of brutal satisfaction that humans may feel when they set a portion of the forest on fire: a desperate attempt to reassert control on a natural world that is perceived as hostile and overpowering. Burning a small section of forest is a long process: first one must cut the trees and lianas and let them dry for months; then a trench is traced to delimit the area; finally, dozens of people gather around and start the fire, which is like an explosion. In a few minutes the land is turned into a brazier and on the remaining ashes either rice or corn is planted, so that humans may establish their precarious dominion.

When the author arrived in San Paolo, she had the impression of being in an Italian city. Surrounded by gentle hills, like Florence, it was a great commercial and industrial center where the many Italian dialects fused together, as people had adopted the Italian national language as their official idiom. All is Italian in the city, including wine, bread, books, and automobiles; there are over fifty Italian schools, in addition to several musical and fine arts institutes. When Guglielmo and Gina arrived, on a special train made available to them by the Brazilian government, thirty thousand people came to greet them, tossing flowers and chanting, because their presence reawakened in them a sense of *italianità* and reminded them of the glories of their motherland. The laws of Brazil, she writes enthusiastically, had been modified according to the theories developed by her father, whose name had become as popular as those of Mazzini and Garibaldi (35). Many celebrations were organized in their honor, with splendid banquets and astonishing flower arrangements. Unfortunately, Gina writes, the Italian government does almost nothing to support the local Italian community, which feels abandoned and neglected. This is a criticism that was made repeatedly by Italian travelers at the turn of the nineteenth century, regardless of political affiliation: it is as if the Italian government were ashamed to acknowledge and support its many citizens living abroad.

After San Paolo, the author visited the coffee plantations, which are organized like modern factories where the workers are not expected to have any initiatives: they must only perform determinate tasks. Until recently, enslaved people brought from Africa worked in the *fazendas* and lived next to the *fazendero,* in an enclosed area. Enslavers and the enslaved had lived in close proximity and ate a simple diet based on the products of the land. The new *fazendas* are organized differently: the colon is something between a sharecropper and a day laborer. In addition to the pay, workers also receive a house as well as a parcel of land where they may cultivate corn and other products and pasture their animals, usually cows. Every *fazenda* is like a small village, with a chapel and a priest, a square with a fountain, and a small hospital with a doctor. In some cases, the owner provided the colons with fresh fruit and milk at no cost. Farmers lived in small houses, which replaced the common dwellings used by enslaved people. Every dwelling has a kitchen, one or more bedrooms, and an open area where they may grow vegetables and keep the animals. Coffee plants in some areas were extremely productive, and the fruits could be harvested up to four times a year. Plants are cultivated in rows, thus making the hilly landscape resemble Italian vineyards. Farmers have to keep the soil free from invasive herbs, which in the tropics are often very difficult to control. Their life is not much different from the one they led in the Italian countryside, with the traditional Sunday mass, weddings, First Communions, and other typical festivities. Gina and her husband were received with enthusiasm by the colons, who were excited to see illustrious representatives of their homeland. Most of them were from Veneto, and some had met Gina's father when he was a young doctor, investigating pellagra epidemics in the region. The way they were received is reminiscent of De Amicis's encounter with the Piedmontese colons in Argentina: women invited Gina and her husband into their houses, showed them their chickens and pigs, and offered them coffee, eggs, and bananas. The Italians live simply, but they seem to have everything they need, and some had achieved a relative prosperity. Most importantly, the author remarks that the colons managed to maintain a sense of community, continuing in the new land many of the traditions from their own native regions. Unfortunately, the salary they receive is very low, and the economic crisis made the situation even worse. The author includes in her volume two "libretti" that contain detailed family budgets, and she concludes that to make a good living and save some money in Brazil it is necessary to have a large family in which everyone contributes. Children usually start working in the farm at the age of six or seven. She emphasizes that the role of women is essential: all families that have achieved some degree of financial security were guided by intelligent and active women who had to perform multiple tasks: cultivate and maintain a vegetable garden, care for the animals, make their own soap and cured meats, and take care of the family. A man alone would have serious difficulties surviving in these regions. Until recently, when owners relied exclusively on the labor of enslaved people, they made good profits, but as the price of coffee on the international market collapsed and the cost of labor increased, many *fazenderos* were forced to close their operations. In Lombroso's opinion, the traditional large *fazenda* is guaranteed to disappear, to be replaced by smaller farms owned directly by colons, who often abandon the traditional coffee cultivation and start their own vineyards, which are much more profitable. Some colons bought the land from the original owners, got together with other farmers, and formed authentic "Socialist villages" (60).

Lombroso seems to have been especially fond of the state of Minas Geras, whose landscape is comparable to Switzerland. A beautiful railroad connected Rio de Janeiro with the state capital, Belo Horizonte, going through a landscape similar to the Italian Alps but with a luxuriant vegetation that astonished travelers with its splendor. Unfortunately, this region underwent massive exploitation that negatively impacted both the environment and the native population. In the sixteenth century, the first veins of gold and precious stones were discovered, attracting people from all over the world. Presently, most mines were abandoned because they were no longer productive, but Lombroso got to visit one, whose tunnels reached almost a mile underground. The author was horrified by the conditions in which the miners worked, particularly the unbearable heat. Their condition was even more absurd considering the surrounding magnificent territory, where people could live happily without much effort. Instead, she writes, the thirst for gold prevailed, turning this wonderful land into a hellish landscape. Italians were numerous in Minas, albeit scattered throughout the territory. In Lafayette, the Italian couple received a wonderful welcome from the Italian community, whose leader was an old man from Calabria who had participated in the famous Bandiera brothers' expedition: an old *garibaldino* whose only dream was to go back to Italy one day. Many inhabitants of the region adjusted to the decline of the mining industry and started cultivating the beautiful and fertile land. In Minas there were no large *fazendas*, as in San Paolo; people lived more simply and were less dependent on the price fluctuations on the global markets. The region constituted a small oasis of tranquility in a country where everyone was obsessed with making money fast. Although the people of San Paolo made fun of them, the inhabitants of Minas Geras, in Lombroso's opinion, were making slow but more definitive progress, and in the long run it seemed they would end up being more successful than those living in metropolitan areas.

Since the original capital of the region, Ouro Petro, was in the middle of the mountains and thus difficult to reach, it was decided to create a new capital, Belo Horizonte, in a more accessible area. In about a decade, the new city prospered and expanded with a rapidity that was typical of the young American nations. Interestingly, when describing the material progress brought about by Europeans, the author uses the same military metaphors that were present in De Amicis, Barzini and other European Italian travelers who preceded her. The advance of the great "army of modern civilization" is lightning quick and cannot be stopped:

In a few years, the wooded highland was transformed into a large, spacious city, surrounded by beautiful parks, shaded by wide boulevards that all converge on the central park, which provides air and cool to the city. Nothing is missing in the new capital: boarding schools, schools, hospitals, churches, prisons, barracks, soldiers, firefighters; every army of modern civilization has its house, actually. its palace in Belo Horizonte.[9]

As many other American cities, Belo Horizonte was characterized by a great diversity of architectural styles reflecting the cultures that contributed to shape it. Whereas other Italian observers criticized this plurality of styles as chaotic and kitsch, Lombroso is appreciative and sees it as a sign of freedom: "La libertà assoluta domina negli edificii, come nelle istituzioni" (absolute freedom reigns both in the buildings and the institutions; 78). In Belo Horizonte, the penal code and the prisons were based on the principles theorized by Cesare Lomboso aiming at the rehabilitation and reintegration of criminals, not merely their punishment. Although the local Italian community was not rich, it was very united, and they showed their appreciation for Gina and her family by decorating their wagon with flowers and fruits of the region.

In the surrounding countryside, the government experimented with a new type of colony that turned out very successfully. In fact, Lombroso writes that many enterprises in the Americas failed because farmers were not provided with the financial means and the knowhow to succeed. Even when the land was gifted to the colons, they could fail because of the many adversities that the settlers had to overcome. Thus, the state of Minas Geras instituted a new method: not only were the colons given land, seeds, and tools for free, but they were assigned an expert, called "Maestro di colonia," who lived in the colony and advised them. The local government also built railroads to facilitate the transport of products and provided machinery and technicians who showed the colons how to use them properly. This system may seem expensive, but ultimately the investments paid off because most families permanently settled there, thus contributing to the economy. The author concludes the section about Minas Geras on a positive note:

> The alacrity of the inhabitants together with the fertility of the soil will convert in the near future the lands of Minas Geras into mines more profitable than those of gold and silver, that generated in the State of Minas Geras so many hopes and disillusions.[10]

Lombroso maintains that Brazil could not have grown so rapidly without enslaved African people and thinks that their quality of life in the new country improved with respect to the way they lived in Africa. According to her, the enslavers did not despise the people they enslaved. As she points out, they often adopted the children they had with them and sometimes even married them. Lombroso claims that when they arrived in Brazil enslaved people were treated fairly and were protected by the law. For instance, family unity was respected, and wives and children could not be separated due to a change in owners. They were permitted to profess their own religion and maintain their traditions. Young girls were taught domestic work by their female enslavers; if enslaved people escaped from their household, they could be adopted by the new enslaver, who had to reimburse the previous one. Lombroso claims that the conditions for the enslaved in Brazil were much better than in North America, which explains why slavery lasted so long in the South American nation, and it did not end because of revolts but for economic reasons. Lombroso also remarks that the conditions for the enslaved were not as bad as the abolitionists claimed. The enslavers adopted many cultural habits from the people they enslaved, including games, sports, cuisine, and even agriculture. Reciprocally, the African people they enslaved incorporated many European practices, and interracial unions were very common. The author argues that the close relationships that developed between different races caused people to love and appreciate each other. When Gina visited the region, she noticed a large number of professors, doctors, and engineers with African physical features. Racial discrimination was rare, she concluded, because interracial unions deeply permeated Brazilian society, preventing the problems that segregation generated in North America. These observations reflect, in my opinion, Lombroso's "paternalistic" vision of society, where class conflict is ideally replaced by mutual collaboration between hegemonic and subaltern groups. The same vision inspired, as we shall see, her analysis of Uruguay.

Lombroso writes that Black influence in Brazil was enormous, and she argues that the impact that Black people had on society was more beneficial because African slaves were selected from among the healthiest and strongest subjects, while European immigrants often were "scarti e rifiuti delle nazioni—condannati, reprobi, turbolenti o inetti" (rejects and waste of the nations—convicted, despicable, unruly or inept; 107). Furthermore, Africans found in Brazil a similar climate and adjusted more easily than Europeans, who, according to her, acquired from Africans mental habits that were disappearing in Europe, like "l'immaginazione, il cuore, la pazienza" (imagination, heart, and patience; 108). Finally, Lombroso observes that Africans were responsible for enhancing the poetic, artistic, and literary components of Brazilian culture, which are stronger in the north, where the African influence was more pervasive. The author applies the usual Eurocentric racial stereotypes when analyzing Brazilian culture, observing that in the south, where northern European influence was more widespread, rational thinking was predominant. Other characteristics that Brazilians attributed to Africans were kindness, generosity, and attachment to the family, which Lombroso claims were not found to the same degree among the whites. Ultimately, Lombroso maintains that the constant mixing of the two races in Brazil contributed to the renewal of European culture, making it more dynamic. The fear of decadence and degeneration was very common in Europe at the turn of the nineteenth century; therefore, for her, the interaction with African individuals represented an opportunity for physical and moral renewal, bringing Europeans more in touch with their natural instincts, which were invariably associated with developing countries. Another characteristic that Lombroso attributes to Brazilians is their sense of hospitality and generosity. This, however, could have negative consequences, because sometimes people go too far trying to help others, at the expense of their own economic situations. The author, however, is very appreciative of the generosity she witnessed in Belo Horizonte and elsewhere in the country. She argues that since so many individuals had to leave their families behind to come to Brazil, friendship is considered very important. Therefore, people are never completely alone, because they can count on the help and support of their friends and neighbors. Another psychological feature that the author attributes to African influence is the extreme timidity that she noticed even among cultivated people. The Brazilian poets and intellectuals she met did not like to talk about their accomplishments, as if they perceived themselves as inferior to Europeans. The most prominent characteristic of Brazilians is their imagination, which is "fertile like the air of Africa" (119). They seemed like dreamers, even when it would be more advisable to take a more logical, practical approach. Nevertheless, Lombroso was fascinated by what she saw as an idealistic and juvenile enthusiasm permeating civil society. The term used by Lombroso is "encyclopedism," meaning that Brazilian culture did not seem as compartmentalized as in Europe. Individuals (usually male) pursued multiple interests while holding important public offices, and it was not uncommon for a general or a statesman to do historical or scientific research. Their authentic love for culture found its temple in the splendid Garnier Library in Rio de Janeiro, where educated people gathered to read and discuss the most recent books, browsing through the beautiful rooms, indulging in the pleasure of learning for its own sake.

Lombroso laments that in Italy the idealism of the Risorgimento was forgotten, and people pursued their own individual careers with no concern for the common good: "Il soffio di idealismo, di patriotismo, di altruismo, di fratellanza che esso aveva acceso nel cuore dei nostri nonni, si spense con essi" (the breath of idealism, patriotism, altruism, and brotherhood that it had ignited in the hearts of our grandparents, was extinguished with them; 121). In Brazil, instead, encyclopedism was prospering, as reflected in the names that parents choose for their children: Eloise, Washington, Ulysses, Franklyn, Iphigenia, and many more, showing a genuine admiration for the great men and women of the past. In Lombroso's narrative, Brazilian culture embodied the values and passions that Italy and Europe in general had lost. Brazilians would move forward, she thought, because they had faith in humankind and showed a sincere appreciation for the natural world and its beauty. The idealism that Italy experienced in the first half of the nineteenth century and that inspired the struggle for unifying the country continued to exist in Brazil, safeguarding it from the cynicism "che va allagando tutto il mondo moderno e preservando gli intellettuali da quella unilateralità negli studi che sterilizza la scienza e l'arte nella vecchia Europa" (that is flooding the entire modern world. Idealism protects the intellectuals from that unilaterality in the studies that is sterilizing science and culture in old Europe; 127).

Another important consequence of Brazilian encyclopedism, according to Lombroso, was the role that women played in society. Traditionally, upper-class women were confined to the domestic sphere: enslavement forced them to learn management skills, since they had to oversee many servants, both enslaved African and Native Americans. The ideas of the Enlightenment made women more aware of their rights, but in Lombroso's opinion, women in Brazil did not embrace feminist ideology. Instead, they preferred to remain next to their men, guiding and inspiring them in a discreet way. Therefore, although very few women studied at the university and pursued professional careers and were only recently allowed to sit at the same dining table with men, the author writes that women were present "in tutte le opere dell'uomo più assai che nei paesi cosiddetti avanzati e femministi" (in every man's work much more than in the so-called developed and feminist countries; 132). The typical example of a strong and audacious Brazilian woman is Anita Garibaldi, who sacrificed her life for her husband. The author claims that most of the male prominent figures she met in Brazil had next to them women who supported, helped, and inspired them and were reciprocally beloved and protected by their male companions.

After enumerating the positive effects that she thought Africans had on Brazilian culture, Lombroso acknowledges that European immigrants often found it difficult to work with Black and biracial people, especially when they held a superior position. When both parents were Black, according to Lombroso, individuals accepted their condition without showing any resentment and maintained their own traditions, but when one of the parents was white, they tended to develop a sense of hatred against whites and did everything possible to humiliate and prevail upon them. Thus, the relationships between whites and biracial people were very tense. Lombroso claims that biracial people rarely married Blacks, because their goals were to become "whiter" and to move as far as possible from the Black community. "Whiteness" was supposedly both the object of hatred and the goal toward which one aspired. In the author's opinion, biracial individuals perceived their hybrid condition as "transitory" and she remarks that the country "va imbiancandosi" (137), is becoming increasingly whiter, precisely because of the psychological mechanism that she described.

Lombroso characterizes Brazilians as "indolenti" (lazy). In her opinion, that is the greatest defect they inherited from enslaved Africans. Brazilians lacked even the concept of being exact, punctual, and reliable, she claims. They did not refuse to work but would not perform any job that was out of the ordinary. They lack any initiative and prefer to follow a daily routine instead of exploring new venues. Although Lombroso does not say it explicitly, she seems to imply that the repetitive nature of enslaved labor, in which individuals are forced to perform the same tasks every day, was ingrained into the culture, preventing it from developing in a dynamic way. She does admit, however, that the negative stereotypes about Brazil may be due to the simple economic fact that the nation ceased to be the promised land of plenty that it had once been: the extinction of gold and silver mines that once attracted people from all over the world, the abolition of slavery, and the recent fall of coffee prices have impoverished it: "Il Brasile presentemente non è ricco. Ecco forse il difetto che più lo infama alla faccia dell'avido mondo europeo" (Brazil at the moment is not rich. Here is the defect that defames it in the eyes of the avid European world; 142). When a country does not have the resources that it once possessed, it ceases to interest Europeans, who do not care about natural beauty. Since the time of the Spanish conquest, their gaze has been fixed on one thing: gold. Lombroso is hopeful, nevertheless, that Brazil will find the strength to prosper once again while maintaining the idealism that is, in her opinion, the true motor of progress.

After visiting Brazil, Gina and Guglielmo traveled to Uruguay. The chapter devoted to that country is short but insightful. While other contemporary Italian observers classified Montevideo as sad, because of the many conflicts the city had to face during its brief history, Lombroso's assessment of the capital and the country in general is remarkably positive. Montevideo, in her view, was not as obsessed with modernity as other American cities. It could not compete with the astonishing natural beauty that surrounds Rio de Janeiro; it did not have grandiose theaters and enormous boulevards like Buenos Aires. Its appeal was more subtle and reflected an internal harmony that derives from being constructed on sound principles. Solidarity comes to mind as the most quintessential value: in the author's view, Uruguay did not display the economic disparities typical of modern capitalist societies. There were not many extremely affluent persons, but absolute poverty was absent as well: "Non si vede da alcuna parte il miliardario ma da nessuna parte la miseria nera. Dappertutto una ricchezza sana, media, equamente distribuita" (One does not see anywhere neither the billionaire nor extreme poverty. Everywhere a healthy and average prosperity, equally distributed; 156). The level of education was high, and there was a good balance between religious and lay schools. In fact, Uruguay managed to limit the influence of the clergy in civil society and public institutions, and the nation's budget was in solid shape because the government wisely channeled its workforce toward agriculture. As a result, the country had the highest percentage of cultivated land in South America.

As a physician, Lombroso admired the way the authorities dealt with tuberculosis: instead of creating specialized hospitals, a special foundation offered individual assistance to patients, so that they could remain at home, eat a good diet, and receive the care they needed from their own family. This system was costly, but in the long run it saved money because it prevented the spread of the disease. Another institution praised by the author was the Montevideo orphanage, where children were well treated, living in an environment that Lombroso describes as luxurious when compared to similar institutions in Europe. Natural mothers could remain in touch with their children and even reclaim them if they wished to do so. Maternal schools, "scuole maternali," were also well organized and generously funded, showing that the government invested generously in the welfare of children, thus preventing the emergence of problems in the future. Interestingly, Lombroso does not talk much about Italian immigration in Uruguay, except for Signor Castro, a "patriarch" who had fought with Mazzini and Garibaldi and lived in a large mansion surrounded by his many children. Although he had not returned to Italy for over fifty years, he kept up on all the political events, like a good father who has given some of his blood for his son. The country had experienced a decline in immigration from Europe in the previous twenty years, thus preserving Montevideo from "quell'aria di modernismo e provvisorio che hanno frequentemente le città sud-americane" (that semblance of modernism and precariousness that often characterizes American cities; 157). I would argue that the reason Lomboso was so appreciative of Uruguayan culture is because it seemed to embody a social model based on class solidarity and simple good sense. Thanks to the enthusiastic collaboration of its inhabitants, according to her, the Republic managed to reach "il massimo benessere generale colla massima economia sociale" (the highest level of general well-being with the highest social economy; 171).

On the other side of the Rio de la Plata, Buenos Aires offered a totally different spectacle, both through its architecture and the lifestyle of its inhabitants. While in Montevideo streetcars and automobiles were rare and life flowed calmly, the Argentine capital seemed to Lombroso as the apotheosis of modernity. "La febbre del nuovo" (the fever of new; 180) was visible at every corner, with splendid, imposing buildings all illuminated by electricity, while entire neighborhoods were continually being demolished to make room for new developments. Lombroso, unlike other Italian travelers, turned her gaze toward the "dark side" of the modern metropolis, represented by the shantytowns that preceded the so-called *villa miseria*, which unfortunately continued to grow in every major Argentine city.[11] The author writes that thousands of families lived in minuscule dwellings where three or four people had hardly enough space to lie down, built with oil barrels flattened and roughly tied together, as well as straw, cloth, wood boxes, in short with any scrap material they could find: "vespai fittissimi di insetti umani sparsi tutti come un branco di pecore disordinatamente tra il fango e la mota" (very dense wasps' nests of human insects disorderly scattered in the mud and sludge; 186). This enormous shantytown unfolded for many kilometers outside the capital. The author wonders how people could accept to live in such conditions, where it would seem impossible to raise a family. The answer, she argues, is because people in Buenos Aires did not dwell in the present but were constantly projected into the future: they lived in the illusion of moving away, changing profession and social status: "ammantano i poveri abituri degli smaglianti colori del benessere avvenire" (they adorn their miserable dwellings with the dazzling colors of future prosperity; 187). The illusion of social mobility, in other words, is what prevents people from facing the harsh reality and fighting for better living conditions.

In her book, Lombroso focuses on another marginal place, the cemetery of Chacarita, the largest in Argentina, an authentic city of the dead, quite different from the magnificent cemetery of Recoleta, where many of the wealthiest and most iconic Argentine figures are buried, from the *caudillo* Facundo to Evita Peron. Chacarita consists of long boulevards flanked by small white houses, separated by a minuscule garden, inside which people recreated a typical domestic interior, with tables, chairs, and portraits of their loved ones. A parallel city, as if the inhabitants felt the need to create a quiet, peaceful space removed from the chaotic frenzy of the metropolis. One may be tempted to use Michel Foucault's notion of "heterotopia" to conceptualize the "other places" singled out by Lombroso. The "other places" described by Foucault in his famous essay include cemeteries, prisons, and mental institutions: the same ones privileged by Lombroso during her journey in South America. These "institutional" places usually occupy a marginal position within the urban landscape, but through them one may gain new insights into society as a whole.[12] In her wanderings through Buenos Aires, Lombroso paused to observe an "other" marginal place, called "La quema de la basura," where the trash generated by the city was disposed. Lombroso defines this location as "exotic" and "picturesque," not aware that such marginal places would become a common feature in postmodern, neoliberal metropoles. The *quema* was an immense white plain with hundreds of hills that were constantly burning. An "ocean of ashes" lingered over the entire area, where small pieces of glass and metal shined in the middle of *basura*. At the bottom of each hill, hundreds of individuals, many of whom were children, searched for whatever is saleable. Lombroso was surprised to see how many reusable things one could find there: clothes, shoes, kitchen utensils, bottles, even furniture. At around one in the afternoon, the area turned into an open-air market.

Next to the *quema,* an authentic industrial town was born, where clothes were washed, shoes polished, and metal melted down and prepared to be reutilized. Like the inhabitants of Italo Calvino's haunting "invisible city" Leonia, where people constantly discard objects they just bought, Buenos Aires did not like old things and seemed to Lombroso to want to reinvent itself by discarding what was perceived as old.

> The city of Leonia refashions itself every day: every morning the people wake between fresh sheets, wash with just-unwrapped cakes of soap, wear brand-new clothing....It is not so much by the things that each day are manufactured, sold, bought, that you can measure Leonia's opulence, but rather by the things that each day are thrown out to make room for the new.[13]

What Calvino did not envision in his fictional city, however, is that for every item that the wealthy residents discard, there is a multitude of dispossessed people, hidden at the margins of society or in remote, underdeveloped countries, who survive (barely) thanks to what the rich world constantly throws away.

Lomboso writes that Buenos Aires had wonderful schools, state-of-the-art hospitals, and modern prisons and mental institutions, but the most important thing for its residents was the theater, because the metropolis was not just the political and economic capital of Argentina, it was the place everyone went to have fun. The epicenter of entertainment was the theater, a microcosm where spectators saw themselves being portrayed on stage, as in a mirror. There were over thirty theaters in the city when Lombroso visited it, where world-renowned artists regularly came to perform. But people don't go to the theater just to watch the actors: in the splendid Opera Theater, the *parterre* and *foyer* became stages where the upper classes could display their wealth. Lombroso observes that the Opera was a temple dedicated to women; they all seemed young and beautiful, because in the many *institutes de beauté* scattered throughout the city, even "la signora più vecchia, rugosa ed ingiallita, provincialmente vestita, può uscire dopo qualche ora trasformata interamente dai piedi alla testa" (the oldest, wrinkly, and faded lady may go out a few hours later entirely transformed from head to toes; 202). Theaters also are places to learn about history and other cultures, as it happened with Lombroso's husband, Guglielmo Ferrero, who was invited to present his research on ancient Rome at the prestigious Teatro Colón. The author observes that when they arrived in the port, they were welcomed by a committee composed of notable politicians and intellectuals. In their honor, that day all the public schools were closed so that students and teachers alike could greet the prestigious guests as they passed through the city. The parade was so large that it had to be redirected to wider streets to avoid potential disruption. With this demonstration, the author comments, Buenos Aires showed that it was eager to absorb and appreciate the highest forms of culture, even when they did not have an immediate practical application. I would argue, however, that while in Montevideo the need for culture originated from a genuine desire to create and partake in a practice "che sia al di fuori dei propri interessi personali" (that is beyond personal interests; 161), in Buenos Aires ostentation seemed to prevail, even in the world of high culture.

Lombroso was very impressed with the Argentine public school system, which Faustino Sarmiento considered the backbone of the new nation, and for which he invested huge resources. The school buildings were very modern and equipped with the most modern devices, like projectors and all kinds of scientific laboratories. Teachers were carefully selected and meticulously trained, and the pedagogical methods were extremely modern and hands-on. Students learned by doing and their instructors strove to keep them engaged with creative activities. The author observes, though, that by trying to entertain while teaching, children did not get as accustomed to abstract thought and would become less willing to learn independently: "Direi quasi che a furia di far studiare divertendo, disabituano a studiare" (I would almost say that by making students learn while entertaining them, they become unaccustomed to study; 212).

Lombroso especially admired the female professional schools of Buenos Aires, where the supervisor, Laura Rossen de Mitre, devised a system whereby the instructors were paid through the work of their students, whose manufacts were sold to local stores. In their final two years of school, girls were encouraged to seek potential customers on their own, thus facilitating the transition from school to the real world. Lombroso also writes that although the academic quality of public schools in Argentina was higher, upper-class families preferred to send their children to religious boarding schools, where they learned proper manners and rules of conduct, which the public system neglected. In Italian, the words *educazione* and *istruzione* denote different practices: schools do not teach "buona educazione," because good manners are expected to be learned at home. Lombroso thinks, on the contrary, that rules of conduct should be taught in public schools as well, otherwise religious institutions could become hegemonic and end up shaping the behavior of the emerging ruling classes: "Questo monopolio della educazione sociale lasciata interamente in balìa del clero ha per necessaria conseguenza che la sua morale deve diventare la morale ufficiale" (This monopoly of social education entirely left to the clergy necessarily ends up making its moral laws the official ones; 222).

One of the most "beautiful" Argentine institutions, in Lombroso's view, was the Penitenciaría Nacional, that she did not consider a place of detention but a real house of moral, physical, intellectual, and psychical redemption (223) for which she regretfully could find no equivalent in Italy. From the outside, the building did not have the gloomy look of traditional penitentiaries, and upon entering one did not see guards but only ample, luminous hallways decorated with palm trees. Each cell had electricity, its own bathroom with running water, a window, and a table with a chair and writing utensils. The building was structured as a panopticon: the hallways with the cells converged into a vast glass room, "donde il sottocapo può sorvegliare tuti i raggi del suo dominio" (where the supervisor can control all the branches of his dominion; 224). As Michel Foucault argued in his seminal work on the history of the carceral system, modern prisons are no longer built to "punish" but to "discipline." *Surveiller et punir* was the book's original French title, as the same verb used by Lombroso in Italian: *sorvegliare*.[14] But the real keystone of the Penitenciaría, which made possible the "redemption" of the inmates, was work. As Lombroso writes, the prison was also "uno dei più vasti opifici della Repubblica" (one of the largest factories of the Republic; 223). Work, in the institution, was mandatory, and individuals were "initiated to the art" they preferred or the one considered most suitable to them (224). On the redemptive function of forced labor, both Gina Lombroso and Pietro Gori seem to agree: in the penal colony, criminals acquire a normal, virile appearance and lose that "poisonous ferocity" that is so common in Italian prisons. Most of all, through work they would supposedly learn again how to be useful members of society. A complex system of gratifications encouraged the inmates to discipline themselves. A series of "prizes" marked their road to redemption: being able to see family members several times a week; permission to grow facial hair; the possibility of physical exercises once

a week in the garden, and more. The most coveted prize by the prisoners, however, was not having a number imprinted on their hat and jacket,
being called by one's name, and being treated like "normal" people (227).
Lombroso was moved when she saw the excellent results achieved by the
director, Antonio Ballvé, who was for the prisoners an authentic "spiritual
father." He confessed to her that he rigorously applied the precepts theorized by Cesare Lombroso: "Un nodo mi veniva alla gola, all'idea che egli
fosse così lontano...che egli dovesse continuare a vivere in un paese che gli
è sempre così ingrato" (I got a lump in my throat when I thought of him,
so far away...having to live in a country that is always so ungrateful to him;
230). Paradoxically, Lombroso's theories found a better implementation in
Argentina than in his own country.

An important aspect of the Penitenciaría and the other "exemplary"
facility visited by Lombroso, the mental hospital "open doors," was
their medicalization. When Lombroso visited it, the head of the Polizia
Scientifica was Doctor José Ingenieros, Pietro Gori's friend and collabo-
rator and one of the most prominent Argentine Socialist intellectuals. In
his office, the new inmates were analyzed, both physically and mentally,
including their supposed hereditary defects, and their progress toward
"normality" was meticulously registered. The psychiatric institute was
situated in an immense plain, where the patients built an entire village
with bricks produced on site. Although most of the inmates were destined
to work in the fields, there were workshops as well, where a multitude of
goods were produced and sold on the market, thus making the institution
entirely self-sustainable. Patients raised chickens, pigs, sheep, and cows,
and they even produced and sold their own butter and milk. Contrary to
similar facilities in Italy, the Buenos Aires hospital had no walls, and family members could visit their loved ones whenever they wished. Moreover,
it kept expanding, because with the income generated by the sales, patients
were building other houses for the new guests who kept arriving at the
"open door" institution. Patients of the mental hospital, like the inmates
in the Penitenciaría, received a small salary that was deposited in their
account, to be retrieved when they got out or else distributedto their
families.

What I find most intriguing about the "other places" described by
Lombroso is that they seem to have developed into mini-utopian societies based on coercive work and self-discipline. Italian immigrants had
dreamed of a land of plenty, but when they arrived in Argentina, they

realized that it was just a mirage. Life in Buenos Aires was hard, often unsustainable, living conditions in the *conventillos* unsanitary, and as a result many resorted to crime, which was very high in the capital at the turn of the century. Unable to solve the social problems caused by an unjust economic system, in which a small oligarchy had almost total control of the country's natural resources, social reformers ended up creating parallel, disciplinary "other" spaces where an ideal, artificial order held sway. By living under a strict disciplinary system, madmen and criminals metamorphosed into ideal citizens, ready to be reinserted into society. It is paradoxical that so many immigrants who had dreamed of a better life in America would end up living in shantytowns, whereas penitentiary institutions became the places where their dreams were materialized, albeit in a nightmarish way. The mentally ill individuals observed by Lombroso in Buenos Aires lived isolated in small houses separated from each other by ample gardens, with large dining rooms, where they could gather to eat, listen to music, watch movies, and read books and newspapers. The locations where the American dream was finally realized are places of confinement: prisons and mental hospitals, where everyone was free to move around and yet constantly under surveillance, forced to choose (another oxymoron) one's favorite "art." Lombroso writes that the guests of these model institutions were in high demand when they finally got out, since in prison they learned not only a trade but a way of life. Employers constantly sought "reformed criminals" because at the Penitenciaría they were thoroughly disciplined, as in the religious schools where upper-class parents preferred to send their children. One could argue that the "educazione" (in the sense of learning good manners and self-discipline) not provided by Sarmiento's public schools was accomplished instead in the Argentine penal and mental institutions, producing citizen-workers whose path to redemption was inscribed in the booklets that social reformers like Ingenieros were carefully annotating.

Gina and her husband traveled extensively through Argentina, visiting all the major cities, but her observations on the interior of the country are not as insightful, probably because she spent less time there and did not have as much time to talk to people as she did in the capital.[15] She writes, however, that as one followed the river Paraná, which at that time was the main route to the *pampa gringa,* there were fewer interactions between Italians and other ethnic groups, although they often belonged to the same affluent classes (250). A "fusion" with other nationalities would have been beneficial, in Lombroso's view, because when Italians lived too isolated from the larger community, they became nostalgic and desired to return home, where they would end up being disoriented because they no longer fit in the society they had left.

It is surprising to learn that even in 1906 Argentina still lacked a good transportation network: Lombroso writes that the roads ended just outside Buenos Aires, and in the rest of the country only the main streets were paved. As a result, when it rained, all the activities were suspended. To transport merchandise and products of the land, the traditional wagon with huge wheels pulled by six pairs of horses was still the only reliable means of transportation. Railroads were being built, but they did not reach all the small communities scattered in the *pampa*.

Lombroso presents the interior of Argentina as a land full of contrasts. While Rosario, situated along the Paraná River, is described as a modern city comparable to Buenos Aires, Cordoba still maintains "l'aria grigia, austera di una città medievale sotto l'incubo del giudizio universale" (the gray, austere look of a medieval city facing the nightmare of the universal judgment; 283). The presence of Jesuits who founded it was noticeable everywhere. While in Buenos Aires there was an abundance of theaters, in Cordoba the main forms of entertainment were religious processions. Young women, however, were fighting to liberate themselves from the domination of the church, and when they could not be regularly enrolled at the university, they started auditing courses. Lombroso writes that when she visited a women school in Cordoba, one of the teachers gave an inspiring, courageous speech, one of the best she heard during her voyage to Latin America. In the city, however, Italians were viewed with suspicion by the residents, as those who have taken Rome away from the Pope (288).[16] The author writes that Cordoba was poor, like all the cities that live on religion. By contrast, Tucumán, which she visited during her tour of the interior—surrounded by hills and mountains—was one of the most liberal and thriving cities of the republic: "a Tucumán, tutto è bello: le case, il popolo, la città, la campagna" (everything is beautiful in Tucumán: the houses, the people, the city, the countryside; 292). The inhabitants reminded Lombroso of Sicilians, with whom they shared a similar revolutionary, enthusiastic character. The revolution that granted Argentina its independence from Spain started there, and the residents were proud of that legacy. Even the native people seemed different from those she encountered elsewhere: women were always active cooking, washing clothes, and taking care of the house and the garden, like Italian housewives. When harvesting sugarcane, the most important crop of the region, native men and women showed a dexterity that Europeans did not possess, according to Lombroso. The countryside surrounding Tucumán was very fertile and one of the most picturesque of Argentina, with citrus trees, flowers of every sort, and forests where precious tropical trees grew spontaneously. Sugarcane was everywhere, but Lombroso remarks that before cultivations were more diversified to satisfy the needs of the inhabitants. As one moved north, toward Santiago del Estero, the soil got drier and the landscape more desolate. Only the natives ventured into the forests to cut the valuable trees, like the *cabil, quebracho,* and *algarrobo.* Water was so scarce that the main function of the railroad that went through the town was to bring large cisterns of water to its inhabitants. Nevertheless, Italians settled even in this remote, inhospitable region, and they welcomed Gina and her husband with great enthusiasm: the whole community gathered to greet the famous guests, adorned the buildings with flowers and prepared a banquet in the Italian Club, also attended by the governor. Lombroso does not show any concern for the native workers: they were used to the harsh environment, she seems to have thought, and could survive just on sugarcane, the little water they extract from plants, and their *mate.* She does express concern, however, for the future of the forest: if the clear cutting continues at the same pace, she writes, the *pampa* will soon be transformed into a desert. Interestingly, though, the author does not blame the whites, who profit from the clearcutting, but the indigenous people, "che spietamamente va tagliando i boschi" (who ruthlessly continue to cut the trees; 306).

In Mendoza, the Argentine capital of the wine industry, Lombroso found the same urge to accumulate wealth as rapidly as possible, as in Buenos Aires. Until recently, it was a quiet town, where the *criollos* lived a simple life: they produced little, but their needs were minimal as well. When the European immigrants arrived, they started building canals for irrigating the vineyards, and the region was completely transformed. At the time of Gina's visit, the cost of living in Mendoza was higher than in Buenos Aires and the *nouveaux riches* were mainly interested in material things and cared very little about culture. This attitude, the author argues, must change, because culture is as necessary as eating and drinking for the upper classes, and only when culture "diventa un piacere per la maggioranza dei membri di una società, il paese comincia a diventare veramente civile" (becomes a pleasure for the majority of the population does the country start to become truly civilized; 321). Before the boom of the wine industry, Mendoza had intense commercial relations with Chile, but then they became competitors, and the plans to extend the railroad connecting the two countries vanished. Thus, the only connection across the Andes was provided by *troperos,* who resembled the *gauchos* of the *pampa* and transported merchandise on their mules, even in winter. A railroad across the Andes would have been beneficial to all the South American nations, but political conflicts always prevented it from becoming a reality. Lombroso's statement, "La ferrovia non sarà mai definitivamente costrutta" (The railroad will never be definitely constructed; 332) is prophetic. When I visited Valparaiso in 2016, all the passengers going from Mendoza to Chile had to get off the bus and wait for hours at the border, in a deserted area situated at very high elevation. A tunnel across the mountains would be relatively easy to realize and would shorten considerably the journey, bringing the two countries closer to each other, but as Pietro Gori and his Anarchist comrades argued, nationalism, the great enemy of progress, continues to push people further apart.

The most controversial chapter of Lombroso's book is the final one, devoted to the position of women in Argentine society, a topic that she continued to reflect upon, often in conflict with the rising feminist movement. The Italian scientist met many accomplished female professionals in Argentina, including doctors ("medichesse"), composers, and artists, many of whom also had a family and never encountered serious obstacles during their career. Nevertheless, instead of rejoicing for their success, Lombroso was very critical of the "masculinization" that she thought was causing serious communication problems between men and women and was leading women away from their own "natural" inclinations. The author noticed a difference between Europe (especially southern Europe) and America. European women in her experience were constantly next to their men, regardless of their social class: the woman was the adviser, the supporter, the associate of her husband, son, father, and brother. She exerted a great influence on the important decisions concerning the family and the nation, but always in conjunction with the male figures (336). In Argentina, on the contrary, men and women were becoming increasingly separate and fearful of each other. During her journey, Lombroso observed that in Argentine public life women, when not entirely absent, preferred to position themselves far from their men: "non vogliono mescolarsi agli uomini" (they don't want to mingle with men; 337). When the author was invited to social events, she always found herself in the company of women. Even at the theater, the favorite pastime in Buenos Aires, husbands and wives often sat in different boxes. Married couples led separate lives, made important family and personal decisions without informing each other, and this was considered normal. In Lombroso's view, this separation had negative consequences on society at large, because in Europe the ideas expressed by politicians "non sono degli uomini soli, ma la risultante delle proprie idee, modificate già da quelle donne con cui stanno a contatto" (do not belong exclusively to men, but are the product of their ideas, modified by those of the women with whom they live; 345). The reciprocal influence and constant conversations helped smooth the contrasts and contributed to making society more stable and harmonic. Lombroso thinks that one of the great accomplishments of the French Revolution was bringing women into a public sphere that had previously been reserved to men. In northern Europe, however, they began creating separate women associations that seem "copie delle associazioni maschili" (copies of the male associations; 346). The result, according to her, is a progressive "masculinization" of women, who are expected to behave like men. Instead of forcing men to share with women the public spaces that were their exclusive domain, learning how to be more courteous toward women, barriers are being created that protect women but also isolate them (347). Lombroso maintains that women are "organically" different from men. Thus, according to her, they should not try to imitate them but trace their own path with "solchi vigorosi e profondi" (with vigorous and deep grooves; 348).

How did Argentine women move away from the domestic sphere? According to Lombroso, that phenomenon should be attributed to the negative influence of Native American women: indigenous women were usually seen crouched in front of their houses, smoking their pipes, and drinking *mate*. Except in Tucumán, where they were more active, "la donna *criolla* non lava, non cuce, non tesse; la cucina si riduce per lei ad arrostire la carne o a farla bollire" (the creole woman does not wash, saw, and weave; cooking for her amounts to nothing but roasting or boiling meats; 351). Bread and other items that require careful preparation were not common in traditional Argentine cuisine. The author writes that the female arts of patching, picking fruits, and preparing preserves were almost unknown in Argentina. Rags were difficult to come by, and paper mills had to import them from Europe, because Argentine women were not used to mending clothes and other household items. Interestingly, she remarks that in Argentinian hotels one could find sheets and napkins with holes that had not been mended. Disposable paper products were already replacing traditional ones: "tovaglie, tovaglioli, sacchetti, tutto è di carta" (tablecloths, napkins, bags, everything is made out of paper; 352).

The availability of inexpensive industrial products contributed to the erasure of traditional domestic arts, where upper-class women often worked together with their servants, thus diminishing the distance between social classes. I would argue that in the final section of her book on Argentina Lombroso is beginning to articulate a critique of industrialism or "macchinismo," which would be the subject of one of her last and most important books, *Le tragedie del progresso meccanico*, published in 1930. In that book Lombroso argued that industrialism was causing moral and intellectual decadence and was also having serious impacts on the environment.[17] Contrary to most Marxist and Anarchist thinkers, who embraced technological innovations because of their potential to liberate humans from repetitive, alienating work, Lombroso dreamed of an impossible return to a society with no class conflicts, where upper-class individuals, "naturally" more gifted and educated, would govern in a paternalistic fashion, helping the poor cultivate the values of hard work and frugality. In this context, the role of female domestic work is essential because of its role in preventing the disaggregation of the social fabric. In the last pages of her book, the author praises those "enlightened" privileged women who were creating, both in Italy and Argentina, "scuole del focolare" and "escuelas de l'hogar" (hearth schools) where girls were instructed in the traditional female arts that were being forgotten. This new feminine (and not feminist) movement would help fill the social and racial gap because, as Lombroso has it,

> female work is always collective, consisting of intellectual and manual parts. When higher class women engage in domestic work and home economics, they necessarily collaborate with women who are inferior for their intelligence and social position; from this temporary association the empathy and harmony between social classes was born.[18]

The Italian social scientist saw women as a "natural" barrier against the class and racial conflicts that modern capitalism was exacerbating, both in Europe and the Americas. Instead of condemning a system based on the systemic exploitation of its workers and the disintegration of their families, as Anarchist thinkers like Pietro Gori did, she called upon women to find imaginative ways to restore an imaginary harmony within the household, concealing from its male members the great sacrifices they had to sustain to create a fictional and ultimately unsustainable facade of happiness. Faced with the tragedies of two global wars and a dictatorship that lasted almost twenty years, Italian women responded to the call for national cohesion and sacrifice that made it possible for their families to endure and survive. Under the watchful gaze of Mussolini, symbolic father of the motherland, Italian women were forced to return to the domestic sphere, accepting a regime of autarchy and simulating a normality that did not exist.

With World War I and the advent of Fascism, immigration to Argentina declined, but the anti-Fascist struggle did not, and during the Italian Resistance (1943–45) women played a major role in overthrowing the regime and liberating the country from the Duce's fatherly, oppressive control. When the war ended, Italians started leaving again.

EPILOGUE

*If presently you and I, and all our companions, were not
on these ships, in the middle of this ocean, in this immense
unknown solitude, in an uncertain and risky condition; in
what other life condition would we be?*
— Giacomo Leopardi, "Dialogo di Cristoforo
Colombo e Pietro Guiterriez"

In this book on Italian emigration and travel writing, I have examined
how emigrants were perceived and represented, but the reader has hardly
heard their voices. The problem is that most Italian emigrants during the
period I chose to study were illiterate. When they learned how to write
and reflected on their own experiences, they often did it in Spanish, the
language they had learned in the new country. Camilla Cattarulla, professor of Latin American Studies in Rome, recently published an anthology
of autobiographies written by Italian immigrants in Argentina.[1] Some of
the excerpts I found extremely interesting, but since the scope of my book
is the analysis of Italian travel writing, I decided to leave them for a future,
possibly collaborative project. Recently, historians have begun to study
the letters of Italian emigrants to Latin America. Emilio Franzina, one of
the leading experts of Italian migration studies, has published a collection of such letters.[2] The Center for Migration Studies in Genoa, housed
in the Museo del Mare e delle Migrazioni (MoMa), has created a web page
devoted to this epistolary. Some letters are quite touching and offer original
and contrasting views of Argentina. For instance, in April 1878, Vittorio
Petrei wrote to his family from Cordoba that the living conditions were
good, and one could earn in two days what he made in two months in his
native town. He also encouraged them not to listen to the "Signori," who
say that America is full of ferocious beasts: "I Signori di talia diceva che in

America si trova bestie feroce. In talia sono le bestie che sono i Signori"
(The gentlemen of Italy say that in America one finds ferocious beasts.
The ferocious beasts are the Signori who live in Italy).[3] On the same year,
Luigi Basso, who was living near Santa Fe, gave his wife a dreary description of his life in the *pampa gringa*: locusts have been coming for the last
five years and destroyed the harvest. Working as a laborer in other farms
is not a good option, because the pay is insignificant and the workers are
treated worse than animals: "Si deve dormire al campo al lustro dele stelle
come le bestie che sono più bene allogiate le bestie in Italia che i cristiani in
americha" (One must sleep in the field under the stars like the animals. In
Italy, animals are treated better than common folks in Argentina).[4] Luigi
is planning to move either to Montevideo or Brazil, but he cannot travel
because he does not have enough money.

These letters are quite valuable for historians, but the information they
provide is anecdotal and usually limited to the migrants' material existence.
It was rare for them to achieve the level of education that would enable
them to reflect on their own experience and produce texts with a complex-
ity comparable to the ones I have examined in the book. One important
exception is Vanni Blengino's memoir, published in 2007, at the end of a
long and successful academic career. In a bio-bibliographic essay, his colleague Camilla Cattarulla defines him a "pioneer" in the interdisciplinary
field of literature and migration studies.[5] Blengino constituted an important model for my research too, because he built his academic identity on
his own experience as emigrant. As he recounts in his memoir, throughout
his life he went through a series of displacements, from the Langhe countryside of northern Italy to Turin, then to Argentina. Every time he moved
from one location to another, he also crossed complex social stratifications.
Since his childhood, Blengino occupied an "in-between position," interacting with the most marginalized individuals, like the little boy Pirro, whose
family had recently migrated from southern Italy to Turin, and was constantly hungry, and "Madama Barone," owner of an elegant apartment,
where little Vanni entered all dressed up as if he were going to his First
Communion. In the Langhe, leaving one's village was considered a sin, and
the author's great-grandfather was excluded from the family clan when he
opened a *trattoria* in a nearby town, thus losing his rights to his portion
of inheritance. During World War II, Vanni's family was forced to leave
Turin because of the Allied bombings, and returned to the Langhe, which
in 1943–45 was one of the major areas of resistance against Nazism and

Fascism. The Piedmontese peasants usually protected the partisans from the occupying forces, often risking their life and property, and Vanni saw people he knew well being executed by the Nazis in the central square. His family was anti-Fascist, but Vanni was sent to a religious boarding school belonging to the Salesian fathers, the same missionaries who went to Patagonia, attempting to convert the natives during the conquest of the desert. In his memoir, Blengino compares the taverns in the Langhe to the *pulperias* of the Argentine *pampa*, situated next to the Indian territory: general stores where one could buy all sorts of merchandise, including alcohol. Thus, the author implies that the partisans of the Langhe were, like the Native Americans, attacked and ultimately exterminated by the Argentine army.[6] The outcome of the Italian Resistance was different, and the bands of rebels, many of whom were associated with the Communist Party, ended up being the winners. The illusion of real social and political change, however, did not last long. As soon as the American troops arrived, they disarmed the partisans: Carlo, a young man from Vanni's village who was found in possession of a gun that he had been given by the patriots, was sentenced to prison. He was among those who left for Argentina after the war. During the conflict, the boundaries were clear: Fascists and Nazis were on one side, partisans and their supporters on the other, but afterwards it became difficult to distinguish between them. As Blengino recounts, "i buoni e i cattivi si mimetizzavano nella normalità" (the good and the bad ones camouflaged themselves in normality; 25).

The author points out that post–World War II migration to Argentina differed from previous iterations: those who left were no longer poor peasants but mostly members of the lower middle classes who had enough savings to pay for the trip and sometimes a small capital to invest, like Vanni's father, who had a small bakery and relatives in Buenos Aires. Vanni was only fourteen when his family migrated. It was a slow and painful process: first his uncle, then the father followed by two aunts; finally, he left with his mother. The author describes the feeling he experienced in the months prior to his departure as *straniamento,* "estrangement," as if he were looking at familiar, everyday objects for the first time, observed from afar: "La tecnica di osservare, come se si vedessero per la prima volta, oggetti che ci sono familiari…li sentivo e li visualizzavo interiormente come se li vedessi da lontano" (the technique of observing, as if one saw them for the first time, familiar objects…I felt and visualized them internally as if I saw them from far away; 96).

Paradoxically, when leaving one's country, the sense of belonging to it is intensified, a sensation that Blengino experienced when he was on the ship. After leaving Genoa, the liner stopped in Naples, where most passengers boarded. The boy noticed a clear social stratification on the ship: Neapolitans were perceived by the Piedmontese as inferior, even dangerous: "All'orizzonte, come una minaccia, c'era Napoli e i napoletani" (At the horizon, like a threat, was Naples and the Neapolitans; 77). As a natural reaction, during his first period in Buenos Aires, Vanni's sense of regional belonging increased: "Nella nave avevo rafforzato il mio nordismo: per maggior precisione il mio regionalismo piemontese" (On the ship, my Northern identity had strengthened; more precisely, my Piedmontese regionalism; 87).

Although the young author had lived in Turin, one of the most industrialized and modern Italian cities at the time, Buenos Aires was a truly cosmopolitan metropolis, with bars and restaurants open until three in the morning, crowded with people of different nationalities. Furthermore, there was a widespread sense of wasteful abundance, which for someone coming from Piedmont was hard to accept: "Io venivo dalle Langhe...non poteva quindi non suscitarmi un culinario disprezzo lo spreco di cibo che caratterizzava l'Argentina di quegli anni" (I came from Langhe...thus the waste of food that characterized Argentina in those years could not but cause me a culinary abhor; 90). The young Vanni, however, is the one who adjusted more easily to the new culture, even linguistically, becoming a cultural mediator for his parents. The author realized the importance of a proper education, and although he took several part-time jobs, his goal was receiving his high school diploma and eventually enroll in the university. While Vanni's father was perfectly at ease in his new bakery, where he enjoyed a certain success and supervised many assistants, Vanni found his co-workers too vulgar and could not relate to them. The bourgeois environment of the Italian newspaper *Il Corriere degli italiani,* where he landed a job as office boy after completing evening classes, disappointed him too: "I nostri borghesi, i borghesucci rampanti, trasudavano spocchia e presunzione" (Our bourgeois, the ambitious petty bourgeois, oozed arrogance and presumption; 118). Vanni realized that there was a world out there to be discovered, while the Italian migrants he encountered seemed to remain enclosed in their petty, provincial enclave. He missed the social cohesion and sense of dignity of the dock and factory workers he had met in Savona and Turin and found something analogous only when he got to know a group of Argentine anarchists. Increasingly distanced from his parents, absorbed by their new commercial activities, the young man found comfort in literature and philosophy. The Argentine capital had a rich intellectual life: movie theaters and bookstores were open until late at night and offered films and books from around the world.

Vanni had grown up in a working-class environment where books were looked upon with suspicion, as something not suitable to him. His uncle Franco yelled at him when he saw him reading and studying: "Testone, lo sai che a forza di leggere si diventa scemi!" (Idiot! Don't you know that one may go crazy by reading too much?; 42). In the public library of his small town there were only "edifying" books, and his mother and aunts only read "pink" romance novels by Liala—the nickname of a popular female author—and the magazine *Grand Hotel*, famous for its "fotoromanzi," photo stories featuring attractive, fashionable ladies and their romantic lovers. When the priest in his hometown found Vanni reading Dumas's *The Three Musketeers,* he took it away from him because it was considered a banned book. In middle school, he had read *The Iliad, The Odyssey,* and *The Divine Comedy,* and his favorite hero was the Trojan hero Aeneas who had been forced to leave his homeland, but his first important encounter with serious literature took place in Buenos Aires. In one of the apartments where he lived with his family, he found a book by Dostoevsky and developed a passion for Russian literature. One day, one of the renters, a man named Elías, saw him reading a book by Maxim Gorky and started talking to him. For the young emigrant it is a revelation: Elías was a free thinker, an individualist anarchist who introduced him to his circle of friends and became his cultural mentor. When Vanni confessed that he had read only a few books he exclaimed, "Beato te! Quante belle soddisfazioni ti riserva ancora la vita!" (Lucky you! How many beautiful satisfactions life has in store for you!; 135). Elías was a taxi driver, and his friends were bricklayers, dockworkers, and plumbers, but they all despised popular culture—especially soccer and tango—and cultivated a passion for the arts, literature, and classical music. They strongly opposed Peron, who had managed, in their view, to coopt a large sector of the working class with his populist politics. Although Elías and his comrades did not engage in any political activities, their "aristocratic anti-capitalism" fascinated Vanni and enhanced his desire to study at the university, where he eventually majored in philosophy, with a thesis on Antonio Gramsci. The choice was quite appropriate, because of the importance that the Italian philosopher placed on education as a necessary tool to achieve a cultural hegemony, without which any revolutionary project would be bound to fail. Elías and his Anarchist friends opposed communism, and Vanni's mentor did not hesitate to kick out of his house his old friend and comrade Spivavski, who had recently joined the Communist Party, when he criticized them for being too isolated from real working-class issues. For Vanni, the encounter with Elías was an important moment in his intellectual development, one that continued at the university, which at that time was going through major changes: with the fall of Peron, professors who had studied in the United States and Europe got teaching positions and began spreading new ideas. Vanni was especially impressed with his female peers. Whereas in Elías's circle, women were either excluded or confined to secondary roles—like preparing food for the men during their interminable discussions—once he got to university, he discovered "il piacere di parlare con le compagne, di avere amiche donne" (the pleasure of talking with classmates, of having female friends; 152). When he returned to Italy, his old friends asked him about sex life in Argentina, and when he told them that he had relationships with his female friends, they replied: "Sono tutte puttane, allora?" (So they are all whores, then?; 165).

From a purely economic viewpoint, Vanni and his family's journey to Argentina may be considered a failure, because they returned with less money than when they departed. While they were away, the Italian economy was experiencing an important economic boom. The region of Piedmont and the city Turin had become the destination of a massive migration from the South, and the living conditions had improved dramatically. If Vanni's family had hoped to go to Argentina and "fare l'America," paradoxically, they found out that "l'America l'avrebbero fatta coloro che sono rimasti" (those who had remained had found America in Italy; 161). The author remarks, nevertheless, that although Italy had a more solid democratic foundation, Argentine society was much "più evoluta nei rapporti sociali, interpersonali, più aperta nei confronti del mondo, meno condizionata dalla famiglia, con meno pregiudizi" (more developed in its social, interpersonal relations, more open toward the world, less conditioned by the family, with less prejudices; 164).

Blengino's memoir stands out among the texts I analyzed in the book for the emphasis he placed on the cultural component of emigration. Although his family did not find in America the economic success they were seeking, they all benefited from their experience, even though not all of them were fully aware of it when they returned. For Vanni's mother, her stay in Buenos Aires were the happiest years in her life. Blengino writes that she became a more unselfish and open person, but when she went back, she turned out to be even more Piedmontese, probably because she wanted again to feel an integral part of the community she had left. The father continued working in bakeries, while singing and drinking in the same old *osterie*. Their native region of Langhe, however, was undergoing a profound metamorphosis: as the wines of Piedmont acquired international prestige and tourists began to pour in, the traditional farmers rapidly disappeared, replaced by large global corporations that hegemonized the wine industry. As Blengino writes, the *osterie* kept their old name to attract tourists, but the clients who used to go there "per bere un bicchiere e intonare un coro" (to drink a glass of wine and sing with their choir; 163), like Vanni's father, were marginalized. Soon they would no longer be able to find a table available to them.

The family member who was most profoundly affected by the experience of emigration was Vanni. As he ventured away from the Italian enclave abroad and intermingled with migrants from other parts of the world, he began reflecting in a more self-conscious way on the original sense of estrangement that he experienced when he left his native town. As he points out toward the end of the memoir, "potevo sdoppiarmi in un io argentino, in un io italiano e forse un terzo, più occulto, più difficile da far emergere, un io che osservava gli altri due" (I could split into an Argentine I, and Italian I, and perhaps a third I, more concealed, more difficult to reveal, an I that observed the other two; 152). What makes Blengino's experience so intriguing is his keen desire to immerse himself in the host culture while remaining solidly anchored in the culture of his parents. His condition of "betweenness" is beautifully articulated in one passage in which he explains that Italy represented the past, but a past that had to be reinvented every day through the act or remembering. Persons, stories, and landscapes of their past would have been forgotten if they had not retold them to their new interlocutors. Argentinians were eager to listen to their stories, and the act of storytelling allowed Vanni and his family to evoke the past while fully living in the present. Thus, remembering became "un'avventura della memoria" (an adventure of memory; 153). Other Italian migrants chose different paths: they either erased their past, hoping to achieve a more complete and rapid assimilation, or refused any possible form of integration and remained stubbornly attached to a crystallized set of rituals that prevented them from interacting with people of other nationalities. Vanni's family, instead, demonstrated a rare ability to adopt new practices by grafting them onto the ones they had brought from the old country. In the Langhe, for instance, there is a long tradition of choral singing, and many family members, particularly his father, were excellent singers. That tradition was preserved and became a way to communicate with other ethnic groups: "il canto si era rivelato un mezzo di comunicazione privilegiato, fra il mio clan familiare e gli argentini" (singing turned out to be a privileged means of communication between my family clan and the Argentines; 30). Operatic arias were often newly arranged with Piedmontese expressions, and the family members did not hesitate to experiment with traditional Spanish songs, even though their command of the language was not perfect. This openness allowed Italians and Argentinians to meet somewhere in the middle, where the encounter between the languages and regional dialects produces creative "contaminations" and promotes mutual understanding. The Argentine tradition of popular theater that originated at the turn of the nineteenth century, with actors performing in *cocoliche*, a mix between Italian regional dialects and Spanish, is an example of just such a creative contamination. A similar process took place in the Argentine bakeries where Vanni's father worked. Piedmontese cuisine is one of the most prestigious, especially its patisserie. Buenos Aires bakeries were enormous compared to the ones in Piedmont, and although the quality was not at the same level, there was a great variety of breads and sweets, representing the many migrant communities in the city. As Vanni recalls, "ogni prodotto veniva arricchito con sperimentazioni spregiudicate" (every product was enriched with daring experimentations; 101), and although the family members were astonished by the abundance of ingredients and the size of the products, Vanni's father adjusted well and did not hesitate to change his traditional recipes and learn new ones: "si esploravano tutte le varianti…la forma di un pane o di un grissino italiano si modificava con l'impasto di un pane tedesco e viceversa" (we explored all variations…the shape of an Italian bread or breadstick was modified with the dough of a German bread or vice versa; 101).

Popular music and gastronomy are two social contexts where the cross-contaminations happened in a mostly natural way, but when Vanni started attending the university and interacting with other young intellectuals, he became more self-reflective in his daily interactions. His Jewish peers fascinated him the most because their people had been living for a long time in the same diasporic condition that he was just discovering. At that time, there were about a half million Jews in Argentina; Vanni's first important love relationship was with a Jewish girl. Through her, he came to understand and appreciate that sense of displacement ("spaesamento") that he had experienced:

> The common sense of uprooting from every context, they, eternal emigrants, the sensation to find oneself in a place while you are somewhere else with your thought, a universality that cohabits with atavistic identity roots…living, as a result, in a constant marginality that stimulates hyper-criticism of the world.[7]

The last time I read Blengino's memoir, as I prepared to write this epilogue, I realized why I was so fascinated with his writing: in a certain way, my experience in North America has been similar to his. We both came from working-class families, and although I was born in Genoa, I spent many summers in the Langhe region, where I got to know and appreciate the traditional culture of Piedmontese farmers. Like Vanni's father, y own father was a man who worked hard but also enjoyed spending time with his friends. His long militancy in the Community Party made him aware of international issues and open to other cultures, although I don't think he ever completed his elementary education. My mother was a generous woman and an avid reader of "pink" novels and *Grand Hotel*, like Vanni's. In my family, we never had a lot of money, but everyone had a strong work ethic, and any form of waste was perceived as a sin. Contrary to Vanni's family, I was the first one to migrate, on my own. One of my father's eight siblings tried, without his mother's consent, but he returned from North America right away and was promptly disowned.

I left Italy in the mid-1980s at the age of twenty-nine, when the big wave of revolutionary politics that had characterized the two previous decades was vanishing, replaced by the consumerism of the so-called yuppie generation. Like the postwar period, it was a moment of disappointment and disillusion for many young people of my generation, who had been hoping for radical political change. Although I had earned a university degree while working full-time as a usher at City Hall, my real intellectual formation took place abroad, like Vanni's. The Department of Comparative Literature at the University of Oregon, where I studied for six years, was extremely stimulating, with graduate students from all over the world and a curriculum of studies strongly based on critical theory. In Eugene, I was introduced to feminist philosophy and postcolonial studies, made my first gay friends, and experienced the same sense of estrangement and displacement that Vanni describes in his memoir. I always liked to meet people of other nationalities and explore other cultures, and I shared Vanni's feeling toward Italian bourgeois abroad: "era meglio perderli che trovarli" (better to lose them than to find them; 157). Like Vanni, I have become an "Atlantic commuter" and developed a sense of hypercriticism that makes me look at political and social issues from contrasting perspectives. I always felt estranged in the world of academia because it is so far from the one where I grew up, and I have never fully identified with many of its rituals and conventions. Finally, as I matured, I found myself choosing, often unconsciously, research topics that indirectly reflect my own past. I don't know if I will ever write a memoir, like Blengino did, although sometimes I am tempted. I believe, however, that my life story is already contained, as in a kaleidoscope, in the books and essays I have written, including this one, which started with an investigation of my native region's forgotten diasporic past and took me to remote places that at times seemed like its disjointed reflection.

NOTES

Introduction: From Genoa to Le Havre with a Pot of Chestnuts

Epigraph: "Perché io c'ho già vissuto in Argentina / Chissà come mi chiamavo in Argentina / E che vita facevo in Argentina?"

1 The Rio de la Plata basin includes parts of southeastern Bolivia, Uruguay, Paraguay, and Argentina, making up one fourth of the continent's surface.

2 Cisiano in Val Lentro is the village where my father was born. See my book *La civiltà del Castagno: Storia, cultura, memoria del borgo di Cisiano in Val Lentro.* (Genoa: Fratelli Frilli, 2006).

3 See De Amicis's short story "Santa Margherita Ligure," in *Pagine allegre* (Milan: Treves, 1906), 124–36. He also wrote a memorable piece about the dock workers in the port of Genoa, titled "I lavoratori del carbone del porto di Genova" (16–31).

4 The much-contested statue of Vittorio Emanuele II was placed in Piazza Corvetto, although some Genoese would like to have it removed, because in 1849 the king was responsible for the brutal repression of a rebellion against the House of Savoy.

5 See Mark Choate, *Emigrant Nation: The Making of Italy Abroad* (Cambridge: Harvard University Press, 2008).

6 Johnathan Boyarin and Daniel Boyarin, *The Powers of Diaspora: Two Essays on the Relevance of Jewish Culture* (Minneapolis: Minnesota University Press, 2002).

7 See Donna Gabaccia, *Italy's Many Diasporas* (Seattle: Washington University Press, 2000). The volume is part of a series titled Global Diasporas, edited by Robert Cohen.

8 See my essay "From Diaspora to Empire: The Nationalist Novels of Enrico Corradini," *Modern Language Notes* 119, no. 1 (2004): 67–84.

9 See Walter Mignolo, *The Idea of Latin America* (Oxford: Blackwell, 2008), 70–94.

10 "Creoles of Spanish and Portuguese descent lived under the illusion that they were Europeans too, although they felt their second-class status." Mignolo, *Idea of Latin America*, 66.

11 Maria Luis Ferraris, *El Malón y otros relatos* (Buenos Aires: Editorial Dunken, 2015).

12 Laura Malosetti Costa, "Commentary on The return of the Indian raid (La vuelta del malón)," Museo Nacional de Bellas Artes, Buenos Aires, available at www.bellasartes.gob.ar/en/collection/work/6297/.

13 Jacopo Virgilio, *Delle migrazioni transatlantiche degli Italiani e in ispecie di quelle dei Liguri alle regioni del Plata* (Genoa: Tipografia del Commercio, 1868).

14 See especially Nicoletta Pireddu, who wrote several essays on Mantegazza and even argued that he should be considered a precursor of "Italian Cultural Studies." See her essay contained in the volume *Italian Cultural Studies*, ed. Ben Lawton and Graziella Parati (Boca Raton, FL: Bordighera Press, 2001).

15 Fernando J. Devoto writes: "Pochi decenni della storia argentina furono più 'italiani' della decade del 1880" (Few decades in Argentine history were more "Italian" than the 1880s). Devoto, *Storia degli italiani in Argentina* (Rome: Donzelli, 2006), 45.

16 Fernanda Elisa Bravo Herrera used the term "anti-emigrationista" in her book *Huellas y rocorridos de una utopia: La emigración italiana en la Argentina* (Buenos Aires: Editorial Teseo, 2015).

17 Mignolo, *Idea of Latin America*, 84.

18 See Eugenia Scarzanella, *Italiani malagente: Immigrazione, criminalità, razzismo in Argentina, 1890-1940* (Milan: Franco Angeli, 1999).

19 See Emanuela Minuto, "Pietro Gori's Anarchism: Politics as Spectacle (1895-1901)," *International Review of Social History* 62, no. 3 (December 2017): 425-50.

20 See: Peter D'Agostino, "Craniums, Criminals, and the 'Cursed Race': American Anthropology in American Racial Thought, 1861-1924," *Comparative Studies in Society and History* 44, no. 2 (April 2002): 319-43.

Free to Leave: A Liberal Economist Looks at Emigration

Epigraph: "Tanti sum li Zenoeixi, e per lo mondo si desteixi, che dund eli van e stan un'aotra Zena ghe fan."

1 See the book by Osvaldo Raggio, recounting the story of the bandits in Fontanabuona who attacked the caravans of merchants transiting through the interior. Raggio, *Faide e parentela: Lo stato genovese visto dalla Fontanabuona* (Turin: Einaudi, 1990).

2 See De Amicis, *Santa Margherita*, in *Pagine allegre* (Milan: Treves, 1906), 122-33.

3 "potente mezzo provvidenziale, diretto a proporzionare le popolazioni...e a diffondere presso le genti meno colte i germi di progresso e di civiltà." Jacopo Virgilio, *Delle migrazioni transatlantiche degli italiani e in ispecie di quelle dei liguri* (Genoa: Tipografia del Commercio, 1868), 9. The translations are mine, with assistance from Ben Faintych.

4 "non solo non fu fecondo, ma anzi cagionò quasi sempre ruine e sciagure" (10).

5 "La Fenicia, possedeva su di una striscia di terreno una fitta popolazione arricchita dalla navigazione e dal commercio, aveva bisogno di disseminare su di un campo più esteso il soverchio delle sue multitudini" (10).

6 "L'emigrazione succede allora libera, spontanea, sebbene con lenta progressione; ed i risultati che si ottengono sono infinitamente più vantaggiosi e durevoli" (10).

7 "quanto più grande è l'autonomia, più si facevano sentire vivamente i vincoli d'affetto" (11).

8 "la vivace intelligenza, l'affabilità, lo spirito di economia, d'ordine e di sobrietà" (15).

9 "squadre di suonatori ambulanti che non contribuiscono certo ad acquistarci stima, presso i popoli seri e laboriosi" (15).

10 "lasciar libero campo alla migrazione....Essa si compie dalla località ove la vita è diventata più difficile verso le contrade nelle quali essa è più agevole" (25).

11 "l'atto più iniquo e dannoso che si possa perpetrare da un Governo" (26).

12 "Vi hanno purtroppo paesi ove le bocche sono soverchie ai mezzi di sussistenza, sterminate contrade imputridiscono sotto l'ingombro della nativa loro fecondità e innumerevoli popolazioni urbane allibiscono in angusto spazio e nelle strettezze dell'inopia. Questi due fatti innegabili ed evidenti bastano di per sè a palesare tutta l'incalcolabile importanza dell'emigrazione. La quale serve oggidì ed è destinata a servire maggiormente in futuro di veicolo alla propagazione della ricchezza e della civiltà sul terrestre pianeta....Tutto ciò che il governo deve fare è di togliere gli ostacoli che alle emigrazioni si frappongono, deve favorire societ protettrici di emigranti e lasciare perfettamente libero chi emigra e chi immigra ed abbandonare alla individuale responsabilità le conseguenze della scelta e dei modi di questa economica emigrazione" (26–27).

13 "più di 60 mila operai senza lavoro [che] vivono nell'ozio e nella più squallida miseria" (29).

14 "sono rese più dure e insopportabili dalla carestia in molte di quelle contrade e dal cholera" (29).

15 "un uomo può quando meglio gli piace andarne nel mondo che egli ravvisa più opportuno, dove meglio gli talenta, poiché facendo questo esercita uno dei diritti più semplici, ma eziandio più fondamentali della personalità" (33).

16 "l'emigrazione d'Italia per via di mare si compie pressochè tutta dal porto di Genova" (41).

17 "La Liguria con vantaggio proprio e comune in tutta Italia creava in varii luoghi, e soprattutto nella vasta regione del Plata, una vera colonia importantissima sotto molti aspetti, e destinata a bello avvenire, benchè non abbia la forma politica delle colonie che una volta si fondavano e rispetti l'indipendenza degl'indigeni ispano-americani" (42).

18 "non sono neppure in grado di provvedersi d'una sana e sufficiente nutrizione" (47).

19 "tane sudice e malsane, più degne di bestie che d'uomini. Il loro vestito poi, non è che un lurido ammasso di cenci" (48).

20 "Non le baionette e le sommarie esecuzioni potranno mondare quelle province da così terribile lebbra" (48).

21 "un'onda di popolo irrequieta, perché disoccupata, che va cercando ove possa con qualche profitto prestare la propria opera" (52).

22 "i salari si accrescerebbero equilibrandosi all'aumento del prezzo di ogni cosa...il commercio tra i nostri porti e quelle terre alle quali volgono di preferenza i nostri migranti si accrescerebbe, determinando un maggior consumo di prodotti nazionali, agricoli e manufatturieri, vantaggerebbe la marina mercantile, una delle poche nostre vigorose, crescerebbero le somme che ogni anno i coloni inviano in patria e diverrebbe in ultimo maggiore il numero di coloro che ritornerebbero in Italia a godersi il frutto delle loro onorate fatiche."

23 "tale fatto spiega i ragguardevoli trasporti che i bastimenti genovesi fanno di prodotti del Piemonte e della Lombardia, nei porti dell'America meridionale" (55).

24 "Remittances and trade from emigrants became the keystone for the Liberal vision of emigration colonialism." Mark Choate, *Emigrant Nation: The Making of Italians Abroad*, 72–73. Choate quotes from "The New Ten Commandments of Italian Emigration," *La Patria degli Italiani*, May 1913, which reads: "You shall always buy and sell, consume and distribute goods and merchandise from your fatherland."

25 "L'emigrazione funge nei popoli l'ufficio che compie nel corpo degli individui la circolazione del sangue; essa non è solamente sollievo alle popolazioni troppo numerose, ma è anche condizione essenziale di prosperità, di ben'essere e di ricchezza" (55).

26 "alleviano il nostro paese, troppo abitato in proporzione dei mezzi di sussistenza, attivano il commercio con la patria, rendono prospera la navigazione, spediscono ogni anno più che un milione ai loro parenti, e ritornano ricchi al paese che avevano lasciato poveri" (56).

27 "scendano al livello di quelli che si percepiscono dal *cool* cinese, dal Sudra indiano, dai contadini Russi ed Irlandesi, dai Cafoni dell'Italia meriggiana" (57).

28 "vorrebbero mantenere il contadiname legato alla terra come il servo della gleba nel Medio Evo, ed in una condizione poco dissimile da quella del bruto" (58).

29 "mercanti di carne umana che compiono la tratta dei bianchi" (58).

30 "ragazzi suonatori, contro cui questi infelici non hanno riparo alcuno" (61).

31 "da questa massa che brulicano i vermi che rodono la moderna società. È da questa moltitudine che l'ozio e il vagabondaggio ha perenne vivaio" (63).

32 "Molte migliaia di sudditi sardi hanno in quelle lontane regioni la mente e il cuore rivolto alla madre patria, e con lavoro e colle industrie si procurano pingui patrimoni, finchè, giunta l'età matura, ed ottenute le condizioni di fortuna necessarie, possano ritornare al suolo che li vide nascere e qui aspettare nel riposo ed in una relativa agiatezza che si estingua in pace una vita in parte spesa nelle lontane regioni alle quali emigrano" (68–69).

33 "paesi interi sottratti alla miseria e alla fame...perchè i soccorsi venuti dalle Americhe, ove non vi è famiglia nelle due riviere che non vi abbia qualche congiunto" (69).

34 "la libertà marittima, commerciale ed industriale, la libertà politica, civile e religiosa" (77).

35 "è una cosa meravigliosa scorgere quel brulichio d'operai, intenti gli uni ai *saladeros*, o alle *barraccas*, magazzini di prodotti, altri ancorati al fiume o addetti ai lavori di fucina od a quelli del carpentiere e calafatto, necessari per la

riparazione e costruzione di quelle flottiglie sempre in moto, spinte ora dal vento, ora dalla corrente ed ora trascinati dai cavalli" (76).

36 "se ne vanno fidenti nelle nuove terre, e vi trovano la ricchezza e la felicità" (81).

37 "quei germi di attività continua, di calcolo commerciale, di oculatezza industriale che sono propri degli uomini vissuti sempre in mezzo agli affari" (87).

38 "avrà una ragguardevole influenza nel temprare più convenientemente la razza italiana" (88).

39 "dai legni d'altura ai cannotti del porto, dagli armatori, consegnatari e spedizionieri, ai capitani, marinai e mozzi maestri d'ascia, calafati...tutti appartengono all'una od all'altra delle riviere della Liguria" (91).

40 "le industrie, contentandosi di accumulare con poca fatica le ricchezze che provengono dai doni naturali di quel paese" (93).

41 "slancio alla costruzione navale, industria che gratifica di larghi salari coloro che vi sono addetti" (101).

42 "Fu essa che dapprima valse, col nolo dei passeggeri, a rendere possibile i viaggi di andata, allorchè la richiesta dei nostri scarsi prodotti era ancor minima" (106).

43 "Non vi è solido commercio marittimo, se prima non vi ha emigrazione e numerosi stabilimenti di concittadini all'estero" (107).

44 "Senza colonie non vi ha vero commercio, non vi ha florida marina, non vi ha attività delle industrie, nè quindi prosperità dello Stato" (109).

45 "Quando l'Italia avesse un diretto dominio su Montevideo e Buenos Ayres tutta la prosperità di quelle colonie, tutti i vantaggi che la nostra nazione attualmente vi ricava, sfumerebbero" (110).

46 "la gloria, l'utile delle nazioni madri, non istanno nel tener le figliole in dipendenze politiche e commerciali ma appunto in quell'aver in esse sangue, nomi, lingue e costumi comuni" (112).

47 "se andiamo di questo passo, mancheranno gli uomini necessari per lavorare i terreni e sviluppare l'industria" (118).

48 "L'assistenza si riceve gratis ed è più che soddisfacente" (132).

49 "Gli stranieri godono nel territorio della confederazione di tutti i diritti del cittadino...non sono obbligati ad accettare la cittadinanza e...ottengono la cittadinanza dopo due anni di residenza ininterrotta nella confederazione" (133).

The Anthropologist as Entrepreneur: Paolo Mantegazza's Real and Imaginary Journeys to South America

Epigraph: "Povero quel paese che non abbia una terra lontana e quasi sua, dove possano trapiantarsi i violenti e gli impazienti; dove possano errare le comete della società civile; dove possano guarirvi gli ammalati nel sangue o nel cervello."

1 See: Diego Stefanelli, "Italian Scientists in South America: Argentina as Constructed by Paolo Mantegazza and Pellegrino Strobel," in *Transnational Perspectives on the Conquest and Colonization of Latin America*, ed. Jenny Mander, David Midgley, and Christine Beaule (New York: Routledge, 2020), 125–37.

2 See: Fredric Jameson, *The Political Unconscious* (Ithaca: Cornell University Press, 1981).

3 *L'Europa alla conquista dell'Argentina* is the title of a book by Ferruccio Macola, published in 1894, that advocated a military conquest of Argentina.

4 I first developed this hypothesis in an article on Enrico Corradini, the founder of Italian nationalism who was strongly opposed to emigration, in an article titled "From Diaspora to Empire," *Modern Language Notes* (2004): 67–84.

5 See Antonella Berzero and Maria Carla Garbarino, eds., *La scienza in chiaro scuro: Lombroso e Mantegazza a Pavia tra Darwin e Freud* (Pavia, Italy: Pavia University Press, 2011).

6 See *Eroi e biganti* (Milan: Longanesi, 1946). Originally published in 1899.

7 "per tentare una speculazione finanziaria da cui spero assai."

8 Quoted in Sandra Puccini's essay "I viaggi di Luigi Mantegazza. Tra letteratura, divulgazione e antropologia," available at https://core.ac.uk/download/pdf/41154666.pdf.

9 "L'Italia è già stretta da lunghi anni colla Repubblica Argentina in vincoli di parentela commerciale e coloniale, e vorremmo vederli fatti ancor più intimi e più caldi. In quel paese vi è un grande avvenire per tutti quelli che fra noi nacquero nei bassi fondi della povertà o che nel mezzo della vita furono schiantati da una bufera economica o morale. Il cambiar clima guarisce molti mali, così come l'emigrazione purga e guarisce molte nazioni. Povero quel paese che non abbia una terra lontana e quasi sua, dove possano trapiantarsi i violenti e gli impazienti; dove possano errare le comete della società civile; dove possano guarirvi gli ammalati nel sangue o nel cervello. Quando l'emigrazione non è fuga, né vendetta sociale, né fame; è un rivellente che mantiene vigoroso ed agile l'organismo delle nazioni; e l'Italia non può trovare in nessun luogo terreno più opportuno ai suoi emigranti quanto nel Rio de la Piata. La bellezza del clima, le vive simpatie degli Argentini per noi, le lunghe tradizioni di più secoli ci chiamano in quelle terre benedette dal genio di Colombo e da uno dei più graziosi sorrisi del cielo australe. E noi vediamo che il quarantacinque per cento dell'emigrazione europea a Buenos Ayres è italiana; e se voi consultate le ultime cifre raccolte nel *Registro Estàdistico del Estado de Buenos Ayres* vedrete come gli Italiani vivano lunga vita in quelle contrade. Molti che qui avrebbero trascinato vita sonnacchiosa, povera o brontolona, rifatti a nuova energia in quei paesi, vivono nel nuovo emisfero vita ricca e benedetta. Non parlo dei pochissimi che malati nel cervello o nel cuore emigrano per fuggire da sé stessi, ma con sé stessi bestemmiano sempre e di sé stessi maledicono in ogni terra e sotto ogni cielo. Il mio libro non è un punto d'ammirazione né uno sprezzo di straniero intollerante; è la semplice e schietta espressione del vero; e alla sincerità più scrupolosa del viaggiatore ci tengo come a diritto di uomo onesto. Odio il panegirico anche quando è diretto al cielo o alla terra; anche quando è inspirato dalla passione e non venduto" (8–10).

10 "Ho due braccia robuste e il coraggio di far di tutto. L'ignoto mi affascina, l'ignoto mi inebbria; il pensare che all'indomani del mio sbarco in America non saprò dove andare, nè come guadagnarmi il pane, mi tenta maledettamente. E poi qui ci starei male; il nostro paese è infelice....Non si può salire in alto senza fare la

corte ai nostri tiranni, e la vita dell'impiegato mi fa nausea, e quella del l'avvocato non mi piace. Ho avuto tante disgrazie in famiglia...ho bisogno di andar lontano lontano" (8).

11 León Sigal, "La Argentina conquistada: Pa(i)sajes de la invasión Itálica," in *L'America degli italiani* (Rome: Bulzoni, 1986), 343–70. The author explains the opposition of Argentine intellectuals against Italian immigration.

12 Tzvetan Todorov, *The Conquest of America: The Question of the Other* (Norman: University of Oklahoma Press, 1999).

13 See for instance his interpretation of the Jesuit missions in Paraguay, defined in the book as a "pastoja di comunismo" (214).

14 "Né soltanto nel commercio incomincia e finisce lo scambio di due nazioni che si conoscono e si apprezzano. Abbiamo ancora lo scambio delle simpatie e degli affetti: abbiamo già in Italia molti cittadini italiani che devono metà del loro sangue a donne argentine; e a Buenos Ayres vediamo nel popolo larga vena di sangue che è nostro e del migliore. Son questi i semi dai quali maturerà ai tardi nipoti la fratellanza universale" (11).

15 See Paul Michael Taylor and Cesare Marino's essay "Paolo Mantegazza's Vision: The Science of Man behind the World's First Museum of Anthropology" (Florence, Italy, 1869), available at https://anthrosource.onlinelibrary.wiley.com/doi/full/10.1111/muan.12209.

16 See: Vittorio Spinazzola, *Verismo e Positivismo* (Milan: Arcipelago Edizioni, 1993). See also Roberto Bigazzi, *I colori del vero: Vent'anni di narrativa, 1860–1889* (Pisa: Nistri Lischi, 1969).

17 In the preface of his masterpiece, *I Malavoglia,* Verga described his novel as a "studio sincero e spassionato" (sincere and objective inquiry) of a simple family of Sicilian fishermen. *I Malavoglia* (Milan: Mondadori, 1988), vi.

18 "Tu hai accolto il buono, tu che hai il cuore più pietoso e più tranquillo, tu che hai trovato l'angelo della bontà. Io son più sensuale, ed ho abbracciato il bello. Dio per Dio; degni l'uno dell'altro. Peccato, che non vi sia un terzo amico o fratello, che adori il vero; perchè in questo caso, sublimando le nostre tre religioni ad un'olimpica altezza di rito, potremmo dire che noi adoriamo un Dio solo, l'ideale, in tre persone: il vero, il buono e il bello" (511).

19 "Nella cuna della società sud-americana v'è un peccato originale, e dopo tre secoli e mezzo se ne sente il fatale influsso: su quella cuna però brillava un raggio fulgidissimo di coraggio e di libertà, e quella gloria risplende sempre nella storia di quei popoli e più che mai rischiara il loro avvenire" (14).

20 See Walter Benjamin's "Theses on the Philosophy of History," in *Illuminations* (New York: Schocken Books, 1968).

21 See Giovanni Verga's introduction to *I Malavoglia* (Milan: Mondadori, 1985).

22 "Chi ha conquistato un nuovo mondo doveva avere la tenacità di volere, tal forza di carattere, tale tenacità di opinioni, da lasciarne ricchissimo tesoro ai figli dei suoi figli....In America ogni uomo è più individuo che da noi e, oso dirlo, v'ha un numero maggiore di uomini d'ingegno che in molti dei nostri paesi europei" (16).

23 Published by Fratelli Bocca in Turin in 1901.

24 *Facundo: Civilization and Barbarism*, trans. Kathleen Ross (Berkeley: University of California Press, 2003), 51.

25 "La mischianza delle umane razze ha in America creato una nuova aristocrazia, ha fondato nuove gerarchie che si appoggiano su una base solida: quella dell'organismo, quella della struttura cerebrale" (27).

26 "il bianco più povero messo a nudo in faccia alla natura può subito persuadere a tutti che egli è superiore al negro prognato e all'indiano fangoso."

27 "un blasone di nobiltà che lo fa uguale al presidente della repubblica e gli rende possibile ogni ambizione" (26).

28 "Quando il continuo intrecciarsi delle famiglie avrà fatto la società americana d'un solo colore, sparirà anche il criterio aristocratico del sangue, e soltanto l'ingegno, il denaro e l'onestà faranno diversi gli uomini gli uni dagi altri" (29).

29 Interestingly, Mantegazza, in the title page, defines his epistolary novel *Il Dio ignoto* as a "poema."

30 And a translator, I may add. His translation of Dante's *Inferno* was published in Buenos Aires in 1893.

31 "il sentimento è la prima molla d'azione politica, come deve essere in ogni società bambina" (39).

32 "si crearono in quei paesi nuovi equilibri e la donna trovò una posizione più dignitosa e più conforme alla sua natura" (31).

33 Buenos Aires was the primary port of South America. Thus, the term *porteño* was applied to all the people who were born in the city.

34 "abbellisce il mondo che la circonda colla lieta gajezza di chi sa di esser potente; innamora colla grazia franca; conquista coll'ardimento e tien salda la conquista con la bellezza. Essa è la venere greca abbellita dalla civiltà moderna" (43).

35 "Gli abitanti di Buenos Aires sono vivaci, leggieri; intrepidi nella lotta e instancabili nel riposo. Amanti di tutto ciò che brilla, si entusiasmano facilmente e con maggiore facilità sanno dimenticare. Di passioni rapide e violente, non conoscono neppur di nome l'avarizia. Sono troppo obbedienti al giogo della moda. Di talenti svegliati, contano già molti uomini di primo ordine nella poesia. La loro pasta, piena di piccoli vizi e di grandi virtù, è di quelle che si prestano alle speranze dell'avvenire" (52–53).

36 "I mediterranei bruni, abitanti il sud-Italia, hanno, come nota principale della loro psicologia, la enorme eccitabilità del proprio *io*. Essi non camminano, corrono; non si muovono, irrompono; hanno sempre furia di cominciare e di finire,—amano la celerità, il rumore, l'instabilità,—esagerano tutto....Hanno tutto in rilievo, il gesto, lo sguardo, la parola, lo stile, l'esclamazione; concepiscono rapidamente, perché il loro *io* guizza celeremente su ogni cosa, quasi in uno stato di sovreccitazione, ma non approfondiscono nulla o quasi nulla; hanno ipertrofico il sentimento e intermittente l'energia." Alfredo Niceforo, *Italiani del Nord e italiani del Sud* (Turin: Fratelli Bocca, 1901), 217.

37 "Buenos Aires mi sembrò una mandra infinita di pecore sporche, che pascolavano in una pianura triste e smisurata" (75).

38 "Qui son tutti più o meno mercanti, repubblica senza libertà e senza giustizia, orgoglio senza scienza, sensualismo senza sentimento. Ovunque non vedo che profanazioni: la chiesa profanata dagli speculatori, il tempio delle lettere profanato dai mediocri e dai mercanti; il santuario del cuore prostituito dal cinismo o dallo scetticismo. Speravo di trovare un altro mondo più poetico, più gaio, più sincero e trovo invece lo scheletro tisico di una società corrotta, che ricopre le ossa spellate col fasto del lusso e la vernice sguaiata del similoro. Anche qui non trovo fede nè entusiasmo...ma l'uomo è dappertutto e sempre un animale così ipocrita e leggero!" (77).

39 "Io sono inerte per natura e per abitudine, ma ad un tratto mi sveglio e sento in me una vera esplosione di progetti, uno più grandioso dell'altro e mi pare che il mio organismo debba schiantarsi, come il cratere d'un vulcano, che ceda all'irromper della lava e dei lapilli. E allora mi getto col capo chiuso alla conquista...alla conquista di che?" (84).

40 "Qui la moralità è molto maggiore che fra noi: le fanciulle, non portando dote al marito, sanno di essere amate per sè sole; e liberamente scelgono lo sposo, senza sentirsi imporre un tirannico giogo dai genitori. Esse amano dopo aver avute molte simpatie, esse scelgono dopo aver veduti da vicino molti uomini, dopo aver studiato molti caratteri; ed è per questo, che dopo aver dato la mano di sposa, sono sempre fedeli al compagno della loro vita. Da noi invece, quante volte si passa dalla feroce verginità del monastero all'adulterio--passando s'intende per la strada del matrimonio" (133).

41 "Voglio gettarmi al deserto in groppa ad un cavallo; voglio conoscere gli Indiani e domarli e farmi loro capo, voglio conquistare la Pampa e la Patagonia e restituirle alla civiltà argentina. Coll'aureola di *cachique* o di generale o di legislatore voglio chieder la mano di Dolores ai suoi genitori" (98).

42 "Qui invece io era in mezzo ad un paradiso terrestre, e gli alberi tutti nuovi per me, eran così belli, ch'io non riusciva davvero a scegliere quello che avrebbe dovuto offrire alla mia meditazione la sua ombra ospitale. Il villaggio sembrava una cosa piccina piccina di mezzo alla natura gigantesca, che lo circondava, e le case degli uomini parevano giuocatoli da bimbi accanto agli *ombus*, ai *talas*, ai *fiandubays* e agli *algarrobos*, che facevan loro da cornice. E anche le erbe del prato eran tutte diverse delle nostre, sicchè il prato sembrava un bosco, e il bosco sembrava una foresta di giganti fatti per un mondo più grande del mondo europeo. E sui fiori di quelle erbe volavano farfalle nuove e luccicavano insetti non mai veduti e sui rami degli alberi posavano uccelli d'ogni colore, e il colibri, vera gemma del mondo aereo, volava rapidissimo per le corolle del *palam palam*, di cui succhiava colla lingua il nettare dolcissimo" (156).

43 "Caro mio signor Attilio, voi siete un grande poeta e andate cercando il Dio Ignoto, dove non lo troverete mai. Per me, senza tanta poesia e tanta fatica, l'ho bello e trovato da un pezzo. Il Dio Ignoto è il denaro, forza di tutte le forze, potenza di tutte le potenze" (180).

44 "Io mi sento invaso dal genio industriale e dalla sete dei sùbiti guadagni; e godo infinitamente di trovarmi in piena armonia coll'aria che mi circonda" (177).

45 "Non vi ha forse che la bellezza che pareggi in potenza la ricchezza, che ne eguagli le seduzioni; ma è troppo caduca; mentre la ricchezza sopravvive alla bellezza e alla gioventù, vive quanto noi e più che noi, perchè a noi sopravvive e sui figli dei figli nostri sparge sempre il calice pieno di un'inesausta dolcezza" (188).

46 For an analysis of the stock exchange culture in Argentina, see Julián Martel's novel *La Bolsa*, published in 1891.

47 "Io adoro l'industria, la grande industria; le manifatture, nelle quali centinaia d'operaj e di operaie sotto la guida d'un mio sguardo e d'un mio cenno trasformano la materia e creano una nuova fonte di ricchezza al paese. Adoro quest'arte di guidare un esercito di operai pacifici e tranquilli, che, cantando in coro, benedicono il lavoro in una sana e ben ventilata officina; adoro l'andare e il venire delle balle, delle commissioni, dei compratori e dei venditori; adoro questa potenza di essere alla testa di una delle prime industrie del paese, di crearla forse, e di generarne poi dieci o cento altre" (190).

48 "come i suoi fratelli, come i suoi padri, e anch'essa avrà figliuoli che continueranno le dolci tradizioni di un ozio splendente, di una felice spensieratezza" (139).

49 "Ed io galoppo, galoppo, galoppo, sprofondandomi tutto in questo infinito deserto di erba gialliccia grulla, che mi circonda per ogni parte" (273).

50 Published by Garzanti Press, Milan, in 1991.

51 The "Conquista del desierto" was a military campaign directed by General Julio Argentino Roca in the 1870s that led to the extermination of the indigenous people in the south of Argentina. I will return to this subject when discussing the travel writings of Edmondo De Amicis.

52 "La razza; che è il criterio più sicuro, più giusto e più tirannico per assegnare i posti agli spettatori nel grande anfiteatro di questo mondo sublunare. La Costituzione argentina dichiara eguali dinanzi alla legge tutti i cittadini della Repubblica; ma ahimè, quante corone d'alloro e di spine non distribuisce il mondo ogni giorno anche senza la legge e all'infuori della legge! Il mulatto e il cholo possono ben vantarsi di essere giudicati dagli stessi giudici, e messi nelle stesse carceri come il bianco americano e l'europeo; ma basta un sogghigno beffardo, un voi, un tu; basta un cenno del capo o un gesto della mano per marcar loro nelle carni, come fosse con un ferro rovente, la sentenza che tacita e inedita sta sulle labbra e negli occhi di tutti: ricordati che tu hai nelle vene del sangue nero o del sangue giallo....Cancellare queste leggi del cuore umano è inutile, perchè stanno scritte a caratteri di fuoco in ogni fibra di esso, e finchè il cuore sarà fatto così come è oggi, le gerarchie umane muteranno forma e sposteranno il loro centro di gravità, ma saranno sempre uno dei cardini fondamentali d'ogni umana società" (190).

53 "Separato da immense distanze dagli amici e dalle città, egli non ha altro mezzo di unirsi al comune consorzio degli uomini che il suo cavallo; vivendo di carne che corre libera e selvaggia nella pianura, egli non ha altro strumento per procacciarsi cibo che il suo cavallo: vero arabo d'America, egli ha in questo nobilissimo animale lo strumento più indispensabile della vita, la fonte delle ricchezze, l'amico inseparabile nel riposo e nel lavoro; nella guerra e nella pace. Il *gaucho*

passa più della metà della vita in arcione e spesso mangia e sonnecchia sulla sella. A piedi cammina male e strascinando i suoi pesantissimi speroni, che con le loro immense ruote gli impediscono di camminare come tutti facciamo, pare una rondine obbligata dal suo aereo soggiorno a scarpinare per terra. Or sono pochi anni ancora i mendicanti di Buenos Aires cercavano la elemosina a cavallo; e a cavallo ho veduto più d'una volta montare il *gaucho* per andare in fondo al cortile ad attinger l' acqua del pozzo" (69–70).

54 "I muscoli lombari e gli altri che tengono eretto il tronco sono così sviluppati da far credere in sulle prime mostruosità ciò che in lui è natura" (71).

55 "Il *gaucho* si risolve spesso all'immenso sagrifizio del lavoro per mettere a parte alcuni scudi e dedicarli a fregiare il suo idolo, sicché spesso la sua casa è senza porte e senza sedie; ma le redini del suo *parejero* (parola onorifica che distingue un cavallo di corsa) sono cariche d'argento" (74).

56 "Para que quiere uno la plata? Lo que yo quiero es la amistad de los hombres....Yo busco la plata para servir a los amigos...La plata es echa para gastar" (75).

57 "La crudele questione della fame è in quel paese una utopia. Il *gaucho* più povero del mondo non mancherà mai di un cavallo e l'ospitalità gli darà in ogni luogo un tetto e *una trincha de asado*" (76).

58 "Juan Manuel Rosas, o come lo chiamarono in vari tempi i suoi sgherri, *el ilustre restaurador de las leyes, el heroe del desierto, el padre de la patria, la columna de la federacion, el defensor de la independencia americana, el Washington del Sud, el principe normando,* è uomo più che robusto, di lineamenti virili e profondamente scolpiti, con occhi infossati e pieni di vita. Ha l'agilità dello scoiattolo e la forza del leone, e la tenacità della vita lo farà morire vecchio e ancor forte. La prepotenza della volontà servita da bassi istinti è la formula morale che lo rappresenta; e in lui l'alto intelletto non coltivato dall'educazione fu tutto e sempre sprecato in servizio della tirannide" (303).

59 "La Pampa vi atterrisce e vi commuove coll'idea sensibile dell'infinito, ma in un modo assai diverso del mare. Quì voi avete quasi sempre innanzi agli occhi una massa sconfinata di acque innanzi a cui vi pare di essere un fuscello di paglia; ma voi vedete pur sempre l'onda, che si muove, or agitata e schiumosa, or lenta e pigra; voi sentite il vento che stride fra le antenne della vostra nave e ne gonfia le vele. Voi vi movete sopra un terreno che si muove e benchè i vostri rapporti con esso siano d' un inesorabile monotonia, vedete pur sempre un quadro di vita entro cui voi siete parte attiva, reagente, battagliera. —Nella Pampa invece voi toccate un infinito che non si muove....Sempre la stessa luce, sempre la stessa erba; la stessa terra; lo stesso circolo infinito che chiude la vostra vista" (331).

60 Parts of the book appeared in 1870 in the newspaper *La Tribuna*. See: María Rosa Lojo, *Una nueva excursión a los indios Ranqueles*, Ciencia Hoy, vol. 6, no. 36, 1996. The book is also available in English: Lucio V. Mansilla, *An Expedition to the Ranquel Indians*, trans. Mark McCaffrey (Austin: University of Texas University Press, 1997). In McCaffrey's words, Mansilla's book is "one of the very few works in either north or south American letters which presents a vivid

and sustained firsthand account of non combative coexistence between American Indians and white civilization, on Indian land, during any period of nation's consolidation" (xii).

61 "Egli è un bellissimo uomo sui 35 anni, con folta e prolissa capigliatura, con occhi grandi e nerissimi; porta due baffi, che si confondono in una barba nera e lucida come la seta, e che gli scende sul petto. È molto fiero della sua bellezza, e porta un uniforme fantastico, mezzo indiano e mezzo europeo, che sembra fatto apposta per far spiccare l'eleganza e l'agilità del suo corpo apollineo. Ha un foulard scarlatto al collo, un poncho bianco, da cui escono le maniche di un uniforme di panno rosso: porta calzoni di pelle e stivali lucidi alla granatiera con due grandi speroni d'argento. Fuma sempre cigarritos e prende mate sempre, in ogni ora del giorno e della notte, non lasciandolo, che quando dorme o mangia" (275).

62 "Il selvaggio faceva piroettare per l'aria la sua lunga lancia e gettava in faccia al cristiano le sue bestemmie; l'altro, l'uomo civile, faceva sentire il suo vigore morale colla sola acutezza e col solo lampo degli occhi" (289).

63 See Massimo Montanari, *Food is Culture* (New York: Columbia Press, 2006), ch. 1.

64 "Volli farmi indiano in tutto e per tutto, sognando la gloria del potere, dopo aver veduto quanto aride fossero le vanità della ricchezza. Sognai di farmi amare e temere dai miei compagni, di dominarli col mio coraggio e la mia intelligenza, di tentare il loro ravvicinamento alle altre tribù vicine, formando una vasta Confederazione della pampa, che indipendente dal Governo argentino, lo trattasse però da amico e si costituisse in una libera civiltà accanto alla Repubblica del Plata. Se il denaro non mi sembrava che uno strumento, il potere mi sembrava tal cosa da bastare a sè stesso e lo scopo a cui miravo parevami abbastanza alto per assorbire tutte le energie del mio pensiero, per spegnere tutti gli ardori del mio cuore" (379).

65 "Quando in quei deserti infiniti io sentiva fischiare il vento nei miei lunghi capelli, stretti solo intorno al capo da una *vincha* indiana, e sentiva fremere sotto di me in un'ebbrezza ardente di moto il *pingo* selvaggio che mi portava, e il suo nitrito e il pestar delle zampe erano gli unici rumori di quel deserto, ampio e melanconico, mi sentiva portato fuori di me e sentiva di essere un uomo doppio, triplo; mi pareva di essere trasformato in uno degli dèi fantastici creati dalla leggenda scandinava" (380).

66 "In mezzo a quella gazzarra infernale, che sembrava un sabato di stregoni, nel cuore di quel campo vi erano quattro uomini, che dirigevano tutti quegli scomposti elementi e nel cui fuoco convergevano tutte quelle energie scapigliate, che pure potevano recar l'incendio della guerra a tutta l'America meridionale o inaugurare un'era nuova di pace e di civiltà. Di quei quattro uomini tre erano indiani, uno era europeo, e senza che l'ingegno segnasse fra di loro troppo diversa gerarchia io mi metteva il primo fra di loro, e li governava a mio talento, contrapponendo le crudeltà dell'uno alla dissimulazione dell'altro e facendo balenare ad ognuno di essi la dolce speranza ch'egli sarebbe un giorno il primo di tutti" (423).

67 "A me non è sembrata neppure una donna, e neppure ora mi sembra una creatura umana, per cui si possa provar tenerezza o la voglia di stringere fra le braccia: mi pare piuttosto una gazzella, una guanacca, una cerviatta: tutto fuorchè una donna. Quel suo sguardo timido e feroce nel tempo stesso, quel colore di bronzo, quelle pitture rosse sulle guancie e sul mento, quei néi nerissimi sul pomello della faccia me la fanno parere una bambola, un idolo fantastico, qualche cosa di curioso e di strano...null'altro" (326).

68 "Quando fra un uomo e una donna il pensiero non può darsi la mano nè stringersi insieme come si stringono insieme i corpi, dell'amore non rimane che la voluttà e questa è cosa caduca; e quando è eccessiva, anche noiosa. Altre volte però, per dirti tutta la verità, devo aggiungere che la grandezza morale della mia Katriel, l'ambizione grandissima del potere, che meco sentiva, e a cui portava tanto ardore di sentimento e di pensiero, me la rendevano cara" (415).

69 "il terreno più propizio e più fecondo per una delle tirannie più inaudite e mostruose dei tempi moderni" (201).

70 "il sangue libero e orgoglioso del castigliano si diluì nel Paraguay col sangue pallido e snervato del Guaranì, nati per servire e pascolare mandre e armenti" (189).

71 "E perchè mai si occuperebbero di agricoltura e d'industria, quando la natura per essi semina e coltiva, per essi riscalda l'aria e prepara il cibo?—Finchè l'*algarrobo* si carica di frutti, essi non mancheranno mai di alimento e di bevanda" (351).

72 "Dopo tanto andare e tanto succedersi di colli e di piani, di valli serpeggianti e ristrette o aperte in liberi campi; dopo un lungo silenzio di voci umane, ecco che ti appare inaspettata la capitale di una provincia, un vero trovante di civiltà, che ti sembra posato dalla mano capricciosa del caso di mezzo alla natura vergine e selvaggia. Difatti, entrando per quelle vie polverose, senti ad un tratto il rumore attivo delle aspre officine e i clamori confusi d'un alveare umano, e al trombettio del tuo postiglione vedi escire dalle porte, vezzose signore vestite alla foggia che loro imponevano la vanità femminile e gli inviolabili precetti della lontanissima metropoli francese" (370).

73 "L'*arribeno* è un boliviano argentino, o un argentino boliviano, per cui, servendo di passaggio a questi due tipi americani, in sè li riunisce e confonde. La sua impassibilità, la sua aria cupa e tenebrosa ti sembrano un paradosso di mezzo a quel paradiso di cielo e di fiori che lo circonda. Ti senti ad ogni momento invitato a cantare e a schiamazzare, a benedire la natura, a baciare una terra così lieta di luce e di profumi, e ti vedi innanzi una creatura immobile che sembra sempre scontenta, con un piglio di diffidenza perpetua. Davvero che in quel momento sei trascinato a dire che l'uomo della campagna di Salta è la pessima fra le creature di quel paese" (381–82).

74 "Intanto piacciavi di ricordare che quell'uomo è un prodotto bastardo degli indiani che ubbidivano all'impero degli Incas e che la goccia di sangue europeo, che colò nelle sue vene, si può appena indovinare" (382).

75 "Nella provincia di Salta i bianchi sono spagnuoli o quasi spagnuoli, e in essi trovi coltura, buon cuore; tutte le virtù e i difetti dell'uomo iberico da cui derivano" (383).

76 "Salta è una città antica che conta forse diecimila abitanti e che ci porge un aspetto alquanto diverso delle altre sue sorelle Argentine per le case di due piani, coi barocchi balconi spagnuoli, coi tetti coperti di tegole e non fatti a terrazzo, colle contrade un po' meno regolari e che si permettono di violare la monotona eterna quadratura delle altre città della confederazione....Salta si vanta con ragione di avere nella sua provincia tutti i climi del mondo riuniti da piccole distanze; sicchè a dieci leghe dalla capitale si trova il ghiaccio con cui si fanno i gelati e alla stessa distanza verso il sud il Campo Santo offre ad essa lo zucchero, la banana e la deliziosa *chirimoya*" (387-88).

77 "La plebe di Salta è una delle più brutte ch'io abbia mai vedute. Sembra che i peggiori esemplari delle razze europee, indiane e negre si sian data la mano per formare una famiglia rachitica e mostruosa...tu vedi dinnanzi grame creature che ti sembrano destinate dalla natura a trascinare una vita povera di energia e di piaceri e che sarà tronca innanzi tempo. Eppure, entrando nelle case agiate, si vede venirsi innanzi gentili e belle *senoritas* dalle lunghe ciglia e dagli occhi andalusi, e sei presentato ad onorevoli *caballeros* dal portamento nobile e sdegnoso; e in tutte le famiglie leggi la fisonomia di una vita piena e robusta" (391-92).

78 "Davvero che in Salta la plebe e i ricchi formano due nazioni diverse che vivono sotto lo stesso tetto, ma che hanno scritto sul volto origini diverse e diversi destini."

79 "Dove il sangue spagnuolo si è mantenuto puro e dove l'agiatezza ha combattuto contro le cause perturbatrici, trovi salute, e vita: dove invece fermentarono in un impuro crogiuolo molti sciagurati germi di sangue umano, ne nacquero l'atrofia fisica e morale, foriere di una morte sicura della povera razza che n'è sorta" (392).

80 Mantegazza seems to be aware of the contradiction implicit in his discourse and speculates that the reason for the racial inferiority of the natives may be attributed to the first Europeans who settled there: "In Salta tutto il male che vediamo al giorno d'oggi nella classe povera, è forse dovuto ai primi abitatori che infermi ed esausti tramandarono un mal seme alle generazioni future e forse la statistica dei morbi e della mortalità ci parla con maggior eloquenza sulla ragione tutta fisica di questa atrofia" (In Salta all of the suffering that we see today in the poor class is perhaps due to the first inhabitants who, sick and exhausted, passed on a bad seed to the future generations and maybe the statistics of disease and mortality speak more eloquently to us on the physical reason of this atrophy; 393).

81 "Art. 1. Si obbliga il dottor Paolo Mantegazza a condurre alla provincia di Salta, nel termine fisso di due anni contati dal 1.° gennaio 1858, trenta famiglie lombarde o piemontesi tolte dalla classe agricola. Ogni famiglia consterà di quattro individui almeno d'ambo i sessi. Art. 2. Queste famiglie saranno scelte fra le più sane e le più morali e fra quelle che si dedicano specialmente alla coltura

del gelso, del frumento e degli altri cereali. Ogni famiglia partirà dall'Italia con un capitale di mille pesos (5000 franchi) che apparterrà ad una società agricola lombarda o piemontese. Art. 4. Questa somma sarà impiegata per il trasporto. Da Montevideo all'imboccatura del Bermejo corrono 300 leghe e 227 da questo punto ad Oran, in tutto 3030 chilometri, tutti navigabili con vapori e navi di discreta portata. Ecco dunque come dall'Oceano si possa portarsi per acqua ai piedi delle Ande nel cuore del continente americano delle famiglie e per incominciare i lavori agricoli nel luogo dove si stabiliranno. Art. 5. Il governo della provincia concederà alla colonia secondo la legge sulle terre pubbliche, 54 leghe quadrate di terreno, delle quali sei almeno sopra l'una o l'altra riva del Rio Bermejo. Art. 6. Di queste si darà una per ogni famiglia, rimanendo due di fronte per due di fondo al dottor Mantegazza, il quale potrà scieglierle da tutta la superficie del terreno concesso alla colonia. Art. 7. La Società anonima del Bermejo (società di navigazione) si obbliga a trasportare gratuitamente la colonia da Buenos Ayres fino alle rive del Bermejo, a condizione però che il supremo governo nazionale le conceda il privilegio esclusivo che ha domandato. Art. 8. Il governo della provincia si obbliga a consegnare al dottor Mantegazza, o a chi lo rappresenti, la somma di 2000 pesos (10 mila franchi) per le spese di viaggio, appena compia ciò che ei propone di fare, cioè appena faccia giungere alla provincia le trenta famiglie, delle quali parla l'articolo 1. Art. 9. Se, passati i due anni, il dottor Mantegazza non adempisse alle stipulazioni anzidette, questo contratto rimarrà senza valore nè effetto alcun, e si potrà prorogare per due anni, quando avesse dato ragione al governo dei giusti motivi che gli hanno impedito di eseguirlo nel termine di tempo indicato, ciò che dovrà fare prima che questo sia trascorso. Art. 10. Si firmeranno due copie di questo contratto. Una rimarrà negli archivii della segreteria generale e l'altra sarà consegnata al dottor Mantegazza. Salta, 19 dicembre 1857. Martin Guemez, Governatore. Pio Josè Tedin, Segretario. Dottor Mantegazza" (399).

82 "Da Montevideo all'imboccatura del Bermejo corrono 300 leghe e 227 da questo punto ad Oran, in tutto 3030 chilometri, tutti navigabili con vapori e navi di discreta portata. Ecco dunque come dall'Oceano si possa portarsi per acqua ai piedi delle Ande nel cuore del continente americano" (408).

83 "L'educazione dei bestiami è un'immensa risorsa per il paese, ma il terreno che dà erba a cento vacche e mantiene una famiglia può coll'agricoltura dare alimento a cento uomini per cento secoli" (410).

84 "Solo gli arcadi e i metafisici sentimentalisti, gente malata di mente e di corpo, ponno aver ribrezzo alla cucina: per il medico ed il filosofo si passa per essa per andare all'officina e al gabinetto e all'ospedale; e nel movimento generale che avvicina i popoli e dà si largo corso all'umana attività, v'ha pure una fratellanza gastronomica che arricchisce le mense dei tesori di tutta la terra" (404).

85 "L'argentino del nord è carnivoro, ma non dimentica ch'ei vive nella terra degli Incas, agricoltori infaticabili ed abilissimi. Egli non disprezza i legumi e le radici, e le verdure, come il suo fratello del mezzodì" (426).

86 "Un vero museo dei tre regni voi avete nella zuppa nazionale di Salta e della Bolivia, il *chupi*. E' l'eclettismo e il panteismo della pentola: voi vi trovate infatti come rappresentanti del regno inorganico il sale e l'acqua; il regno vegetabile vi dà la zucca, il peperone, il cavolo, la rapa, il prezzemolo, il coriandoro, la mela, la cipolla, il porro, il pepe e non so quante altre piante; mentre la vita animale vi è degnamente rappresentata da molti pezzettini di carne fresca o di *charqui* (dal quichua charqui, carne secca o persona molto magra) e di grassumi. E tutto questo olimpo gastronomico, caldo, aromatico, pizzicante è sicuramente una delle glorie della cucina saltena e boliviana" (429).

87 "Legge agraria più rigorosa e più semplice si vide in nessun luogo e in nessun luogo vi fu comunismo, più dispotico. Nessun era povero in quell'impero, nessuno mendicava; ma il progresso era chiuso in una crisalide, era arrestato. Era spenta la sacra favilla dell'umana famiglia, la libertà....Sul vasto territorio dell'Impero peruviano si agitano cinque repubbliche, piene di vizi e di passioni, ma con germi fecondi di un avvenire senza fine. Il circolo magico che rendeva immobili tanti milioni di uomini è spezzato; e se l'anarchia più sanguinosa agita e divide i discendenti di Pizarro, sono però uomini che vanno innanzi e progrediranno indefinitamente. La libertà guarisce sempre e di per sè le proprie ferite, anche quando sembrano gravi e crudeli. Il dispotismo sotto tutte le forme spezza invece la molla più potente che anima e muove l'umana famiglia" (444).

88 "L'indiano dell'America meridionale è un uomo di poca sensibilità, poco contento di sè stesso; cupo, silenzioso, diffidente, freddamente crudele; qualche volta tenero e appassionato; tenacissimo e amante della libertà; poco intelligente, poco attivo; temperante per necessità o per inerzia, come per opportunità vorace; che dalla civiltà non impara che i vizii; appassionato dei piaceri dell'ebbrezza. Superstizioso senz'essere religioso; poco morale perchè poco intelligente; incapace di per sè a raggiungere un alto sviluppo di coltura e destinato ad essere travolto e a confondersi col gran torrente della civiltà europea" (453).

89 "L'indiano è più in alto del negro nella scala umana; è più intelligente di questo e i suoi sentimenti sono più ricchi di forme; ma il nostro fratello africano ci inspira maggiore simpatia, perchè più lieto schiamazzatore; perchè più espansivo cicalone. Il negro è una scimmia umanizzata; l'indiano è un bianco che medita sul dolore del passato o sopra una vendetta dell'avvenire. Il negro ci diverte senz' intenderci; l'indiano ci fa paura o ci fa compassione. Dinnanzi all'uno ed all'altro sentiamo di essere parenti lontani, fors'anche cugini; non mai fratelli" (454).

90 "I filosofi che sopra un'elastica poltrona, fra la studiata lussuria della vita civile, rimpiangono la libera e nuda civiltà del selvaggio, dovrebbero fare una corsa nella Pampa argentina o recarsi a Corrientes....Vorrei domandar loro se quelle povere creature del color del fango, nude o coperte di luridi cenci, coi muscoli sottili, coi capelli sciolti e sucidi, e divorati da una folla d'insettucciacci, sono i rappresentanti della primitiva innocenza e della libertà: vorrei conoscere se quei volti stupidamente tristi aspettano un raggio di luce dal cielo o dalle opere dei loro fratelli filosofi d'oltremare" (454).

91 See the Carlisle Indian School Digital Resource Center, https://carlisleind ian.dickinson.edu/.

92 "E di questi uomini che occupavano tanta vastità di continenti, e che in tanta ricchezza di natura erano le creature più povere, cosa ha fatto la civiltà europea? Ha fatto un vasto cimitero. Gli indiani, col venire in contatto con noi, dovevano subire la tirannide di questo dilemma: *o essere educati o spenti*" (461).

93 "I più fortunati fra tutti son quelli che per la flessibilità della tempra si piegarono alla servitù e per il loro numero sopravvissero a tante cause di distruzione. Questi si confusero coi vincitori, dando loro larga onda di sangue e talvolta anche la lingua" (465).

94 "E chi non legge anche al giorno d'oggi sulla fisonomia triste, seria, riflessiva e apatica dei Quichua la storia del loro passato, di quel comunismo forzato che si riduceva poi ad una forma molto ingegnosa di dispotismo, copiato più tardi con molta fortuna dai Gesuiti nelle loro missioni del Paraguay e del Brasile?" (504).

95 "Il tempo e le vicende della vita scrivono i loro ricordi. Nessuna fisonomia è più vivace e più mobile di quella del negro; nessuna è più immobile e fredda di quella di un indiano della pampa. Il negro guineo alla menoma scintilla di gioia o di dolore che lo scuota, muove tutti i muscoli della sua faccia e gli agita e gli contorce, e grida e schiamazza come una scimmia; il pampa invece sta seduto e curvo all'ombra del suo cavallo, e colle mani sulle ginocchia e il capo fra le mani rimane immobile ore ed ore in mezzo al deserto erboso che, quasi un oceano di terre, lo circonda per ogni lato" (512).

96 "In nessuna razza l'espressione del volto è più nobile e più elevata che in quella che regge e indirizza in questi tempi l' umana civiltà. In essa nè le spasmodiche contrazioni, nè i moti telegrafici del negro, più scimmia che uomo; nè l'impassibilità desolante degli indigeni americani. Le passioni si dipingono sulla nostra faccia dalle più violenti fino alla menoma oscillazione di un sentimento soave, e sempre in un modo opportuno che misura l'intensità e il modo d'azione. Le creazioni del genio, le amarezze del dubbio, le mille varietà de' bisogni morali creati dal lusso della civiltà trovano un linguaggio perfetto nella fisonomia europea" (513).

97 "Io credo fermamente in una bellezza assoluta, e senza voler far qui una dissertazione sulle origini e sul criterio del bello, mi appellerò a molti e molti indiani d'America, i quali senza aver mai studiato l'estetica, trovano assai più belle le nostre donne delle loro mogli, e ne fanno prigioniere quante possono, e spesso tagliuzzano loro le piante dei piedi, perchè non abbiano a fuggire" (515).

98 "L'idea di imbarcare in una nave infetta una giovane sposa che aveva sempre vissuto in paesi dove la malaria e la febbre gialla non son conosciute che di nome, mi faceva più che paura; orrore" (549).

99 "La valle ridente dell' Orotava che ci sta d' innanzi, e il Picco e l'Oceano formano un quadro, dove il contrasto di una natura tutta dolcezza chiusa fra il gigante dei monti e l'infinito piano dei mari non ci lascia parlare, ma ci fa sospirare di quando in quando, quasi le parole fossero di troppo in quel paradiso.

Talvolta involontariamente e quasi di muto accordo i nostri cavalli s'arrestano e stringendo la mano alla nostra compagna di viaggio ci pare che in quel paese nessuno possa essere infelice" (583–84).

100 "Le piante e i giardini fanno lieta corona alle case e queste sembran solo costrutte per abbellire il paesaggio. In molti punti la classica architettura delle vie non si trova, e case, chiese ed orti s'intrecciano e si confondono in mille modi in mezzo a quell' eterna primavera" (586).

101 "Di fronte alla perfezione siamo assorti, e la mente non può far altro che ammirare; Il nostro amor proprio è quasi confuso. Dinanzi al bello abbozzato, il nostro pensiero si fa parte viva di quel quadro, e lo corregge e lo compisce a suo modo, voluttuosamente s'incarna con la natura quasi volesse involare un raggio della sovrana voluttà del creare" (493).

102 On the concept of Mantegazza's aesthetics, see Nicoletta Pireddu's insightful essay, "Paolo Mantegazza: ritratto dell'antropologo come esteta," in *Paolo Mantegazza: Dalle Americhe al Mediterraneo,* ed. Alessandra Atzei, Orlandini Carcreff, and Tania Manca (Monaco: LiberFaber, 2014).

American Tears: Edmondo De Amicis and the Remaking of Italians in Argentina

Epigraph: "Dell'Italia nei confini / Son rifatti gli italiani; / Li ha rifatti Mussolini / Per la guerra di domani / Per la gloria del lavoro / Per la pace e per l'alloro, / Per la gogna di coloro / Che la patria rinnegar."

1 Paolo Mantegazza, *Rio de la Plata e Tenerife : Viaggi e Studi* (Milan: Brignole, 1867).

2 For an insightful analysis of this poem, see Luigi Cepparrone, *Gli scritti americani di Edmondo De Amicis* (Bergamo: Rubbettino, 2012), ch. 1.

3 A famous *sceneggiata* and a movie were produced later, based on the same song, starring the king of the Neapolitan genre, Mario Merola. See www.youtube.com/watch?v=--uYLkyVTcs.

4 I am quoting from Cepparrone's volume, *Gli scritti americani di Edmondo de Amici,* 53.

5 Zola was the most successful novelist of the time. He also exercised a strong influence on Mantegazza. See Ternois's essay "Deux admirateurs italiens d'Emile Zola: P. Mantegazza et S. Sighele," *Cahiers naturalistes* 28 (1964): 162–73.

6 See: Giovanni Asserreto and Marco Doria, *Storia della Liguria* (Bari: Laterza, 2004). The authors write that between 1876 and 1901 almost two million people left from the port of Genoa, adding that in those years 15–25% of the population were emigrants transiting through the city. Virgilio founded the Genoese journal *La Borsa* (The stock exchange) and was active at the local and national level.

7 The poem also recalls the famous passage in chapter 8 of Alessandro Manzoni's novel *I promessi sposi,* where Lucia is leaving her native village by Lake Como, starting with the words: "Addio monti sorgenti dalle acque..." (Farewell mountains, emerging from the water...).

8 The text I am quoting from is the one contained in Cepparrone's volume, pp. 53–56.

9 "Mme sonno tutt'e nnotte 'a casa mia / e d'e ccriature meje ne sento 'a voce. / ma a vuje ve sonno comm'a na "Maria" / cu 'e spade 'mpietto, 'nnanz'ô figlio 'ncroce!"

10 "la isotopía de la emigración en los textos antiemigracionistas se construye en un espacio y en un recorrido de sentido pleno de semas negativos que involucran el fracaso, el dolor, la muerte, la pérdida, la traición, el desengaño y la explotación." Fernanda Elisa Bravo Herrera, *Huellas y recorridos de una utopia : La emigración italiana en la Argentina* (Buenos Aires: Teseo, 2015), 79.

11 Edward Worthen, "Edmondo De Amicis. An Italian Hispanist of the Nineteenth Century," *Hispania* 55, no. 1 (March 1972): 78–110.

12 "Je bois à votre santé et à votre fortune, concitoyens fraternisants des deux mondes, je bois à la prosperité et à l'expansion laborieuse et feconde de la jeunesse immortelle du sang argentin, don't je sens les pulsations libres et fortes comme un coeur qui bats dans notre coeur" (98).

13 Cepparrone shows that in 1884 the author was working on a novel whose protagonists would be the Italian emigrants who went to the Argentinean *pampa*, but he could not gather enough background information on the area where the Italian peasants went to live (5).

14 See her introduction to the new edition of the volume *In America* (Vibo Valentia: Monteleone, 1997), 11.

15 Quoted by Vanni Blengino in the book *La Babele nella Pampa: L'emigrante italiano nell' immaginario argentino* (Reggio Emilia: Diabasis, 2005), 117.

16 "un lezzume da metter pietà saliva dai boccaporti dei dormitori maschili nelle giornate più calde." Edmondo De Amicis, *In America* (Vibo Valentia: Monteleone, 1993), 15.

17 Marie Louise Pratt. *Imperial Eyes: Travel Writing and Transculturation* (New York: Routledge, 1992), 118.

18 Pratt, *Imperial Eyes*, 118.

19 "era moto e forza, lotta e coraggio; era la fecondità, era la ricchezza di carne e di sangue, un fremito immenso di vita sulla sconfinata pianura libera, l'aria di un nuovo mondo per me" (35).

20 "conobbi per la prima volta l'animale in tutta la sua bellezza, in tutta la terribilità primitiva della sua forza, dell'orgoglio virgineo della sua razza, nata alla libertà, non contaminata ancora dal servaggio" (33).

21 See the essay "Vico's New Science of Humanity" by T. Whittaker, in the journal *Mind*, April 1926. Vico argues that civilization develops in a recurring cycle (*ricorso*) of three ages: the divine, the heroic, and the human. Each age exhibits distinct political and social features and can be characterized by master tropes or figures of language.

22 "battaglie grandiose invasioni e fughe formidabili di indios...e dall'altra parte avanzarsi l'esercito di lavoratori d'ogni paese d'Europa che verranno a coltivare, a mietere—a mutar tutto—e le signore sotto le pergole di centinaia di ville—e città—e teatri" (64).

23 "Avvezzo al lamentio, al malcontento eterno dei nostri, diffidenti sempre o fintamente ossequiosi coi signori, con qualcosa di contratto e di chiuso, ignari e indifferenti a tutto ciò che non tocca il loro interesse immediato, rimanevo stupito a veder dei lavoratori trattarci da pari e pari con una disinvoltura allegra e cortese, al sentiri ragionar di amministrazione e di politica" (48).

24 Giacomo Bove, *Note di viaggio nelle missioni e nell'alto Paranà* (Genova: Istituto Sordo-Muti, 1887) 42–43.

25 "L'immagine dell'Italia si presenta a loro sotto un nuovo aspetto, illuminata e parlante per la prima volta, e non sotto la forma del villaggio o della provincia, ma dello Stato. E quanto più tempo passa, e tanto più quell'immagine si rischiara e parla più alto" (49).

26 See the speech delivered by the Socialist congressman Andrea Costa at the Italian Parliament on February 3, 1887, available at www.socialismoitaliano1892. it/2018/11/28/andrea-costa-dopo-la-sconfitta-di-dogali/.

27 "E benché quasi tutti fossero partiti forzatamente dalla loro terra, non portando con sé che ricordi di stenti e di dolori, non v'è uno di loro, uno solo, da cui abbia inteso una parola amara contro la patria" (49).

28 See www.monumentos.gob.cl/monumentos/monumentos-historicos/scu ola-italiana-arturo-delloro.

29 See Mark Choate, *Emigrant Nation*, 208.

30 "L'orgoglio di signore primo della sua terra; guarda un po' dall'alto tutta quella povera gente che dovette abbandonar la patria per andar a cercare la vita sopra la sconfinata pianura ch'egli conquistò e le concede; e un vago timor d'essere soverchiato dalla popolazione immigrante gli fa sentire spesso il bisogno di mettere a posto, con una parola altera, i suoi ospiti" (52).

31 "perché dissodano rapidamente e fecondano, e cedono ad altri i terreni, per andare innanzi a dissodare e fecondarne dei nuovi, non badando a disagi e pericoli." Quoted in Cepparrone, 95.

32 *El costo humano de los agrotóxicos*, by Pablo Ernesto Piovano, available at www.youtube.com/watch?v=1o6CujuwoXQ.

33 Originally published in 1912, the poem is collected in the volume *Canti orfici* (Turin: Einaudi, 2014).

34 "E quella povera contadina, vista di lontano, con un bimbo in collo nato sul Paranà, con altri figliuoli attorno nati in Italia, davanti a quella povera capanna su cui sventolava la bandiera nazionale, in mezzo alla sconfinata *pampa* d'America, rappresentava per noi l'amor di patria e la santità della famiglia nella forma più poeticamente dolce, triste e solenne che possa concepire la mente umana" (56).

From Free Emigration to Imperialism: The Debunking of the Argentine Myth

Epigraph: "La grande Proletaria si è mossa."

1 "dove si trovano davanti una razza indigena affine e non preponderante in numero, dove l'avvenire prepari una lenta fusione e non un letale assorbimento."

Luigi Einaudi, *Un principe mercante: Studio sull'espansione coloniale italiana* (Turin: Fratelli Bocca, 1900), 10.

2 Einaudi quotes from Carlo Cerboni's book on Argentina, published in 1898. Einaudi, *Un principe mercante*, 11.

3 "L'Argentina sarebbe ancora un deserto, le sue città un impasto di paglia e di fango senza il lavoro perseverante, senza l'audacia colonizzatrice, senza lo spirito d'intraprendenza degli italiani."

4 See my discussion of Jacopo Virgilio's book in chapter one.

5 "Le colonie libere e non le officiali devono attirare i commercianti desiderosi di creare uno sbocco ai prodotti dell'industria della madre patria" (23).

6 "come un generale sceglie sulla carta il punto migliore per dar battaglia, o la piazza, la cui caduta segnerà la conquista di una vasta regione" (26).

7 "il regno ozioso e spendereccio degli Argentini, e rimaneva il lavoro assiduo e paziente dei capitalisti inglesi e francesi e dei lavoratori italiani" (32).

8 "I figli di quei marinai, cresciuti nel nuovo ambiente, modificarono in parte, è vero, l'asprezza del parlare, ma non tolsero, né potranno togliere a quel luogo, trasformato ora, come per incanto, in un sobborgo popoloso e quasi pulito, quel carattere peculiare che fa credere a chi lo visita di trovarsi in un porto della Liguria. Magazzini, osterie, case di cambio, teatrucoli, negozi di commestibili, depositi di merci, botteghe di ogni qualità appartengono per la maggior parte a genovesi o ai loro discendenti" (36).

9 "tale è la funzione degli uomini grandi, dei ricchi intraprendenti dei paesi nuovi: assumersi il rischio dell'impianto delle colonie, dissodare i deserti ed abbattere le foreste" (39).

10 "Il bracciante del settentrione e il cafone del mezzogiorno d'Italia sono scomparsi dinanzi al tipo del colono energico, padrone di sé e della sua terra, riproduzione italiana migliorata e raffinata di quei milioni di *farmer* che costituiscono l'ossatura sociale dell'Unione Nord-Americana" (46).

11 "Quando è l'epoca della falciatura i campi sembrano percorsi da squadroni di artiglieria a cavallo. È un vero esercito che manovra sotto il comando di capi sperimentati; soltanto che esso non recide vite umane, ma esili pianticelle che...verranno a far concorrenza nell'Europa ai prodotti che i contadini che, pigri e lenti alle trasformazioni tecniche moderne, continuano a falciare, rastrellare e ammucchiare il fieno a mano" (53).

12 "Le ferrovie, i canali ed i porti richieggono imperiosamente l'intervento di capitali dei paesi vecchi, i quali fiduciosi vadano a fornire i paesi nuovi di quelle opere fondamentali senza di cui non è possibile l'espandersi della colonizzazione, l'incremento della popolazione ed il fiorire delle industrie. Dall'Italia non venne il capitale necessario a queste opere; e gli italiani dell'Argentina hanno dovuto perciò contentarsi di ottenere il primato nelle opere di lenta formazione" (72).

13 Choate, *Emigrant Nation*, 50.

14 "Gli intelligenti nelle masse sono come i graduati nell'esercito, una piccola minoranza che guida, non fosse altro con l'esempio, che unisce in un'azione comune. Togliete gli ufficiali ad un esercito d'eroi, ed avrete la fuga più vergognosa.

L'esercito dei nostri emigranti manca di ufficiali, e si sbanda, e si arrende alla spicciolata, subito, cedendo bene spesso a quell'arma potente che si chiama "dignità nazionale." Luigi Barzini. *L'Argentina vista come è* (Milan: Corriere della sera, 1902), 155.

15 "Italy came to rely upon its ethnic expansion to sustain its domestic economy." Choate, *Emigrant Nation*, 75.

16 "Non abbiamo visto i caduti dell'immenso esercito nostro, che ha traversato a squadre l'Atlantico per combattere silenzioso, sotto altra bandiera, la più disperata battaglia" (219).

17 "Infatti la partenza di un emigrante per un lontano paese ha un po' della morte. Egli muore alla sua vita consueta. Muore per i suoi, muore per il suo paese, sparisce verso l'ignoto. Egli forse pensa vagamente ad un ritorno, è vero; la sua morte ha una speranza di risurrezione. Ma nel momento del distacco il turbine del dolore disperde ogni sogno. Egli ha l'occhio perduto e il viso desolato di chi si trova di fronte all'abisso insondabile di un'altra vita" (2).

18 In Edmondo De Amicis's famous novella *Dagli Appennini alle Ande*, the wife emigrates to Argentina as a domestic worker to help the family financially. Her son goes looking for her in Buenos Aires and finally finds her in a city at the foothills of the Andes.

19 The Argentinian migration law, quoted in the *Guida*, defines as "emigrante" any person with good morals who arrives in the country with a ticket of second or third class with the intention to settle there and is less than sixty years old (avendo meno di sessant'anni; 88).

20 "non devono emigrare coloro che hanno studiato, che hanno ricevuto un'educazione più o meno scelta. Costoro formano ciò che si potrebbe chiamare l'epidemia dell'emigrazione, per i danni che arrecano a quelli che emigrano ed alla Repubblica Argentina che li riceve" (45).

21 "L'America è un paese dove si soffre, dove si piange e dove si soccombe, come in tutto il mondo. Laggiù la lotta è meno disciplinata ed è perciò violenta, terribile" (10).

22 "Non è doloroso e umiliante? Questa sottrazione continua delle nostre forze vive, questa trasfusione del sangue nostro per la rigenerazione di paesi lontani, dovuta principalmente alla ignoranza delle nostre masse, non è cosa ben triste?" (11).

23 "Gl'inglesi sono i veri padroni dell'Argentina; essi hanno tutte le ferrovie, il porto, le opere colossali dell'acqua potabile, i *trams*, tutte le principali imprese" (17).

24 "Dal lato opposto della città gli eleganti non vanno mai. Vi è la Boca del Riachuelo, uno strano rione, un paese quasi, dalle piccole case di legno, di ferro zincato, di casse da petrolio; qualche volta anche di mattoni. Dalle vie sterrate, sulle quali il vento solleva il polverone a vortici, si scorgono piccoli recinti pieni d'immondizie...di mobili a pezzi, di cenci, di roba d'ogni genere raccolta certamente per la strada e radunata non si sa perchè, forse per quella strana manìa collezionista che accompagna talvolta la miseria. In alcuni cortiletti al piede di

alberi rachitici bruciati dal sole, vegetano pomodori ed erbaccie fra i quali raz-zolano i polli. In certi punti il terreno è paludoso; le vie sboccano in veri pan-tani. Qui le case sono costruite sopra palizzate, come quelle dei villaggi lacustri; l'acqua marcisce intorno alle abitazioni, tutta coperta da muffe verdi. In alcune strade meno frequentate pascolano liberamente dei buoi, che gettano al vento il loro muggito lamentoso. Per ogni dove piccoli negozî oscuri di *almacen* dove si vende di tutto; povere mostre polverose coperte di mosche; osterie dalle quali esce il tanfo caldo del vino come dalla bocca d'un ubbriaco: loschi caffè dove non si prende il caffè..."

25 See Blengino, *La Babele nella pampa*, 165–85.

26 "esiste un'altra Patagonia, metropolitana, da evangelizzare in Argentina: si tratta degli italiani, degli spagnoli, dei francesi asserragliati in un quartiere per-iferico, territorio sotto il dominio di Satana, si tratta della "Bocca del Demonio." Blengino, *La Babele nella pampa*, 177.

27 The critical literature on *sainete* and *cololiche* is extremely vast. See Blengino, *La Babele nella pampa*, 121–47.

28 Blengino, *La Babele nella pampa*, 97.

29 Blengino, *La Babele nella pampa*, 97.

30 "indefinibile, irregolare, fangosa, che sta fra il torbido e tempestoso Rio della Plata e la città, una striscia di terra che si direbbe la zona neutra fra il pos-sesso delle acque e quello degli uomini" (25).

31 See: Michel Foucault's seminal work *Discipline and Punish: The Birth of the Prison*, originally published in French in 1975.

32 "Nel mezzo all'edificio principale, al gasometro, vi è un cortiletto circo-lare, oscuro, umido, una specie di pozzo, sul quale si aprono le porte delle cam-erate...L'acre odore dell'acido fenico non riesce a vincere il tanfo nauseante che viene dal pavimento viscido e sporco, che esala dalle vecchie pareti di legno, che è alitato dalle porte aperte; un odore d'umanità accatastata, di miseria" (37).

33 "Su queste elezioni poggia l'oligarchia che strema le forze dell'Argentina e ne prostra le promettenti energie. Dalle elezioni nasce la piovra governativa, e viceversa: come la storia dell'uovo e della gallina. È un circolo chiuso, la cui anacronica esistenza è spiegata dalla esclusione della vita politica di quella grande parte della popolazione che più lavora, produce e paga, la quale avrebbe precisa-mente il più grande interesse ad una politica onesta: alludo agli stranieri. Con questa straordinaria organizzazione, elettorale viene a mancare completamente il controllo del popolo nel complesso organismo governativo. Una macchina senza regolatore" (78).

34 "E poi il sangue argentino è sangue andaluso con un pochetto di sangue indiano, e perciò l'argentino è cortese, cavalleresco, generoso forse anche, ma bene spesso impetuoso e violento. il revolver e il pugnale sono endemici, e per un niente s'ammazza, come vuole l'uso *criollo*. La rivoltella è nelle tasche di tutti."

35 See Scarzanella, *Italiani malagente*, 30. I will return to further discuss her book in the next chapter, dealing with the influence of Italian Positivism and Criminology in America.

36 "Gettai un'occhiata sulle fisionomie; una raccolta di tipi risoluti, una collezione di occhi fieri, di baffi e di barbe dal taglio poco comune, e qua e là dei nasi adunchi, degli zigomi salienti e delle bocche larghe tagliate come con un colpaccio di ascia, caratteristiche non dubbie della razza meticcia. Vi era anche un negro" (85).

37 "Queste corrispondenze potranno fare più bene della malsana massa di altre pubblicazioni la cui schifosa adulazione eccita sospetti. Siccome il paese è commercialmente, politicamente e socialmente malato, il Barzini fa bene a dirlo, dissipando così malintesi e disperdendo illusioni. Noi non crediamo che abbia calcato le ombre, poichè queste crescono invece di diminuire; l'incauto emigrante che crede di trovare integrità di governo e di giustizia è messo in guardia. Togliendo di mezzo le false idee, egli ci rende un buon servizio. I nostri migliori amici non sono quelli che ci adulano, e la stampa indigena dovrebbe porsi bene in mente ciò nel pesare il valore delle opinioni del Barzini" (50).

38 "L'argentino porta la sua carta moneta insaccata nelle tasche dei pantaloni. Qualunque somma è portata così, come il fazzoletto. Per pagare si tira fuori un pugno di biglietti, se ne getta uno tutto spiegazzato al venditore con un'inimitabile aria di disdegno, e si ripone il resto con noncuranza nella solita tasca" (104).

39 "Il lusso infesta tutti i campi, come una splendida ortica, e vegeta persino sul bilancio di Buenos Aires....Si fanno *boulevards* perfettamente inutili perchè Parigi ne ha. È il lusso sterile di chi spende per spendere, per 'figurare,' di chi poco conosce il costo del denaro" (104).

40 "A poco a poco tutto tende a diventare giuoco, dalle imprese alla politica; la via del lavoro è sempre più schivata come mezzo per raggiungere la prosperità e la ricchezza, perchè è una via troppo lunga e aspra e difficile in confronto delle altre. Si spende rapidamente; è necessario guadagnare rapidamente. Ne viene uno squilibrio nelle manifestazioni della vita sociale. La compagine morale della società s'indebolisce: e guai quando si rallenta o cessa di funzionare quel potente regolatore delle azioni umane che è la coscienza!" (111).

41 "Gli uomini più intraprendenti e animosi non trovano un campo dove applicare le loro iniziative; parrebbe che l'Argentina vigorosa e piena d'energia sia stata trasformata in un paese estenuato, esaurito, avente appena tanta vita da fornire lo scarso pane quotidiano" (119).

42 "È che noi italiani siamo le api operaie di quel grande alveare; è che l'Argentina esiste e vive in virtù del lavoro italiano. Senza di noi non avrebbe produzione, non avrebbe nè agricoltura, nè industria, non avrebbe teatri, palazzi, porti, ferrovie. È il lavoro dei nostri connazionali che ha veramente creato l'Argentina d'oggi, la quale senza di esso non avrebbe nessuna potenza economica, come un Guatemala od una Bolivia qualunque" (144).

43 Blengino, *La Babele nella Pampa*, 37–60.

44 "Non sono molti anni che rappresentava un'ingiuria mortale, ma poi i *gringos* sono diventati tanti che la parola ha perduto molto dell'acerbo significato, restando una semplice espressione disprezzante" (163).

45 In one of the founding texts of Argentinian literature, José Hernández's *Martín Fierro*, the homonymous protagonist is a gaucho who has been forcibly enrolled in the army to fight the natives who periodically attack the colonizers. Although Martín Fierro is a destitute individual, marginalized from society, he treats the Italian soldier as inferior, makes fun of the "cocoliche" idiom he speaks, calls him a "pappolitano" and characterizes him as a coward, unfit to be in the army, because he does not know how to ride properly and cannot endure the hard life in the pampa. In another instance, Martín meets a "gringo" who plays an organ grinder accompanied by a monkey and makes everyone laugh. The image is stereotypical and represents a reoccurring *topos* in popular literature and theater. Jorge Luis Borges, in a famous essay on *Martín Fierro*, remarks that the conflict between the *gaucho* and the *gringo* reflects the hostility that shepherds always showed toward farmers—Cain versus Abel. The *gaucho*, although poor and marginalized, embodies the sense of superiority that the knight feels toward those who work the land. In Borges's view, as agriculture gradually replaced animal husbandry, the relationship was inverted, but I would argue that the Argentine elites continued to identify with the *gaucho* and the cultural values he represented. Although Martín Fierro is marginalized, his total disregard for material wealth and generosity endows him with noble features that the greedy, awkward, and materialistic *gringo* will never acquire, even when he becomes economically successful. See Jorge Luis Borges and Margarita Guerrero, El "Martín Fierro" (Buenos Aires: Emecé Editores, 1979).

46 "Siccome i poveri emigranti meridionali, calabresi, abruzzesi, napoletani, siciliani, sono i più miseri e i più incolti, la parola *tano* poco a poco è venuta a designare l'ultimo gradino dell'umiltà umana. Dire *tano* è come dire "miserabile!" L'Argentino irritato vi dice in faccia *gringo*: irato vi grida *tano*. Ciò significa che le parole equivalenti a *italiano* e *napoletano* occupano un posto nel vocabolario delle ingiurie. E il nostro orgoglio non ne può essere lusingato" (121).

47 "è burlato da tutti, parla a strafalcioni; è un po' il 'servo sciocco' delle antiche scene italiane, ma più servo e più sciocco, per di più ladro e....bastonato" (163).

48 See Devoto, *Storia degli italiani in Argentina*, 161–235.

49 See Devoto, *Storia degli italiani in Argentina*, 234.

50 When I was in Rosario in 2015, I visited two of these associations, one representing the northern region of Liguria and the other Abruzzi, in the Mezzogiorno. Although rooted in specific regions and traditions, their activities went far beyond the local boundaries and included Italian language and cooking classes that were attended by many Argentinians of Italian descent, regardless of their regional affiliation. The president of the Ligurian association, a physician who spoke perfect Italian, set up a visit for me to the Scuola Dante Alighieri. Located in a beautiful building in the most prestigious boulevard in Rosario, it offers Italian classes from kindergarten to high school. The Scuola Cristoforo Colombo in Buenos Aires, which I also visited during my trip, is considered one

of the best in the capital, and their graduates' knowledge of the language, literature, and culture of Italy is comparable to that of any Italian high school student.

51 "Una gran parte dei nostri emigranti dispersi per la Repubblica Argentina si maritano con delle donne del paese, con delle *criollas*, spesso con delle brune *chinitas* figlie della Pampa, misere e fiere come i cardi delle loro pianure. Nulla d'italiano nella casa, e i figli crescono ignari della patria del padre, se non sdegnosi" (178).

52 "Ogni donna che emigra porta con sè chiuso nel cuore un piccolo lembo della Patria. Ne parlerà ai suoi figli, sempre; imparerà loro le preghiere che ella vi ha imparato; conterà loro le leggende che essa vi ha appreso; farà sì che l'amino, poichè essa l'ama" (178).

53 *Innocentes o culpables : Novela naturalista* (Buenos Aires: Imprenta del Courrier de la Plata, 1884), 6.

54 Blengino, *La Babele nella Pampa*, 68.

55 Quoted in Blengino, *La Babele nella Pampa*, 73.

56 "Il *peon*—italianizzato in *peone*—è l'essere più umile che esista. È qualche cosa meno di un uomo: è una macchina da lavoro della forza d'un uomo. Il peone fa di tutto: è facchino, manuale, spazzino. Vive alla giornata, oggi trasporta le pietre nei cantieri, domani trasporta i covoni sui campi. Gira sempre in traccia di lavoro; passa da colonia a colonia, da provincia a provincia, ben felice quando un'occupazione lunga lo fissa in qualche parte. Viaggia quasi sempre a piedi come l'Ebreo Errante, ma senza le scarpe leggendarie, perchè le sue si logorano" (204).

57 "si preoccupano solo di ricavare da essa (la terra) il maggior profitto possibile, seminando un anno dopo l'altro lino o grano turco, lasciandola impoverita dopo alcuni anni" (43).

58 "Non riportavo certo delle storie segrete: chi vive e chi ha vissuto nell'Argentina le conosce bene pur troppo. Si tratta di una situazione nota a milioni di persone, della quale centinaia di giornali locali scrivono ampiamente e uomini politici discutono" (218).

59 "Le riforme forse non verranno, ma se ne parla, e questo per l'Argentina è già un bel risultato dovuto tutto al controllo dell'opinione pubblica straniera, che per gli argentini è una cosa tanto nuova quanto fastidiosa" (224).

60 "che cosa avviene di questo *esercito* di nostri lavoratori che abbandona la Patria per dare l'immensa sua forza ad un altro paese" (iv, emphasis added).

61 "L'esercizio delle armi è stato da noi sempre riconosciuto come fra i più eletti, e l'esercito è divenuto poi oggetto di ogni onore e di ogni amore quando il popolo tutto è stato chiamato a combattere nelle sue file le più sante battaglie; l'esercito è divenuto tutta una cosa, tutta una carne col popolo" (95).

62 See: Gabriela Anahí Costanzo, *The Inadmissible Turned History: The 1902 Law of Residence and the 1910 Law of Social Defence. Sociedad (Buenos Aires)*, No. 26, 2007. Translated by Marta Inés Merajver.

63 See www.treccani.it/enciclopedia/giuseppe-bevione_(Dizionario-Biografico)/.

64 "Immersa nelle pelliccie preziose, scintillante di gemme, la portegna con-
duce in giro sotto gli occhi della gente la sua molle bellezza. Ha lineamenti regali
e forme opulente, ma la pinguedine l'insidia e spesso l'offende" (wrapped in precious furs, sparkling with gems, the *porteña* lady carries around her soft beauty
under the gaze of people. She has regal features and opulent forms, but her plump-
ness undermines and even offends her allure; 24).

65 "ma il deserto li impaurì, e la dura opera delle prime seminagioni fu più
grande del loro cuore: e se ne stettero nelle città popolose ad aspettare il passaggio della ricchezza, per attrarne qualche rigagnolo ai loro *almacenes* ed ai loro
boliches" (87).

66 "Mi sentivo gonfiar l'anima di entusiasmo al pensiero che erano stati figli
d'Italia coloro che avevano dissodato e donato alla civiltà quell'immensa con-
trada. Mi riempiva d'orgoglio la certezza che quella grande oasi verde che si dilata
nel deserto argentino sarebbe ancora per tre quarti pampa selvaggia ed incolta
se gli Italiani non ci fossero venuti, e in cinquant'anni di lavoro coraggioso non
ne avessero fatto un giardino. Quando si dubita delle qualità della nostra razza,
non si conoscono le sue propaggini pel mondo. Quando si dice che abbiamo nel
sangue la luce di troppi secoli e di troppe civiltà, non s'è visto ciò che questa nostra
decrepita e avariata gente è riuscita a fare nell'America del Sud" (87).

67 The assassin was Gaetano Bresci, an Italian anarchist who had migrated to
the United States and returned to Italy to avenge the killing of the workers during
the protests that took place in Milan in 1898.

68 "La quistione vitale era ed è di non restare sommersi sotto le cataratte
degli stranieri arrivanti a milioni dai paesi civili d'Europa, ma di renderli innocui
alla stirpe stabilita, anzi di assorbirli nel minor tempo possibile" (98).

69 "I nostri connazionali che lavorano nella Repubblica, rappresentano miri-
adi di monadi isolate e disperse, che s'ignorano a vicenda, e non fanno il più leggero sforzo per conoscersi, intendersi, organizzarsi, e creare, dalla fusione della
collettività, la forza specifica che deve difenderla. L'Italiano che va in America
diventa di un egoismo cieco e feroce. Lavora con un'energia tremenda, dall'alba
a notte, per conquistare al più presto la fortuna: ma perde immediatamente passione ed interesse per ciò che non ha rapporto diretto e visibile colla ricchezza. Si
direbbe che l'Italiano, anche di buona razza, finchè sta in America, è un cittadino
in aspettativa, un dimissionario di tutte le cittadinanze e di tutti gli obblighi. Si
cura poco di ciò che succede in patria e nulla di ciò che succede intorno a lui, nel
paese che l'ospita" (176).

70 See Antonio Schiavulli, *La guerra lirica* (Ravenna: Pozzi, 2009).

71 "Come tutti i grandi fenomeni sociali, la emigrazione è intessuta di vantaggi e di danni, ma i danni sono preponderanti, e per di più di carattere perman-
ente, ed offendono beni collettivi insurrogabili, mentre i vantaggi sono transitori,
e si concretano in conquiste, che è possibile raggiungere per altra via" (162).

72 "Il gravissimo problema terriero, che è alla radice di tutti i problemi della
Repubblica, non potrà essere risolto se non mediante una politica energica e, se è
necessario, autocratica, di espropriazioni forzate, sulla base della restituzione del

prezzo d'acquisto, e l'assegnamento scrupolosissimo ai piccoli coloni della terra ritornata libera nel demanio nazionale" (232).

73 "Il paese deve trionfare o morire, l'Argentina deve elevarsi al novero delle nazioni libere e dominanti o cadere irreparabilmente nel gregge delle nazioni sfruttate e schiave. Ora, io ho la convinzione assoluta che la natura vincerà, che il suolo feracissimo plasmerà l'uomo a sua immagine e somiglianza e che l'Argentina giuocherà col Canadà e l'Australia un ruolo capitale nella storia dell'umanità futura" (223).

74 On Corradini's journey to Brazil and Argentina, see Erminio Fonzo, "Un intellectual Italiano en América Latina: el viaje de Enrico Corradini de 1908 y lor origines del nacionalismo en Italia," in *Ensayos americanos*, vol. I, ed. Maria Rosa Coluciello, Giuseppe D'Angelo, and Rosaria Minervini (Bogotà: Penguin Random House, 2018), 533–59. In his article, the author quotes extensively from a series of articles that Corradini published in *Corriere della sera* in 1908.

75 Enrico Corradini, *La Patria lontana* (Milan: Treves, 1910), 23.

76 "C'era il rifiuto della feccia delle città, cacciato dalla cupidigia della avventura, c'era il rifiuto della miseria delle campagne, cacciato dalla fame; del vecchio mondo...navigavano verso l'ignoto del nuovo mondo...la notte scendevano giù nelle stive e facevano tutt'un carnaio fermentante e suppurante...e poi toccata la riva d'America si sarebbero disperse, usciti dall'ignoto, un'altra volta nell'ignoto" (15–16).

77 "Lo guardi, come parla a tutti e tutti gli parlano! Sono i suoi nuovi amici. Si fa raccontare la loro vita, i loro disegni per l'avvenire ignoto, dà loro dei consigli, vede in tutti, anche nell'ultima abiezone, una nobile forza da rialzare, indirizzare a uno scopo....Accorrono da tutte le parti! È una turba!" (18)

78 I analyzed Corradini's nationalist novels in "From Diaspora to Empire: Enrico Corradini's Nationalist Novels," *MLN* 119 (2004): 67–83.

79 "Perché potessero restare italiani, nazionalmente parlando, bisognerebbe che la terra sulla quale lavorano e s'arricchiscono, diventasse italiana" (7).

80 In 1912, Ricciotto Garibaldi—son of Giuseppe and Anita—a controversial figure who started his military career as a democratic fighter but ended up supporting Mussolini, gathered twelve thousand volunteers and clashed with the Turks in Macedonia. See the article in the *Treccani Encyclopedia*, available at www.tcani.it/enciclopedia/ricciotti-garibaldi/.

81 "al pari della musica, dell'arte, della religione, è uno sforzo dell'uomo per uscire dell'individuo e propagarsi nel tempo e nello spazio" (244).

82 "Bisogna morire a noi stessi per rivivere in una vita più grande. I cristiani dicevano per rivivere in Cristo, noi per la patria" (251).

83 Terry Eagleton, *Criticism and Ideology* (London: New Left Books, 1976), 77.

The Whole World Is Our Homeland: Italian Transnational Anarchism in Argentina

Epigraphs: "I proprietari e i governi possiedono 'la patria' materiale, il suolo, il capitale, tutto; l'operaio è scacciato dalla terra che l'ha veduto nascere. Non ha

niente da difendere, niente che possa chiamare 'suo bene' e quindi non ha 'patria.'
Nel suo padrone o governante c'è un suo nemico, mentre al di là delle frontiere
tutti quelli che lavorano e soffrono come lui sono suoi fratelli." The *Almanaque
Popular de La Questione Sociale* was an Anarchist periodical directed by Errico
Malatesta in Buenos Aires, printed in Italian and Spanish.

"Che danno si risentirebbe se sparissero i padron i? Sarebbe come se fossero
sparite le cavallette." *Fra contadini* was a pamphlet published by Malatesta in 1884
that was translated into many languages.

1 See Marco Manfredi's volume *Emozioni, culura popolare e transnazional-
ismo* (Florence: Le Monnier, 2017).

2 See: Osvaldo Bayer, "The Influence of Italian Immigration on the Argentine
Anarchist Movement," available at https://libcom.org/library/influence-italian-
immigration-argentine-anarchist-movement-osvaldo-bayer. The essay was first
pubished in the volume *Gli italiani fuori d'Italia: Gli emigrati italiani nei movi-
menti operai dei paesi d'adozione* (Milan: Franco Angeli, 1983).

3 Emanuela Minuto, "Pietro Gori's Anarchism: Politics as Spectacle (1895–
1900). *Internationaal Instituut voor Sociale Geschiedenis*, 62 (2017) 425–450.

4 The English translation from which I am quoting was published by
Elephant Editions and printed in Catania in 1981, with an introduction by Alfredo
M. Bonanno, 7–8, available at https://libcom.org/files/Errico%20Malatesta%20-
%20Fra%20Contadini.pdf.

5 Quoted in Minuto, "Pietro Gori's Anarchism," 425. From Fabbri's preface
to Pietro Gori's volume *Conferenze politiche* (Milan: Editrice Moderna, 1948).

6 See Minuto, "Pietro Gori's Anarchism."

7 See Minuto, "Pietro Gori's Anarchism," 433. Many of Gori's court speeches
were collected and published in the anthology of writings *Scritti scelti*.

8 See: Antonio Gramsci, *Quaderni dal carcere* (Turin: Einaudi, 1975), 778–79.

9 "In popular memory, the Italian Anarchist was remembered as an angel, an
exceptionally good man, all heart, all heart for everyone." Minuto, "Pietro Gori's
Anarchism," 444.

10 Gori, "La nostra utopia," in *Scritti scelti*, 26.

11 See Francesco Rotondo, *Itinerari alla periferia di Lombroso: Pietro Gori e
la "Criminalogia moderna" in Argentina* (Naples: Edizione Scientifica, 2014), 11.

12 The news appeared on the front page of the Anarchist periodical. In the
following months, the editors gave ample summaries of Gori's conferences in
Buenos Aires and other Argentinian cities.

13 The periodical is available at http://americalee.cedinci.org/portfolio-
items/la-protesta/.

14 See   www.lanacion.com.ar/turismo/10-teatros-buenos-aires-perdio-nid
2243890/.

15 On Pietro Gori and his fight for freedom of speech, see Emanuela Minuto,
"Gli anarchici nella crisi di fine '800: L'attività di Pietro Gori in difesa della libertà," *Storia e Futuro*, No. 52, February 2021.

16 The entire collection of the feminist periodical was reprinted in 1997 by
the Universidad Nacional de Quilmes, with an introduction by Maxine Molyneux,

professor of Latin American Studies at the University of London. Her essay originally appeared as "No God, No Boss, No Husband," *Latin American Perspectives* 13, no. 1 (1986): 119–45.

17 The text of the conference is contained in the first volume of *Scritti Scelti*, published by *L'Antistato*, Cesena, 1968, 168–83.

18 See Maxine Molyneux, "No God, No Boss, No Husband," 125.

19 Ana Ruth Giustachini, *La dimensión verbal en el teatro anarquista: la columna de fuego de Alberto Ghiraldo*, Buenos Aires, October 1990, available at www.teatrode lpueblo.org.ar/sobretodo/05_sobre_autores_y_obras/giustachini001.htm.

20 See Martín Albernoz's article "Pietro Gori en la Argentina (1898–1902): Anarquismo y cultura," 32.

21 For a thorough analysis of Gori's journal, see Rotondo, *Itinerari alla periferia di Lombroso.*

22 "...este joven país, al que transmigran no solo las actividades creadoras en el bien, sino también las actividades criminosas del hombre contra el hombre" (this young country, where not only the good, creative activities migrate, but also the criminal activities of man against man).

23 See: Scarzanella, *Italiani malagente*, 13.

24 Quoted by Scarzanella, *Italiani malagente*, 31.

25 See: Rotondo, *Itinerari alla periferia di Lombroso*, 26.

26 See: R. D. Salvatore and C. Aguirre, eds., *The Birth of the Penitentiary in Latin America; Essay on Criminology, Prison Reform, and Social Control, 1830–1940* (Austin: University of Texas University Press), xi.

27 See: Francesco Rotondo, *Itinerari alla periferia di Lombroso*, 27. Rotondo is a legal scholar who studied Gori's journal and the impact it had on the judicial system in Argentina.

28 Lila Caimari observes that Gori's objectives were different from Ghiraldo's: "El espíritu que guió a Gori era muy diferente: no podía hallarse en sus escritos ni la caridad del religioso, ni la curiosidad del periodista, ni el sadismo del vulgo, ni la vanidad del diletante" (The principle that guided Gori was very different: one could not find in his writings neither the compassion of the religious man, the curiosity of the journalist, the sadism of the uneducated masses, nor the vanity of the dabbler.). Quoted in Albernoz, "Pietro Gori en la Argentina," 39.

29 "Las líneas durísimas de su fisionomía asumían un aspecto más feroz: las enormes mandíbulas tenían el aspecto de las bestias carnívoras, las cigomas prominentes, las orejas asimétricas y en forma de asa, los arcos supraciliares pronunciadísimos, resumían en forma más acentuada, todos los caracteres degenerativos" Albernoz, "Pietro Gori en la Argentina," 41.

30 See: Scarzanella, *Italiani malagente*, 13.

31 "El gaucho malo era una derivación ambiental del simpático "beduino de la Pampa," que puede volverse de repente bestial y feroz bajo el influjo del licor. Le tocaba al preso número 218 ser la encarnación típica de ese tipo sarmientino" (41).

32 "un reducido grupo de intelectuales y académicos podía resultar una discusión progresiva, habilitaba los comportamientos más reaccionarios en "la

generalidad de la masa social," ya que ésta "cuando oye gritar guerra al delito se arroja sobre el primer gañán desharrapado o pervertido, sobre el primer vago o náufrago de la vida, y ayuda al esbirro a aplicarle cadenas o apalearlo" (35).

33 See "Biografia de un Tribuno Libertario" y su paso por la Regíon Chilena (1901)." *Revista Acontratiempo,* August 19, 2012, available at https://archivohist oricolarevuelta.wordpress.com/2012/08/14/pietro-gori-biografia-de-un-tribuno-libertario-y-su-paso-por-la-region-chilena-1901/.

34 "El anarquista Gori, antes de abandonar (por suerte) nuestra anarquizada república, fue a saludar a los anarquistas Roca y Mitre, y estos anárquicamente le han entregado dos autógrafos anárquicos que Gori exhibirá en las asambleas ácratas como testimonio evidentísimo de la apoteosis de la anarquía por los anarquistas más grandes de América Latina." *La vanguardia,* January 18, 1902. Quoted in Albernoz, "Pietro Gori en la Argentina," 40.

35 David Turcato, "Italian Anarchism as a Transnational Movement, 1885–1915," *International Review of Social History* 52, no. 3 (December 2007): 416.

36 « Les socialistes, en acceptant un jeu parlementaire faussé à l'avance, se rendaient complices de la classe dirigeante; l'unique alternative, à la fin du XIXe siècle, dans le cadre d'une démocratie frauduleuse, consistait à refuser totalement le système." Zongalo Zaragoza Ruvira, "Anarchisme et mouvement ouvrier en Argentine à la fin du XIXe siècle," *Le Mouvement social,* no. 103 (April–June, 1978): 8.

37 Their journals were: *La Miseria* (1890), *Lavoriamo* (1893), *La Liberté* (1893–1894) *and El Perseguido* (1890–1898). *El Perseguido* was by far the most important and arrived at publishing 1,500 to 2,000 copies, but its influence ended with the financial crisis of 1890.

38 In 1896 there were twenty-six workers' organizations in Buenos Aires, and in most of them Anarchists and Socialists worked together. See Ruvira, "Anarchisme et mouvement ouvrier en Argentine," 140.

39 See Choate, *Emigrant Nation,* esp. 189–218.

40 See Livio Sansone, "Hiperbólicos italianos: as viagens dos integrantes de Escola Positiva de Antropologia da Itália pela América meridional, 1907–1910," *História, Ciências, Saúde—Manguinhos* 27, no. 1 (January–March 2020): 265–74.

In the Shadow of "Great Men": Gina Lombroso's Travels to South America

1 One of the best studies on Gina Lombroso and her sister Paola is Delfina Dolza, *Essere figlie di Lombroso: Due donne intellettuali tra '800 e '900* (Milan: Franco Angeli, 1990).

2 The book was translated into English and published with the title *The Soul of Woman* (New York: E. P. Dutton & Company, 1923). Mary Siegrist published a critical review in the *New York Times* on July 19, 1923, titled "Woman's Place in the Background. Dr. Gina Lombroso Condemns the Whole feminist Movement."

3 Benedetto Croce strongly criticized Ferrero's work as an "invented history," without solid scientific foundations. See Dolza, *Essere figlie di Lombroso,* 145.

4 Sansone, "Hiperbólicos italianos," 266.

5 *Nell' America meridionale (Brasile, Uruguay, Argentina): Note e impressioni.* (Milan: Treves, 1908), vi–vii.

6 "Quando dentro lo spazio ristretto la vita si accumula, si sovrappone così furiosamente come in una foresta vergine, non è piu il senso dell'infinito che vi penetra, ma quello della solitudine, della sfiducia nelle proprie forze" (27).

7 "Davanti, di dietro, di sopra, di sotto, liane, uccelli, fiori, alberi che vivono per sè, fra sè, che non ti chiamano, che non ti invitano, che ti ricacciano lungi da loro, come un intruso" (27).

8 I refer to Charles Baudelaire's famous poem, *Correspondances,* where he anticipated many themes that will be developed by Symbolism at the turn of the nineteenth century. For a critical introduction, see Judd D. Hubert, "Symbolism, Correspondence, and Memory," *Yale French Studies,* no. 9 (1952): 46–55.

9 "In pochi anni l'altipiano boscoso fu trasformato in una città larga, spaziosa, attorniata da splendidi parchi, ombreggiata da grandi viali che convergono tutti nel giardino centrale che dà aria e frescura alla città. Niente ormai manca alla nuova capitale: collegi, scuole, ospedali, chiese, prigioni, caserme, soldati, pompieri; ogni esercito della civiltà moderna ha la sua casa, il suo palazzo, anzi, a Bello Orizzonte" (78).

10 "L'alacrità degli abitanti congiunta alla feracità del suolo convertirà certo in un prossimo avvenire le terre di Minas Geraes in miniere più proficue e più inesauribili che quelle di oro e di argento, a cui lo Stato di Minas deve tante speranze e tante delusioni" (9).

11 On the continuous expansion of shantytowns in Argentina, see https://en.mercopress.com/2011/10/07/half-a-million-families-live-in-buenos-aires-slums-and-keep-expanding-vertically-and-horizontally.

12 Michel Foucault. "Of Other Spaces, Heterotopias," *Architecture, Mouvement, Continuité,* no. 5 (1984): 46–49. Although not reviewed for publication by the author and thus not part of the official corpus of his work, the manuscript was released into the public domain for an exhibition in Berlin shortly before Foucault's death. See https://foucault.info/documents/heterotopia/foucault.heteroTopia.en/.

13 Italo Calvino, *Invisible Cities,* trans. William Weaver (New York: Harcourt Brace Jovanovich, 1978), 123.

14 See Michel Foucault's influential book *Discipline and Punish,* originally published in French by Gallimard in 1975.

15 A manuscript of Gina Lombroso's travel diary, on which her travel book is based, is available at the *Gabinetto Viesseux* in Florence. Many of Guglielmo Ferrero's papers are at Columbia University.

16 Lombroso refers to the capture of Rome, accomplished by the Italian army on September 20, 1870, which made it possible for the capital of the new nation to be moved to Rome.

17 The book was translated into English and published as *The Tragedies of Progress* (New York: E.P. Dutton & Co, 1931).

18 "il lavoro femminile è sempre collettivo, e composto sempre di parti intellettuali e manuali. Quando le donne della società elevata pigliano gusto al lavoro ed all'economia domestica, esse necessariamente associano a questo lavoro delle altre donne inferiori per ingegno o per posizione sociale; da questa associazione momentanea nasce la simpatia, l'armonia tra le classi" (354).

EPILOGUE

Epigraph: "Se al presente tu, ed io, e tutti i nostri compagni, non fossimo su queste navi, in mezzo di questo mare, in questa solitudine incognita, in istato incerto e rischioso quanto si voglia; in quale altra condizione di vita ci troveremmo essere?" Quoted in Vanni Blengino, *Ommi! L'America*, 4, *Operette Morali*.

1 *Di proprio pugno. Autobiografie di emigranti italiani in Argentina* (Parma: Diabasis, 2003).

2 *Merica! Merica! Emigrazione e colonizzazione nelle lettere dei contadini veneti e friulani in America latina (1876–1902)* (Verona: Cierre Edizioni, 1994).

3 See www.memoriaemigrazioni.it/prt_lettere_singola.asp?idSez=252.

4 See www.memoriaemigrazioni.it/prt_lettere_singola.asp?idSez=254.

5 See "Vanni Blengino: un pendolare dell'Atlantico," *Zibaldone: Estudios italianos* 3, no. 1 (January 2015), available at https://redib.org/Record/oai_articulo 2358417-vanni-blengino-un-pendolare-dell%27atlantico.

6 Blengino investigated the conquest of the desert in his excellent book *Il vallo della Patagonia: I nuovi conquistatori: militari, scienziati, missionari, scrittori* (Parma: Diabasis, 2003).

7 "Il comune senso di sradicamento da ogni contesto, loro eterni emigranti, la sensazione di trovarsi in un posto mentre con il pensiero si è in un altro, una universalità che convive con radici ataviche di identità…con il risultato di vivere una perenne marginalità che stimola l'ipercriticismo verso il mondo" (157).